Dynamics of a Social Language Learning Community

PSYCHOLOGY OF LANGUAGE LEARNING AND TEACHING

Series Editors: **Sarah Mercer**, *Universität Graz, Austria* and **Stephen Ryan**, *Waseda University, Japan*

This international, interdisciplinary book series explores the exciting, emerging field of Psychology of Language Learning and Teaching. It is a series that aims to bring together works which address a diverse range of psychological constructs from a multitude of empirical and theoretical perspectives, but always with a clear focus on their applications within the domain of language learning and teaching. The field is one that integrates various areas of research that have been traditionally discussed as distinct entities, such as motivation, identity, beliefs, strategies and self-regulation, and it also explores other less familiar concepts for a language education audience, such as emotions, the self and positive psychology approaches. In theoretical terms, the new field represents a dynamic interface between psychology and foreign language education and books in the series draw on work from diverse branches of psychology, while remaining determinedly focused on their pedagogic value. In methodological terms, sociocultural and complexity perspectives have drawn attention to the relationships between individuals and their social worlds, leading to a field now marked by methodological pluralism. In view of this, books encompassing quantitative, qualitative and mixed methods studies are all welcomed.

All books in this series are externally peer-reviewed.

Full details of all the books in this series and of all our other publications can be found on http://www.multilingual-matters.com, or by writing to Multilingual Matters, St Nicholas House, 31-34 High Street, Bristol BS1 2AW, UK.

PSYCHOLOGY OF LANGUAGE LEARNING AND TEACHING: 9

Dynamics of a Social Language Learning Community

Beliefs, Membership and Identity

Jo Mynard, Michael Burke, Daniel Hooper, Bethan Kushida, Phoebe Lyon, Ross Sampson and Phillip Taw

MULTILINGUAL MATTERS
Bristol • Blue Ridge Summit

DOI https://doi.org/10.21832/MYNARD8908
Library of Congress Cataloging in Publication Data
A catalog record for this book is available from the Library of Congress.
Names: Mynard, Jo, author.
Title: Dynamics of a Social Language Learning Community: Beliefs, Membership and Identity/Jo Mynard, [and six others].
Description: Blue Ridge Summit: Multilingual Matters, 2020. | Series: Psychology of Language Learning and Teaching: 9 | Includes bibliographical references and index. | Summary: "This book presents an in-depth look at a social language learning space within a university context. Drawing on the literature from identity in second language learning, communities of practice and learner beliefs, it demonstrates how psychological phenomena shape a space and how a learning space can contribute to a wider learning ecology"— Provided by publisher.
Identifiers: LCCN 2020016672 (print) | LCCN 2020016673 (ebook) | ISBN 9781788928892 (paperback) | ISBN 9781788928908 (hardback) | ISBN 9781788928915 (pdf) | ISBN 9781788928922 (epub) | ISBN 9781788928939 (kindle edition)
Subjects: LCSH: Second language acquisition. | Language and languages—Study and teaching (Higher)—Psychological aspects. | Language and languages—Study and teaching (Higher)—Foreign speakers.
Classification: LCC P118.2 .M95 2020 (print) | LCC P118.2 (ebook) | DDC 418.0071—dc23 LC record available at https://lccn.loc.gov/2020016672
LC ebook record available at https://lccn.loc.gov/2020016673

British Library Cataloguing in Publication Data
A catalogue entry for this book is available from the British Library.

ISBN-13: 978-1-78892-890-8 (hbk)
ISBN-13: 978-1-78892-889-2 (pbk)

Multilingual Matters
UK: St Nicholas House, 31-34 High Street, Bristol BS1 2AW, UK.
USA: NBN, Blue Ridge Summit, PA, USA.

Website: www.multilingual-matters.com
Twitter: Multi_Ling_Mat
Facebook: https://www.facebook.com/multilingualmatters
Blog: www.channelviewpublications.wordpress.com

Copyright © 2020 Jo Mynard, Michael Burke, Daniel Hooper, Bethan Kushida, Phoebe Lyon, Ross Sampson and Phillip Taw.

All rights reserved. No part of this work may be reproduced in any form or by any means without permission in writing from the publisher.

The policy of Multilingual Matters/Channel View Publications is to use papers that are natural, renewable and recyclable products, made from wood grown in sustainable forests. In the manufacturing process of our books, and to further support our policy, preference is given to printers that have FSC and PEFC Chain of Custody certification. The FSC and/or PEFC logos will appear on those books where full certification has been granted to the printer concerned.

Typeset by Deanta Global Publishing Services, Chennai, India.
Printed and bound in the UK by the CPI Books Group Ltd.
Printed and bound in the US by NBN.

Contents

	Tables and Figures	vii
	Acknowledgements	viii
	Glossary	ix
	Part 1: Setting the Scene	
1	Introduction	3
2	Social Learning Spaces	12
3	The Japanese Educational Context	29
4	Methodology	37
	Part 2: Case Studies	
5	'If some freshman come to us, I said like, "Please join us"': Kokon's Story	51
6	'We see the same people like every day so I feel like yeah it's kind of like a community, Yellow Sofa community kind of thing': Sina's Story	58
7	'Is it okay if I ignore grammar and just speak?': Kaede's Story	65
8	'Don't be afraid of making mistakes': Rintaro's Story	72
9	'I should be more confident in talking with people': Sachiko's Story	78
10	'Just try is I think the most important thing': Sayaka's Story	83
	Part 3: Exploring Concepts Through the Research	
11	Exploring Identity in a Social Learning Space	93

12	Understanding Communities of Practice in a Social Language Learning Space	108
13	Understanding Learner Beliefs and Other Individual Differences in a Social Learning Space	125
14	Lessons Learnt from the Research Methods Applied in This Project	150

Part 4: Implications for the Field

15	Summary of the Findings	159
16	Implications and Practical Interventions	166
	Appendices	176
	Appendix 1: Observation Guidelines	176
	Appendix 2: Interview Procedure and Questions	177
	Appendix 3: My Language Learning History	181
	Appendix 4: Research Preparation Suggestions	182
	Appendix 5: Guidelines for New Teachers on Duty in the English Lounge	183
	References	185
	Index	198

Tables and Figures

Tables

Table 3.1	Perceived obstacles to communicative English teaching in Japanese secondary education	34
Table 4.1	The most frequently observed behaviours	40
Table 4.2	Summary of participants	42
Table 4.3	Analytic framework for understanding the role of key factors	47
Table 11.1	Facets of identity	95
Table 11.2	Trajectory of English Lounge use	106
Table 13.1	Key for reading the threaded analysis	143
Table 13.2	Threaded analysis representing factors, participants and time	144
Table 16.1	An exercise to match actions with beliefs	173

Figures

Figure 4.1	A map of the English Lounge for observers	39
Figure 12.1	Levels of community participation	110
Figure 13.1	Kaede's (RU) core beliefs and nested factors	147
Figure 13.2	Kyoji's (YS Group) core beliefs and nested factors	148
Figure 13.3	Misa's core beliefs and nested factors	148
Figure 16.1	Language policy guidelines for teachers	175

Acknowledgements

We would like to express our heartfelt thanks to all 15 participants in our study. Their stories and insights enhanced our understanding of our social learning space enormously. We greatly appreciate their time and contributions to the project. We would also like to thank series editors Sarah Mercer and Stephen Ryan for their feedback and encouragement throughout, and the anonymous reviewers and Richard Sampson for their feedback, suggestions and insights.

Glossary

Academic Support Area
The place where students can meet lecturers by appointment to either practice speaking English, or get help with writing or presentation skills.

Advisors (Learning Advisors/LAs)
Lecturers working full time in the Self-Access Learning Center (SALC) to support students in achieving their language-related goals.

Building 6
The building housing the previous version of the SALC (from 2003 to 2017).

Building 8 (KUIS 8)
The building housing the current SALC and also 16 classrooms.

Conversation Area
Part of the Academic Support Area where lecturers are on duty to help students with English-speaking skills.

Duty
The shifts that lecturers have in the SALC to support students in developing their English skills.

ELI (English Language Institute)
The institute that employs around 70 full-time lecturers to teach English language proficiency courses and also perform 'duty' (see above) in the SALC and Academic Support Area.

ELI Lecturers
Lecturers employed full time by the ELI.

English Lounge
The official name of the space under investigation. It is a conversation lounge which is part of the SALC.

KUIS
Kanda University of International Studies, a small university in Japan specialising in foreign languages. Established in 1987.

KUIS 8 (Building 8)
The name of the large building housing the SALC.

Lounge
The English Lounge.

Old SALC
The previous facility in Building 6.

SALC
Self-Access Learning Center (American spelling)

Yellow Sofa (YS)
As the furniture in the English Lounge includes yellow sofas, students often refer to the area as 'Yellow Sofa'.

Japanese Terms

eigo
Literally translated into English as 'English'. A type of academic English that is primarily learnt for taking examinations rather than as a communicative tool. *Eigo*-oriented lessons focus predominantly on comprehension and memorisation of grammatical structures and vocabulary.

eikaiwa
Translated as 'English conversation', *eikaiwa* is referred to by some as 'English for communication'. Eikaiwa classes are mainly focused on developing oral English proficiency. Furthermore, *eikaiwa* is usually taught in Japan by non-Japanese teachers.

senpai/kohai
A hierarchical relationship based on seniority that is ubiquitous in group settings in Japan such as education, sports, the arts and the workplace. In exchange for increased power and influence over junior group members (*kohai*), senior members (*senpai*) are expected to pass on knowledge to their *kohai* and aid their integration into the group.

Part 1
Setting the Scene

1 Introduction

Background

This book presents an in-depth look at a social language learning space within a university context. Providing support for language learners through the provision of self-access centres, conversation lounges and other such spaces is becoming more commonplace, but we still know relatively little about the dynamics of them and how they contribute to the language learning process. In this book, the authors present a case study of a social language learning space, share the results of a detailed longitudinal investigation into the space and make recommendations to others who are working in similar spaces related to research and practice.

In April 2017, the institution under examination in this book, Kanda University of International Studies (KUIS), opened a brand-new building called KUIS 8. This building contained the third iteration of the Self-Access Learning Centre (SALC), which is a facility designed to promote target language study and use, and to facilitate the development of language learner autonomy. SALCs (also known as SACs or ILCs [independent/individual learning centres]) are facilities which provide access to resources and services to support learners in their language learning. These resources can include materials such as books, worksheets and audio-visual items; people such as learning advisors and language lecturers; activities such as workshops and classes; and spaces in which students can use these resources. Each time a new version of the SALC is constructed at KUIS, its staff and users improve the facilities and attempt to accommodate the needs of the students by drawing on current theories, research, observations and knowledge from practice. KUIS 8 was conceptualised as a social learning community, so exploring ways to promote the use of the target language within this community was one of the institutional priorities. One of the key features of the new SALC and the previous one in another building (which operated from June 2003 to February 2017) was the conversation lounge, or the *English Lounge*. Although the previous SALC contained materials, offered an advising service, provided courses on self-directed learning and held regular events and workshops, to many students, the conversation lounge was the main feature that they associated with the SALC.

Even before beginning the present research project, it was evident that beliefs, identity and membership of a community all played a role in how learners perceived the lounge and whether they chose to engage with it or avoid it altogether. As we (the authors of this book) work in and around the English Lounge every day, we are able to casually observe the space and make assumptions, but there are several reasons why we decided to undertake more systematic research. Firstly, we wanted to make the English Lounge accessible to all learners who might like to use it. In order to do this, we needed to develop a deeper understanding of what was occurring in the space. This would also include a deeper knowledge of behaviours and views among the different types of users. Prior to this study, with just two exceptions (Gillies, 2010; Rose & Elliott, 2010), no research had been conducted on this social learning space, so we had very little to guide us initially. Secondly, we had just moved into a new space and needed to monitor the English Lounge and the SALC in general more closely than usual and possibly make adjustments in the first year. Finally, taking a broader perspective we could see from the growing interest worldwide in social language learning spaces that other researchers and practitioners were also concerned with ways of creating optimal learning environments for language practice and development. Examples of international interest include symposia resulting in edited volumes (Murray, 2014b; Murray & Lamb, 2018), and a journal column with international contributions published in seven instalments over several years (Thornton, 2015). Murray (2014a) suggests that learners' identities, emotions, feelings and perceptions are key elements which shape spaces and transform them into places for learning, and we were interested in investigating psychological elements in our own context. With this in mind, the study of a micro-space within a larger learning ecology could have much to offer the field. In order to meet these three objectives, we decided to undertake a longitudinal ethnographic study which has resulted in the publication of this book.

The Purpose of This Book

The purpose of this book is to provide an in-depth exploration of psychological phenomena affecting language learning within a social learning space. Drawing on the literature from identity in second language (L2) learning, communities of practice (CoPs), cross-cultural psychology and learner beliefs in conjunction with other individual difference factors, we uncover perceptions and assumptions that language learners have of the space that affect their relationship with it and the people within it. Understanding this micro-space within a SALC will allow us to understand how one learning space can contribute to a wider learning ecology.

Throughout the project, we have kept the following questions in mind, and we hope to provide some answers that will expand the understanding of how psychological phenomena shape a space, and how we might understand a space through the views and actions of participants within it. The versions of the questions below are fairly broad ones and are developed further in the relevant chapters of this volume.

(1) What happens in the English Lounge?
 (a) What communities are formed in the space?
 (b) How do different students perceive and use the space?
 (c) Why do some students choose *not* to use the space? (also considered in Questions 3 and 4)
(2) What is the relationship between the English Lounge and language learner identity?
(3) How do learner beliefs affect participation in the space?
(4) What other factors affect the ways in which participants view and use (or avoid) the English Lounge?

We also attempt to relate our findings to the wider world by considering the following meta questions:

(5) How does an understanding of psychological phenomena benefit users and potential users?
(6) What do we learn that can be applied to the study of social learning spaces elsewhere?
(7) How can language learners best be supported as they navigate the complex processes of language learning within a wider ecology of learning opportunities?

Who is This Book For?

There is growing interest in the field of 'language learning beyond the classroom' (Benson, 2011a, 2017; Benson & Reinders, 2011) as part of a learner's learning ecology, yet language educators are often unprepared to provide appropriate support for learners. In addition, spaces for potential learning beyond the classroom may be available, so educators may benefit from understanding the dynamics within such spaces in order to maximise learning opportunities. There is growing interest in providing and examining social spaces for language learning, yet surprisingly, only one book has been published in this area (Murray & Fujishima, 2016b). Our hope is that our book will be a resource for teachers and self-access professionals such as learning advisors who are supporting language learners mainly outside the classroom, especially if they are interested in exploring what is happening in their own spaces. In addition, we hope that language teachers and university lecturers who may work mainly in classrooms, but who recognise the importance of supporting outside-class learning, will also find this book of interest. We also anticipate that researchers and graduate students will benefit from the thorough and practical examination of three key areas of study (beliefs, CoP, identity) in relation to language teaching and learning, particularly in learning spaces outside of classrooms. Finally, the description of the research may be useful for possible replication in other contexts.

About the Social Learning Community Under Investigation

KUIS is a small, four-year, private university located in Chiba City, about 40 km from Tokyo, Japan. The university has four departments: Department of English, Department of International Communication, Department of Asian Languages and Department of Spanish and Portuguese. All students in the university take English language classes, with students in the first two departments majoring in English, and students in the latter two departments either double majoring or minoring in English. English language instruction is provided to all first- and second-year students by more than 60 lecturers in the English Language Institute (ELI).

At the time of its creation in 2001, the first SALC was the only facility of its kind at a university in Japan, and it continues to aim to be a global leader in the promotion of and provision of support for autonomous student learning, underpinned by ongoing research and professional development. The stated mission of the SALC (2018) is to 'foster lifelong learner autonomy as an international community by empowering learners to engage in reflective practice and take charge of their language learning'. It does this by supporting learners with resources, rooms and spaces for individual or group learning, advising sessions, self-directed learning courses, workshops and community events. A team of 11 full-time language learning advisors mainly work one-to-one with learners to help them understand and take charge of their own learning, and students are further supported by a staff of 7 assistant managers and production designers, plus around 35 part-time student staff who work on the reception counter and as peer advisors.

The SALC offers a variety of areas and services where students can practice speaking in English. Depending on their preferred interlocutor, interactional setting or language learning goals, students may choose to make an appointment for a one-to-one conversation with a teacher, meet with an international student for a one-to-one language exchange, or talk to a learning advisor or peer advisor. They may also choose to join a learning advisor-led discussion group or take part in one of the various student-run study groups or learning communities. However, many students consider the English Lounge to be the 'focal point' of the centre (Gillies, 2010: 199).

The English Lounge has been an integral part of the SALC since 2003 when a second, purpose-built version was created. Although the English Lounge was originally run by the ELI and was organisationally separate from the SALC until the move to the new building in 2017, its location was within the same physical space as the SALC, leading it to be seen as part of the SALC by students. The lounge, which is commonly known as the 'Yellow Sofas' or simply 'Yellow Sofa' due to the colour of the furniture in the space, is an informal area where students can practice English in a relaxed environment. It is accessible whenever the SALC is open (08:45–20:00 on weekdays, 09:00–17:00 on Saturdays). Students are free to come and go as they please whenever they do not have classes, with students spending from as little as a few minutes to as much as several hours there at a time. At most times of the day between 09:00 and 18:00, there are one or two lecturers from the ELI on duty to help facilitate conversations, but students may also choose to talk to other students or to the international exchange students who like to frequent the area. There is no system of checking in or out of the lounge, so it is not possible to give an accurate breakdown of users by year, department, etc., but hourly manual head counts show that over 1000 students visit the SALC each day and almost 200 students use the English Lounge every day. Annual surveys indicate that more than 50% of regular users are first-year students. A study by Rose and Elliott (2010) indicated that the users of the lounge were overwhelmingly first- and second-year students, with very few third- and fourth-year students frequenting the area. They also found no correlation between students' level of proficiency and their frequency of use, a result which accords with a different study by Gillies (2010).

About the Researchers

One of the strengths of conducting this research is the fact that there are seven researchers. Our shared interest in the project evolved from our commitment to understanding and supporting our students. Another strength was the diversity of the team which gives us access to multiple perspectives. During the first year of the project, we discussed the project in weekly meetings, allowing us to carefully consider the research approach and to support each other as we developed appropriate research methods, consulted the literature and collected and analysed our data.

Jo Mynard is the director of the SALC and the initiator and leader of the project. Her motivation for starting the project was mainly to ensure that the new SALC was meeting the needs of the students as the building was a considerable investment for the university. She has over 25 years of experience in the field of language teaching in six countries and more than 20 years of active research mainly in the fields of learner autonomy and motivation within an interpretative paradigm. She has an MPhil in Applied Linguistics from Trinity College, University of Dublin, Ireland and an EdD in teaching English as a foreign language (TEFL) from the University of Exeter, UK.

Michael Burke is a lecturer at KUIS and is actively involved in participating in the English Lounge community. His motivation for joining this research project was a desire to understand and improve the learning environment for students through research. He has 11 years of teaching experience in Japan, five of which have been in the university context. He completed an MA in teaching English to speakers of other languages (TESOL) at the University of Nottingham, UK.

Daniel Hooper is a lecturer at KUIS and has also worked in different TESOL settings in Japan for over 12 years. He has worked as an assistant language teacher in public secondary schools, an instructor in *eikaiwa* (private English conversation) schools and as a university lecturer. He completed an MA in TESOL from KUIS in 2017. He initially joined this research project because of his interest in the English Lounge as a target language social interaction space, and the presence of potential role models for learners beyond the dominant 'native speaker' model.

Bethan Kushida has worked as a lecturer in the ELI for six years. She was initially drawn to this project after forming observations from talking to students about their experiences of the lounge and was eager to find ways as a classroom teacher to better encourage and support students in their out-of-class interactions in English. She holds an MA in Advanced Japanese Studies from the University of Sheffield, UK. She has taught at the secondary and post-secondary levels in the UK, France and the Dominican Republic.

Phoebe Lyon has been a lecturer at KUIS for six years. She joined the project to have the opportunity to learn more about how students interact in the English Lounge and how this affected their identities as English learners. She has over 19 years' experience teaching English in four countries. She completed her postgraduate certification in English (PGCE) in Education at Monash University, Australia and an MEd from Deakin University, Australia in 2012.

Ross Sampson has been in the TESOL field for 10 years and has been a lecturer at KUIS since 2017. He has worked in Japan, South Korea and Thailand and on board a cruise ship. He has an MEd in TESOL from the University of Glasgow. He was motivated to join this research project in order to understand more about the dynamics of the social learning space and the role of identity in language learning.

Phillip Taw is a lecturer at KUIS and has worked in the TESOL field for over a decade. He joined the research project with the aim of exploring the unique dynamics of the English Lounge. He completed a BA in Comparative Literature from the University of California, and an MA in TESOL from California State University.

Overview of the Book

The book is divided into four parts. Part 1 sets the scene by giving background information about the context, participants, approach, theoretical stance and research methods. Part 2 contains six individual case studies from among the student participants in the ethnography. Part 3 contains three research chapters, each considering the data and interpretations from a different perspective. This is a form of triangulation designed to uncover intercepting ideas and explore the psychological processes occurring in a social learning space in greater depth. We also provide reflections and advice on the research methods after the three research chapters. Part 4 brings the findings to a conclusion and offers suggestions and practical interventions. As there were seven authors, we inevitably divided up the work in order to efficiently complete the research and to write this book. Although all seven authors were involved in every chapter, and the chapters present a shared narrative, we have chosen to add the names of the lead authors of each of the chapters in order to acknowledge their considerable work and particular contributions to the book.

Part 1: Setting the Scene

In Chapter 2, we explore the literature on social learning spaces which entails a brief overview of ways in which language learners can be supported outside the classroom, the rationale behind social learning spaces such as the English Lounge and a summary of what research in the field has told us so far in order to situate our own context and study.

In Chapter 3, we give a brief overview of the Japanese context. This includes a description of the education system, insights into the roles and features of schools and universities and an analysis of the role of English language and of language education in Japan. The intention of this chapter is to describe the current situation as a way of understanding our subsequent analysis of the dynamics of the English Lounge within this interesting and unique local context.

In Chapter 4, we provide an overview of the research methods we adopted during this project. The chapter begins with a description of the purpose of the ethnography and a brief description of the systematic observation study we undertook in order to develop an initial understanding of some of the dynamics occurring in the English Lounge.

Part 2: Case Studies

The book includes six case studies, allowing for a deeper exploration of individual learners' identities, beliefs and perceived roles within (or outside) an emergent community. The case studies are presented as in-depth narrative accounts of two participants who were core members of the community within the English Lounge, two regular users of the space and two non users of the lounge.

In Chapter 5, we present Kokon's story. Kokon was a core member of the community who was in her second year of university at the start of the project. Kokon shared her experiences of using the current and former version of the English Lounge over a three-year period.

In Chapter 6, we present Sina's story. Sina was a fourth-year (final year) student at the time of the first interview (first year of the study) and played an influential role as a leader and core member of the community within the English Lounge.

In Chapter 7, we share Kaede's story and explore how, as a regular user, her attitude towards the English Lounge and the anxiety she felt as a language learner were shaped in a number of ways by her past learning experiences. Kaede was a first-year student at the start of the project who was majoring in Spanish,

In Chapter 8, we share Rintaro's story. As a regular user, but not a core member of the community, we can learn much from Rintaro's relationship with the English Lounge over a two-year period. Rintaro was a second-year student at the start of the project who was majoring in Chinese.

In Chapter 9, we explore Sachiko's story, a case study of a non user of the lounge. Sachiko's language learning story is quite unique and, at times, contradictory. In this chapter, we can see how Sachiko approaches language learning and why she chose not to make use of the English Lounge. Sachiko was a second-year student at the start of the project who was also majoring in Chinese.

In Chapter 10, we present Sayaka's story. Despite having an interest in the English Lounge, Sayaka had never used it at the time of the first interview. Her narrative explores the reasons for her reluctance to visit the space and how she eventually overcame them. Sayaka was a second-year student at the start of the project who was majoring in English.

Part 3: Exploring Concepts Through the Research

As part of the ethnography, we conducted in-depth interviews with users and non users of the English Lounge in order to uncover student perceptions, practices and beliefs. We also asked participants to complete a written language learning history prior to the second interview. The data is examined from three perspectives in order to see the multifaceted and complex nature of intersecting influencing factors. Although the three perspectives are presented in three separate chapters, we reflect on the methodology, and later create links which highlight where the three perspectives overlap in order to build up a thorough picture of the phenomena occurring within the social learning space.

In Chapter 11, we explore the data from the perspective of L2 identity, taking a poststructuralist approach drawing on a framework applied by Benson *et al.* (2013). Through a qualitative analysis of our in-depth interviews, we found facets of L2 identity that were influenced by the English Lounge. All but one of the participants were interviewed twice at approximately one-year intervals to examine whether their L2 identities had shifted and the role (if any) the English Lounge played.

In Chapter 12, we explore the data from the perspective of a CoP drawing on work by Lave and Wenger (1991). As a social learning community, the CoP framework was applied in order to understand how *domain*, *community* and *practice* cultivate the community in this context (Wenger-Trayner & Wenger-Trayner, 2015). We found evidence of shared beliefs, imagined communities and artefacts that core group members had created in order to sustain the community.

In Chapter 13, we explore the data from an interpretative perspective in order to examine learner beliefs and other interacting individual differences influencing ways in which participants used the lounge.

In Chapter 14, we return to the research methods, but this time reflecting on the extent to which we answered our research questions and the lessons we learnt during the process. We also offer suggestions for others wishing to explore psychological phenomena in their own contexts.

Part 4: Implications for the Field

In Chapter 15, we bring the themes together and return to our original purpose. We briefly summarise the findings and comment on how the project is situated within the larger research agenda of the SALC as a whole, and may be applicable to other social learning spaces.

In Chapter 16, we comment on the implications of the study and make suggestions for interventions that might help educators in supporting learners to appropriately use a social learning space for language learning.

2 Social Learning Spaces

Bethan Kushida

The English Lounge is an example of a social learning space, a place where learners can gather to learn with and from each other through relaxed and 'informal social interaction' (Murray, 2017a: 117). With a growing recognition of the need to provide opportunities for socially mediated learning outside the classroom, an increasing number of educational institutions are establishing flexible, informal and learner-centred spaces such as learning commons, living learning centres and blended learning spaces where students and faculty can come together to learn in an active, collaborative, participatory, experiential and engaged way (Oblinger, 2006). In the case of language learning, such spaces provide opportunities for target language use in addition to a range of other affordances for learning and growth. Focusing on social spaces for language learning, this chapter will give a brief overview of shifts that are occurring in the study and practice of learning beyond the classroom, together with the rationale behind social learning spaces. This will be followed by a summary of what we have been told so far by research conducted in the English Lounge at Kanda University of International Studies (KUIS) and in the wider field of social language learning spaces. This chapter will serve both to situate our own context and study, and to provide a resource for those who manage or wish to establish a social learning space.

Learning Beyond the Classroom and Social Learning Spaces

For many years, most language learning research was concerned with what happened within the classroom and among classroom learners; however, in the last decade, attention has turned to language learning and teaching beyond the classroom (Reinders & Benson, 2017). With innovations in technology and an increase in global mobility, learners have greater access than ever to out-of-class language learning resources and tools, communities of language learners and users, and opportunities to practice the target language. Benson (2017: 136) urges us to move away from the dichotomy of 'in-class' and 'out-of-class' learning. Instead, he advances the holistic concept of an individual's 'language learning environment', which is made up of a variety of 'settings', only one of which is the classroom. Different settings offer different affordances and constraints for language learning which connect with and complement each other. An effective learner, working as an active agent, will recognise or perceive those affordances (Menezes, 2011) and can then choose whether to engage with the setting, make use of the resources within it (Palfreyman, 2014) and integrate it into their own individual learning environment. Reinders and Benson (2017: 3) describe these '"social ecologies" of language learning' as 'an interconnected web of learning opportunities' (Reinders & Benson, 2017: 14), and when we view second language (L2) development as a complex dynamic system (CDS; Larsen-Freeman & Cameron, 2008), we understand the importance of studying all aspects of a learner's language learning environment, not just what happens in the classroom.

Social learning spaces are one such setting, the philosophy of which draws on social constructivist views of learning, which hold that people make sense of new information as they negotiate meaning and incorporate it into their existing schemata. This negotiation process is facilitated by interaction with the world and the people within it (Lantolf, 2000; Vygotsky, 1987). Social learning spaces promote learning by providing opportunities for interaction with others. In limited class time alone, it can be difficult to provide a learner with enough opportunities for interaction to become proficient, and in monolingual cultures such as Japan, where learners have very few opportunities to use the target language in their daily lives, social learning spaces have an important role to play as places where students can interact with ideas and with other people and negotiate meaning. Although there are examples of informal social learning spaces being set up and managed by the learners themselves in the community, such as English corners in China (Gao, 2009), the English Café in Ankara, Turkey, studied by Balçikanli (2018), and the Language Cafe project in Europe (Davis & Holdom, 2008), most of the literature so far concerns social language learning spaces in self-access learning facilities at institutions of further education, such as the L-café in Okayama University (Murray & Fujishima, 2016b), and the English Lounge at KUIS, the subject of the present study.

Social Learning Spaces in Self-Access Centres

Social learning spaces and autonomy

An important aim of Self-Access Learning Centres (SALCs), including the SALC at KUIS, is to support students in the development of learner autonomy (Gardner & Miller, 1999). There are multiple and varied definitions of learner autonomy, and it is not possible to provide a full discussion here, but one early definition on which much later work is based is by Holec (1981: 3), who defines it as 'the ability to take charge of one's own learning'. This involves holding the responsibility for setting goals; selecting resources and strategies; and monitoring, evaluating and reflecting on one's learning. Benson (2001: 47) later modified this definition of autonomy to 'the capacity to take control of one's learning', with the components of this capacity being the 'ability, desire and freedom' to control learning (Huang & Benson, 2013: 9). Autonomy is not a matter of a learner being either autonomous or not autonomous, rather it is a matter of degrees (Nunan, 1997) and may 'take different forms for different individuals, and even for the same individual in different contexts or at different times' (Benson, 2001: 47). While autonomy cannot be taught, it can be fostered. A learner's use of a self-access centre does not necessarily by itself lead to greater autonomy (Benson, 2001), so SALCs aim to help learners to develop the awareness, knowledge and skills that they need in order to be able and willing to take control of their own learning. With a focus on the learner as an individual, SALCs accommodate 'learners of different levels, styles, goals and interests' (Cotterall & Reinders, 2000: 2), and provide them with the resources, opportunities and support to help them make their own decisions about what, when, where, how and why to learn.

This focus on the individual has often led to the misconception that autonomous learning means learning in isolation (Benson, 2001; Murray, 2014a), and indeed the emphasis in early SALCs was on providing support for learners working on their own. In the last two decades, however, we have seen an increase in the provision of opportunities for social interaction in many SALCs. While early research on L2 acquisition was focused on individual cognitive processes, from the 1990s onwards there has been a movement to broaden the parameters of the field to take into account the social aspects of language learning (Block, 2003; Firth & Wagner, 1997). Social approaches such as situated learning theory (Lave & Wenger, 1991), sociocultural theory (Lantolf & Thorne, 2006) and complexity theory (Larsen-Freeman & Cameron, 2008) have emphasised that language learning and use take place in social, cultural and historical contexts by which they are conditioned and from which they should not be abstracted (Benson & Cooker, 2013a). At the same time, however, there has also been a greater recognition of the social dimensions of learner autonomy as a construct that develops through interdependence and collaboration (Benson & Cooker, 2013a; Murray, 2014a). Oxford (2003), for example, drawing on Vygotsky's (1987: 78) notion of the zone of proximal development, describes autonomy from a sociocultural perspective as 'self-regulation, gained through social interaction with a more capable, mediating person in a particular setting'. The provision of social learning spaces in SALCs gives learners a space in which they can learn with and from each other, developing their autonomy collectively.

Affordances for learning and growth

When learners, working as autonomous agents, come together and interact, possibilities for learning open up that would not otherwise exist. The most in-depth study of a social language learning space to date is by Murray and Fujishima (2013, 2016b), whose five-year ethnographic study of the English Café (later called L-café) at their university in Okayama, Japan, started as a project to identify what opportunities for language learning were available in their space. Initially focusing on communities of practice (CoP), they have since drawn on constructs from human geography, mediated discourse analysis and CDS theory to conclude that 'how learners imagine a space to be, perceive it, define it, and articulate their understandings transforms a space into a place, determines what they do there, and influences their autonomy' (Murray et al., 2014: 81). Viewing places as 'emergent phenomena' – the product of action and discourse – they consider the social learning space to be a complex dynamic ecosocial system in which 'elements on one level of organization interact and self-organize to generate something new on a more macro level of organization' (Murray & Fujishima, 2016a: 8). To allow room for the self-organisation of elements in the process of emergence, autonomy is essential. In this they refer to Davis and Sumara (2006), who write that distributed or decentralised control is one of the components necessary for complex emergence in educational environments, alongside neighbour interactions, randomness, coherence, internal diversity and internal redundancy. To this list, Murray and Fujishima add reciprocity and the design elements of the physical space as further necessary components (Murray, 2017b; Murray & Fujishima, 2016c).

When the elements necessary for complex emergence work together, a social learning space can foster a wide range of affordances which emerge, in unpredictable and unplanned ways, as learners interact with the environment. Drawing on the work of Van Lier (2004), Murray and Fujishima (2016c: 127) define affordances as 'potential for action that are transformed into learning opportunities as students participate in a space'. In addition to the opportunities for the improvement of oral proficiency through social interaction, social learning spaces also afford their users various further possibilities for 'linguistic, intellectual, and personal development' (Murray & Fujishima, 2016c: 146), examples of which can be found in the literature. For example, Acuña González et al. (2015) recount that the spirit of cooperation that has developed between students in their SALC goes beyond the peer conversation sessions in which it starts and extends into collaboration in other language learning activities, such as reading the same book or working on projects together, with the students learning reciprocally from each other. Furthermore, students can offer each other emotional support and encouragement in their learning (Gao, 2009), and motivate each other in their studies (Kuwada, 2016; Miura, 2016).

In addition to fostering a wide range of affordances for language learning, social learning spaces can also provide an intercultural experience through which students can learn new cultures and worldviews (Kurokawa *et al.*, 2013). By acting as 'another society' (Miyake, 2016: 87), social learning spaces can be places where students can learn about other cultures, deepen their understanding of their own culture (Nakamoto, 2016) and develop 'an open mind and a global view' (Fujimoto, 2016: 37). Nakamoto (2016: 83), a student who uses the L-café, describes it as being 'like an airport', where the users have an opportunity to 'visit' other countries and make a 'series of discoveries'. For many, a social learning space is a place to make friends (Miyake, 2016; Tanimoto, 2016), and to give and receive advice, both on matters connected to language learning such as study abroad and language learning strategies, and on issues in daily life (Balçikanli, 2018; Gao, 2009). Such spaces may also help students develop their broader social interaction skills, such as overcoming shyness (Kuwada, 2016) and learning to express their own opinions with more assertiveness (Gao, 2009). By taking part in the organisation of the community, students can also develop valuable skills for their future, such as leadership qualities (Dean & Sugiura, 2017; Gao, 2009). Furthermore, noting the relationship between 'space and place, identity development and self-actualization', Murray and Fujishima (2016c: 128) also see social learning spaces as places that play a role in the emergence of a learner's L2 identity, a process we investigate in more depth in this study.

Finally, Murray (2017a: 124) also contends that 'autonomy is an emergent phenomenon [which arises] from the learner's interaction with the environment'. In the L-café, as in other informal social learning spaces, students can exercise their agency to decide when to come and go and what activities, if any, to take part in, taking responsibility for their own learning and acting, or not acting, on the affordances they perceive. At the same time, the autonomy to interact in the environment in ways that suit them enables learners to take part in the emergence of new possibilities for learning. In other words, autonomy retroacts and produces more autonomy (Murray, 2017a; Murray & Fujishima, 2013).

Future directions in self-access learning

This broad range of affordances can provide a persuasive rationale for creating and supporting social learning spaces. Indeed, the provision of social learning spaces may be necessary for the future survival of SALCs. In order to survive and thrive, self-access facilities need to respond to changes in other settings in their learners' language learning environments. Two recent shifts which might present a threat to physical self-access centres are a greater emphasis on promoting autonomous lifelong learning from within the classroom, and the increased availability of digital or online settings in which language learners can access resources, communities of users and practice opportunities (Mynard, 2016). Reinders (2012: 4) even suggests that the 'need for a physical space [...] seems unnecessary and restrictive' given the access which learners now have to materials for learning and ways to practice in 'new learning environments'. Mynard (2016: 334), however, argues that there will still be a need and purpose for physical self-access centres as long as they retain a 'focus on the social dimensions of learning' and remain 'social hubs' where users can learn collaboratively with fellow students. Hobbs and Dofs (2018) also contend that with the wider adoption of new online and blended learning and teaching pedagogies that require students to act with a greater degree of independence and control over their learning, there is even more need for face-to-face support for students in the development of their autonomy, whether from learning advisors or from peers in informal learning spaces. Mynard (2016) references a study by Hughes *et al.* (2012: 163) which found that the most significant motivational factor for sustained use of their centre was 'social collaborative learning amongst peers'. This correlates with Allhouse's (2015: 133) survey of SALCs in higher education institutions in the UK, which revealed that SALCs which have a focus on materials-based provision have seen declining usage figures, whereas SALCs with a focus on social learning and interaction are often 'thriving'. Therefore, it appears that if SALCs wish to remain relevant in the future, they need to offer more opportunities for interaction.

Student Engagement in Social Learning Spaces

Much of the literature on social learning spaces, including research previously conducted at the English Lounge at KUIS, is concerned with student motivation for using or not using such spaces and how to increase the depth and breadth of student engagement with the spaces. This is perhaps unsurprising given the resources, either financial or human, that educational institutions or groups of learners commit to setting up and running a space. Inevitably, there will be a demand for a return on the investment of time or money, with head counts being one of the blunt statistical measurements most frequently used to evaluate success and, in some cases, ensure continued funding (Bibby *et al.*, 2016; Morrison, 2005; Thornton & Noguchi, 2016). As a relatively recent innovation in, or rethinking of, SALCs, social learning spaces have been through a trial-and-error phase, and the sharing of successes and setbacks by early practitioners has helped establish best practices for those looking to create or improve their own social learning space.

The first hurdle is raising awareness of the existence and the purpose of the space among the target group of learners. A number of papers on social learning spaces have detailed various multimodal methods that have been successfully used for publicising the services available and attracting students, including face-to-face methods such as word of mouth and approaching students outside the canteen; paper-based methods such as flyers and posters around campus (particularly posters featuring people with whom the students can identify); online methods such as e-newsletters, websites and social media; and awareness-raising activities such as orientations, campus tours and class visits (Bibby *et al.*, 2016; LeBane *et al.*, 2016; Taylor, 2014; Uzuka, 2016). In the case of KUIS, for example, all students are introduced to the English Lounge through an orientation to the SALC, and events in the space are advertised through social media and on message boards in the SALC.

Nevertheless, even with attractive publicity that catches students' attention and informs them of the purpose and function of a space, it may still be the case that only a relatively small number of students choose to use it, a situation that causes disappointment for those who have put effort into creating a facility that they believe will be of great educational benefit for the potential users (Taylor *et al.*, 2012; Thompson & Atkinson, 2010). The literature suggests various reasons why students choose not to use such spaces. LeBane *et al.* (2016) report that many of their students do not feel the need for or understand the importance of practicing their productive language skills outside class. Even those who do feel the need may be anxious or shy about entering the space, a situation echoed by Fujimoto (2016) and Uzuka (2016), with anxiety about language level and a belief that one must already have a high language proficiency presenting further hindrances to participation (Bibby *et al.*, 2016). A further issue may be that even if a student becomes a regular user, their usage may wane over time. Both Murray and Fujishima (2016b) and LeBane *et al.* (2016) report a drop in attendance after the second year of university, a trend which is found in the English Lounge at KUIS too (Rose & Elliott, 2010). Furthermore, when a space has few users, it can lack the vibrant atmosphere necessary to attract new users, leading to a negative feedback loop of underuse (Taylor *et al.*, 2012).

In order to attract and retain users, it is necessary for the students to believe that the space can be useful in fulfilling their own language learning needs, for them to have the confidence to take the first step in engaging with the space, for them to feel welcomed once they take that step and for them to experience 'a good balance of success and challenge' in their interactions in the space (Thornton, 2016: 297). When this isn't happening, it is necessary to examine how the space is set up and to determine what factors are deterring students from trying out the space or, once they have experienced it for the first time, from engaging with it more deeply as frequent, repeat users. What is successful in one social learning space will not necessarily be successful in another, however, as Thompson and Atkinson (2010) discovered when they tried to set up a SALC based on the KUIS model in a university where the students had a much lower recognition of the benefits of self-access learning. Davis and Sumara (2008: 42) write that 'given the idiosyncratic characters, recursively elaborative, and ever-divergent possibilities of complex phenomena, accounts of complexity-informed research can never be offered as events to be replicated or even held up as models'. While there is much to be learnt from studying other spaces, it is necessary to remember that each setting has its own particularities. Mynard (2019) reminds us of the importance of gaining an understanding of the particular needs and preferences of the students in a particular context, for example through a needs analysis. When deciding how to create a social environment that is appealing to learners, it is key to listen to student voices and involve them in the process (Acuña González *et al.*, 2015; Mynard, 2016). Taylor (2014), Uzuka (2016) and KUIS's Chen and Mynard (2018), for example, all report on projects in which they successfully collaborated with students in the redesigning of a social learning space. Dofs and Hobbs (2011: 35) state that there is mutual benefit for both the students and the self-access facility when students develop a 'feeling of ownership over the centre', and that current students have a good understanding of the 'likes, dislikes, preferences and interests' of the target learner group. Malcolm (2011: 72) also endorses 'a "bottom up" approach, originating from the students' own ideas', rather than 'a "top down" one, based on "instructors'" conceptions of what is needed to help students on the road to learner independence'. From a complex systems perspective, Murray (2017a) explains that involving students in the decision-making process is a way of distributing control, which supports autonomy and allows for the opening up of new learning possibilities. Students are able to draw on resources from outside systems and bring a 'wide range of diverse resources' to the open complex system of the social learning space (Murray & Fujishima, 2016c: 135).

Previous attention given to social learning spaces, including work done at KUIS, falls into three main areas: (i) exploring the *difference* between the social learning space and the classroom, and the need to create a learning environment that is 'not a classroom'; (ii) exploring the *connection* between the social learning space and the classroom and what can be done to support students' use of the space from within the classroom; and (iii) supporting the formation of a community of users and investigating how to integrate newcomers into that community. The following is an overview of the literature in these three areas.

(i) Differences between the social learning space and the classroom

A principle of KUIS's SALC from its creation, which also applies to the English Lounge, was that the learning environment should not 'feel like a typical university library or classroom' but instead should have a 'relaxed ambience… where students would choose to hang out and speak English' (Cooker, 2010: 8). Gillies (2010) found that this environment, particularly the contrast with the classroom and the perception that it is like being in a foreign country, played an important role in influencing students' attitudes towards the SALC. Using Dörnyei's (2005) L2 motivational self system as a theoretical framework, Gillies (2010: 199) reports that for students with a strong ideal L2 self, regardless of their level of proficiency, being in this study-abroad-like environment which affords 'authentic' English use reduces 'the discrepancy between their current L2 self and their ideal L2 self' and hence increases their motivation for learning English. The creation of a 'different' space involves various aspects, including staffing, the physical environment, the language policy and the level of control given to the students.

(a) Staffing

A significant component in this 'different' environment is the facilitator, whose role in the lounge is very different to that of the classroom teacher. Even in student-run social learning spaces, such as the English corners in China reported on by Gao (2009) and the English Café in Ankara studied by Balçikanli (2018), there is a need for leaders to organise and facilitate conversations and support learners who are new to the space. Within educational institutions, these facilitators may be volunteers or paid staff, and may be one or a combination of language learner peers, international students, dedicated staff or classroom teachers, each of whom allows for the emergence of different affordances. In addition to the above-noted benefits of involving students in the organisation of the space, student staff may also be more comfortable with their peers (Uzuka, 2016) and more understanding of how first-time visitors feel (Miura, 2016). For Acuña González *et al.* (2015: 317), the volunteer student helpers in their SALC brought 'social energy, engagement and imagination' to the community. Taylor (2014), nevertheless, notes the need for careful selection and training of student staff for the lounge to function well.

The participation of 'native' or 'near-native' speakers, on the other hand, can help to create a cultural context which fosters the development of students' sociolinguistic competence, which may be difficult to improve through interaction with peers alone (Rose & Elliot, 2010). As regards the use of teachers as facilitators, Bibby *et al.* (2016) suggest that the relationships between teachers and students can influence if, when and how often students choose to visit their conversation lounge. They recommend that conversation lounges choose staff who are 'approachable, amiable, and easy to talk to' (Bibby *et al.*, 2016: 305). While the opportunity to talk to highly proficient English speakers can be a motivating factor that attracts some students to the SALC, Gillies' 2007 study at KUIS found that not knowing the teachers well enough can be a source of anxiety that demotivates other students from using the lounge. Rose and Elliott (2010) also discuss the misalignment between some KUIS students' expectation that the teacher will be the leader and focal point of the conversation and the teachers' understanding that they should be an equal partner with the student, sharing responsibility for initiating and sustaining the conversation. Gillies (2007) recognises the cultural factors at play here and understands that students who come from an education system that does not encourage autonomy may struggle to adapt to this new ideology.

(b) Physical environment

The physical aspects of a learning environment can both enhance and limit the students' learning experiences. In order to attract users and encourage them to spend time in the space, it is necessary to create a comfortable, 'relaxed, non-threatening mood' (Taylor, 2014: 5), which can help to reduce learners' anxiety and encourage them to take risks. What happens in a social learning space is very different from what happens in a typical classroom or library. In discussing the principles of self-access that were followed in the set-up of the SALC at KUIS, Cooker (2010: 8) explains that the design of the physical space plays an important role in creating a feeling that is 'different' and unlike other institutional settings.

Factors to consider among others are (1) the visibility and accessibility of the location (Bibby *et al.*, 2016; Tahara, 2016); (2) the affordances for individual/collaborative work and privacy/openness allowed by the type of furniture, the way it is laid out and the way it can be moved (Edlin, 2016; Fujimoto, 2016; Taylor, 2014); and (3) the mood created by the colour scheme, lighting, accessories, decorations, background music/noises, etc. (Taylor, 2014). Murray *et al.* (2018: 243) found that attractive and welcoming décor can 'speak to learners' imaginations and help them envisage the possibility of making a place for themselves'. From a complex systems perspective, the physical environment is an active agent of the larger ecosocial system and operates together with the other interrelated elements of the system that support complex emergence (Murray, 2017b; Murray & Fujishima, 2016c). A change in the physical environment will influence how people interact in and with the space and 'can serve to centralize or decentralize control as well as facilitate or inhibit neighbor interactions' (Murray & Fujishima, 2016c: 146). An example from KUIS is the change of the layout of the sofas from forming one enclosed area to being placed in several smaller open clusters, on the recommendation of the student users. This change, which is mentioned in Chapter 5 by one of our student participants as having a positive effect, enabled the area to be used by various groups rather than only one group of regulars, making the space less intimidating and easier for less-confident students to access (Chen & Mynard, 2018).

(c) Language policy

Another important aspect of the learning environment is the language(s) being spoken there. The English Lounge at KUIS is located on the upper floor of the two-storey SALC, which has an English-only policy in order to encourage the practice of the target language. However, this policy is not strictly enforced, and some students complain that other students sometimes use Japanese there (News from the SALC, 2016b). Imamura (2018) outlines how the policy was developed in consultation with students and what actions are being taken to promote the policy. These actions include signage, events, in-class workshops and activities within the lounge organised by student staff. The issue of how to set and enforce the language policy for a target language practice environment can be a polarising one, with both staff and students taking a position somewhere along a continuum from strict enforcement at one end, through a middle ground of encouragement of target language use, to no intervention at all at the other end (see Chapter 16: Figure 16.2 for details, and Chapter 5 for an example of one student's reaction to the policy).

Removing student choice is a contentious decision in learning spaces which aim to promote learner autonomy, yet many social learning spaces uphold such a policy. While a strictly enforced English-only policy can provide the support needed to encourage a hesitant student to use English, it may also have the opposite effect of creating a barrier to entering the space for those students who lack confidence in their English ability (Adamson *et al.*, 2012). Werner and Von Joo (2018), for example, outline their decision to take a translanguaging approach in order to welcome rather than scare students away from their Community Learning International Plaza, where international communication is the main goal. Thornton and Noguchi (2016) also report on a decision to abolish the English-only policy in their Café Space in order to encourage more use of the space by lower-proficiency learners. Although their data shows that study-focused use of the space indeed increased as a result, the amount of English being *spoken* decreased. In response, they have taken a middle route by introducing a '10-minute Active English Time', which takes place every hour. In facilities with a stricter policy, there is the question of who should enforce it; students may find it intimidating and difficult to police each other (Taylor, 2014). The setting of policy in a multilingual social learning space becomes an even more complicated matter. No policy was enforced in Okayama University's L-café, a space where multiple target languages can be practiced, but reciprocity was an issue for international students, who found that English was the dominant language with fewer opportunities for them to practice their Japanese (Ho, 2016; Murray & Fujishima, 2016c; Tangonan, 2016).

(d) Student ownership

Other than the use of English, there are few rules regarding what students may or may not do in the English Lounge at KUIS, allowing students to act on varied affordances that emerge as they participate in the space. Hobbs and Dofs (2018: 214) emphasise the importance of designing learning spaces that are learner centred and flexible so that students can 'take ownership of spaces and thereby create their own places for learning autonomously'. In addition to practicing English conversation, students use the lounge at KUIS for eating lunch, doing homework, giving and receiving advice, meeting friends, playing games and relaxing between classes. Furthermore, the conversations that take place are unstructured, with no requirements or limitations placed on the number of interlocutors, the length of the interactions or the topics of conversation. From the point of view of the locus of control (Benson, 2011a), the students have a high level of decision-making power regarding their participation in the space, although the degree of control they have regarding the activities they do in the space depends to some extent on who else is using the space at the time.

Gillies (2010) found that many KUIS students with a strong ideal L2 self prefer the lounge to the classroom due to the greater freedom of choice, e.g. regarding the topic of conversation. Murray (2017a) highlights the relationship between autonomy and change, writing that students engage in autonomous behaviour (such as integrating the lounge into their language learning environment) because they want to bring about changes in their lives in order to move closer to their vision of what they want their future self to be. However, Gillies (2010) also found that for those students who are motivated by a stronger ought-to self and who lack confidence in their English ability, the absence of scaffolding in the lounge as compared to the classroom can be anxiety inducing. Instead of seeing the constraints of the classroom as a lack of freedom, they instead embrace them 'as shelter, safety, and freedom from responsibility' (Gillies, 2010: 203). Gillies (2010: 204) concludes that some students avoid the SALC because 'it does not meet their "motivational needs"'.

(ii) Connection to the classroom

As noted above, self-directed learning is a difficult concept to adjust to for many students, especially those who have come from a more teacher-directed educational background such as that in Japanese high schools. Creating a link between the learning space and what happens in the classroom is one way to encourage and support students in the process of becoming more autonomous language learners (Gardner & Miller, 1999). Various institutions, or teachers within institutions, have used class project work or assigned speaking homework tasks as a way to familiarise their students with the learning space, train them in how to have positive and enjoyable interactions there, reduce their anxiety, increase their motivation and, hopefully, create longer-term independent learning habits (Croker & Ashurova, 2012; Kanno, 2010; Kiyota, 2018; Mayeda *et al.*, 2016; Taylor *et al.*, 2012; Thompson & Atkinson, 2010). Croker and Ashurova (2012) have reported success in scaffolding their students' journeys towards being active members of the community at their World Plaza. However, others warn that students become less intrinsically motivated when usage of the SALC is made compulsory or rewarded externally, and stop attending as soon as the obligation or incentive is removed (Adamson *et al.*, 2012; Bibby *et al.*, 2016; LeBane *et al.*, 2016).

A principle of KUIS's SALC since its creation has been that students should be free to choose if and how they use the resources and services (Cooker, 2010), with the rationale that 'increased motivation and achievement result from learners' perceptions that they, rather than others, are responsible for their own learning successes and failures' (Cooker & Torpey, 2004: 16). Students may choose to come to the lounge to complete speaking tasks assigned as homework by their class teachers; however, like the rest of the SALC, the current institutional policy is that use of the space is optional and non-incentivised.

As in other institutions, lecturers in the English Language Institute (ELI) at KUIS have discussed how to build a bridge between the classroom and the lounge in order to encourage greater participation. An action research project by Rose (2007) at KUIS found that compulsory use of the lounge as an assignment did not encourage further use of the lounge, and while students reacted positively to activities that raised awareness of the benefits of the lounge, the intrinsic motivation generated was not enough to overcome other factors that hindered its use, such as shyness, lack of confidence in English ability and lack of free time. However, an instrumentally motivated activity (a credit-earning speaking diary that students were encouraged to complete in the lounge) was successful in encouraging greater use of the lounge and created a desire in most students to continue using the lounge in the future, although there was no follow-up to determine whether they did continue or not. Rose and Elliott (2010) also found that increased frequency of usage due to speaking assignments leads to greater levels of comfort in the space and greater satisfaction with the area. They conclude that these tasks can have positive benefits for familiarising students with the space, but that they should not continue to be assigned once this has been achieved. They also recommend scaffolding activities in the classroom to better prepare students to take a more active role in their interactions in the space. Gillies (2010: 205) sees such tasks and activities as a way to 'develop a continuum from reactive to proactive autonomy, from ought-to L2 self to ideal self', helping the students to move from extrinsically motivated to intrinsically motivated use of the lounge.

It should be noted that creating a closer connection between the classroom and the SALC requires not only the reallocation of classroom time but also a shift in the role of the teacher (Cooker & Torpey, 2004). Those teachers who are unfamiliar with the philosophy and pedagogy of self-access learning or who do not recognise its value may be resistant to such changes to the syllabi or unsure of how to implement them, and it may well be necessary to provide guidance and support to them too (Adamson *et al.*, 2012; Dofs & Hobbs, 2011; Mayeda *et al.*, 2016).

(iii) Access and belonging

Whether students first come to a social learning space of their own volition or as part of an assigned homework task, taking the first step of entering the space can be an anxiety-inducing experience. Fujimoto (2016), for example, reports seeing students looking into the L-café at Okayama University with curiosity but being afraid to cross the threshold. Students often report feelings of nervousness, discomfort and worry about their language proficiency levels (Balçikanli, 2018; Gao, 2009; Hughes *et al.*, 2012; Kuwada, 2016), and many of these feelings are connected to the perception that entering a social learning space is entering an already established community.

One framework that has been used to describe the dynamics of a social learning space is Lave and Wenger's (1991) CoP framework, with its concomitant notion of legitimate peripheral participation (Acuña González *et al.*, 2015; Balçikanli, 2018; Bibby *et al.*, 2016; Gillies, 2010; Murray & Fujishima, 2013). Based on the view that learning is a social process in which knowledge is co-constructed, CoP are defined as 'groups of people who share a concern or a passion for something they do and learn how to do it better as they interact regularly' (Wenger-Trayner & Wenger-Trayner, 2015: 1). In social language learning spaces, community members come together to share knowledge and expertise and to support each other, with the common goal of learning a language. Newcomers' participation starts as 'peripheral', perhaps attendance at a cultural event, for example, but through increased engagement with the members and with the shared practices of the group, they can progress to become 'active' members, and then part of the 'core group' (Wenger, 1998; Wenger *et al.*, 2002), taking on, for example, the role of a conversation leader (see Chapter 12 of this volume for a more comprehensive exploration of the literature on CoP and how it relates to social learning spaces).

While the majority of students first choose to visit a social learning space in order to improve their language skills, for many students the reasons for more sustained participation are social, i.e. the students appreciate the opportunities to socialise and make friends, and the ties they create to other users draw them back (Balçikanli, 2018; Hughes *et al.*, 2012). However, the existence of a community of users with close social bonds, the very thing that attracts so many repeat users, can also paradoxically act at the same time as a deterrent and barrier to entry. Some students at the L-café at Okayama University, for example, reported 'a sense of alienation' (Kuwada, 2016: 121), 'an exclusive atmosphere' and an initial sense of feeling that they are an 'outsider' (Hino, 2016: 102). Fukuba (2016), a student, writes that he saw it as a place only for members of the cliques, and after a short period of making an effort to try to fit in, he chose to concentrate on independent study instead.

Gillies (2010) found that KUIS students self-identify early on in their time at the university as users or non users of the lounge, and that factors in non users' avoidance of the lounge include a lack of familiarity with the students and teachers who regularly use the space, and a belief among some non users that one must already have a high level of English proficiency in order to participate in the space. This is corroborated by a survey conducted among the student body by the SALC in 2016 which found that, while those who were frequent users of the lounge overwhelmingly rated it 'Excellent' or 'Good', the overall rating was only 'Satisfactory' (News from the SALC, 2016a). Responses to an open-ended follow-up question showed that the main problems stemmed from issues of accessibility such as the domination of the space by a group of regular users ('same students always use the Yellow Sofa and it is difficult to enter the community if you are not a member'), the difficulty of talking to teachers or a belief that a high level of English ability is necessary to participate ('There's no welcoming atmosphere for students who are not good at speaking in English. The SALC is only for students who have high motivation. I was little disappointed') (News from the SALC, 2016b).

The question of how to welcome and integrate newcomers into the community, then, is an important one. Students report that early use of social learning spaces can be difficult or awkward without a specific reason or purpose for going there (Fukuba, 2016; Hino, 2016; Miyake, 2016); consequently, many social learning spaces use cultural and seasonal social events or classes and workshops as a way to draw first-time users into the space (Bibby *et al.*, 2016; Croker & Ashurova, 2012; Murray *et al.*, 2018). The English Lounge at KUIS, for example, hosts a monthly tea party and larger events in the summer, at Halloween and at Christmas. This gives newcomers a taste of the community and an opportunity to build up relationships with the lecturers and student members of that community. It is also a chance for newcomers to see for themselves that students of all levels of proficiency, not just high-level students, are using the space, and to have interactions with near peer role models (NPRMs) (Murphey, 1998), which will hopefully create the motivation to return again (Bibby *et al.*, 2016). In this respect, Igarashi (2016: 51) celebrates the fluid nature of a social learning space as a 'heterotopia where different identities and interests meet temporarily'. She cites Michel Foucault's (1986) definition of a heterotopia as 'a place that is capable of juxtaposing several spaces in a single real space and creates an illusion of other places that are there or nowhere' (Igarashi, 2016: 51). The ability to use a space in a multitude of ways allows the creation of a variety of pathways or 'initiation rite[s] to enter' (Igarashi, 2016: 58).

How students are welcomed into the space on those early visits can determine whether they become long-term participators. After greeting newcomers and showing interest in them by asking some simple questions, Bibby *et al.* (2016) suggest allowing newer users to participate in conversations as little or as much as they feel comfortable, stating that it is important not to force them to speak. Through such legitimate peripheral participation (Lave & Wenger, 1991), newcomers can gain familiarity and confidence before progressing to deeper levels of engagement with the community. The English Lounge at KUIS has a large collection of board games, for example, and the use of artefacts such as games and musical instruments can be an effective way to allow lower-level or less-confident students to enjoy participating without the pressure of continuous conversation (Acuña González *et al.*, 2015; Taylor, 2014).

As is the case in Japan (see Chapter 3), students from educational backgrounds that have not had a focus on developing communicative ability may need support in sustaining an interaction in a 'non-formulaic way' (Bibby *et al.*, 2016: 308). Lower-level learners may feel intimidated in interactions with higher-level learners, and one option might be to provide separate events or conversation groups for them, such as the 'Beginners' Paradise' mentioned by Croker and Ashurova (2012). However, separating lower-level learners denies them the benefits of interaction with NPRMs. Conversation leaders in Acuña González *et al.*'s (2015: 319) lounge, for example, considered not mixing students of different proficiency levels in order to provide more attention and support to those of a lower level, but ultimately decided that 'mixed levels are an enriching factor of the speaking practice experience as it is closer to reality'. At the English Lounge at KUIS, students of all levels are mixed.

Trying to maintain a community that is both tight-knit and open to newcomers is a difficult balancing act, and L-café manager Fujimoto (2016: 33) had to consider how to 'make the sense of comradeship less visible without destroying the sense of belongingness experienced by the regular visitors'. However, Murray *et al.* (2018: 237) remind us that it is ultimately the student who has to take the responsibility of navigating their way through the various stages of 'entering the physical space, gaining access to the social groups on the inside, making a place for oneself, maintaining one's place and possibly losing one's place'. While there are steps that organisers of social learning spaces can take to support students, we should not impose 'conditions that might impede the emergence of affordances for learning and social engagement' (Murray *et al.*, 2018:

244). Furthermore, CoP are self-organising and self-sustaining. It is worth noting that the managers of the spaces in the Murray and Fujishima (2013) and Acuña González *et al.* (2015) studies did not start with the intention of creating a CoP, rather the community emerged 'from the actions of people within a group as they interact and engage in activities or events' (Murray & Fujishima, 2013: 151). The sustaining of the community is not the responsibility of the manager but of each member of the community, and Murray and Fujishima (2016c: 130, citing Lewis, 2014: 43) remind us that the success of a social language learning space 'depends in large measure on human sociality' which encompasses 'empathy, altruism, reciprocity, a sense of fairness and a predisposition to collaborate'.

An avenue of possible further research in social learning spaces is how the affordances of participatory websites and social media tools could be leveraged to create a digital habitat that complements, supports and enhances the physical space. One smaller-scale example given by Gao (2009) is that of an English club using a web forum to enable discussion outside of club meeting times. Uchida (2016: 71) argues that a digital habitat would 'provide a new "entrance" to the L-café, enhance present participation and ensure that the L-café becomes a more public and sustainable community of learners'. The combination of physical and virtual participation would create synergies and develop further opportunities for learning, while the use of asynchronous and non-location-specific tools would allow students, especially those who are shy or hesitant, new pathways to access, participate in and gain membership of the community.

The Present Study

The move into a new building in 2017 gave us an opportunity to re-evaluate the English Lounge and consider potential interventions to ensure that it continues to meet the needs of the students. No research had been conducted there since Gillies' (2010) and Rose and Elliott's (2010) studies, and we were still contending with many of the same issues as other social learning spaces, as outlined above, such as how to encourage reluctant students to visit and then continue to use the lounge, how best to arrange the physical space, how to set and enforce the language policy and how to make the lounge accessible to all students who would like to use it. We could see that there were some very complex and interesting dynamics at play in the lounge, with identity, beliefs and membership of a community all having an influence on students' perceptions and use (or non-use) of the space. At the same time, we suspected that as the students engaged with the space, they were shaping the space and the space was shaping them. Seeking a deeper understanding of those dynamics, we embarked on this project. The rest of this book will explore how we attempted to answer our questions and what we discovered in the process.

3 The Japanese Educational Context

Michael Burke and Daniel Hooper

As we have seen in Chapter 2, one of the roles of a social learning space includes providing opportunities for interaction in the target language. This is especially relevant for English as a foreign language (EFL) contexts like Japan where there are few opportunities for communicating in English or other languages. This chapter will explore the sociocultural considerations and practices particular to the English education system in Japan in order to explain the relevance the English Lounge has for the learners in our study. We aim to provide readers unfamiliar with the Japanese educational context with the contextual information needed to make sense of what comes in the chapters that follow this one. We begin with a brief explanation of the role of English education in contemporary Japanese society and the significant resources allocated to it. Next, we will detail the lasting impact that certain historical trends and cultural practices have on contemporary English education in Japan and, more specifically, foreshadow how they relate to the specific learners in our study.

English Language Education in Japanese Primary, Secondary and Extracurricular Schools

A focus on English education has gradually increased in both compulsory primary and secondary schooling throughout the past few decades in Japan, with English learning also having a significant commercial presence through the extracurricular education industry. In this section, we provide a brief overview of these educational contexts and discuss the relative place for social learning spaces in the wider landscape. Since 2011, compulsory English education in Japan begins for students in their fifth and sixth years of elementary school, i.e. for children aged 10–12. The amount of English instruction again increases substantially throughout the three years of junior high school up to age 15 (Tahira, 2012). In high school, for students aged between 15 and 18, English is effectively, if not officially, compulsory, not least because it is a vital component for the entrance examination to most, if not all, prestigious universities. According to official government policy, English education in Japan is viewed as a top priority. To reflect this intention, in 2018 the Japanese Ministry of Education, Culture, Sports, Science and Technology (MEXT) announced plans to significantly increase the allocation for English lessons, and they have announced that by 2020 they plan to increase this even further (MEXT, 2017; Nemoto, 2018), while also continuing a push for English classes carried out purely in English in junior high and high school (Machida, 2019).

Another important area for English language education in Japan is extracurricular schools such as *juku* (cram schools) and *eikaiwa gakkou* (private English conversation schools). Empirical data is scant, but the Organisation for Economic Co-operation and Development (OECD) (2015) claims that 53% of Japanese attend extracurricular schools at some point during their lifetime. Furthermore, despite the well-publicised collapse of a number of large chain *eikaiwa gakkou* ('Eikaiwa Gakkou no Jios ga Hasan Shinsei', 2010; Stubbings, 2007), official government data from the Ministry of Economy, Trade and Industry (2019) on the scale of the private language school sector indicates that it maintains a considerable presence, employing over 10,000 instructors across Japan. Based on the above, it appears that English language instruction is still the focus of a significant amount of attention within both the public and private educational sectors. Nevertheless, MEXT recognises that Japanese students' communicative English proficiencies remain insufficient to meet the challenges of globalisation (MEXT, 2014).

A number of studies over the past 20 years have indicated that this lack of communicative proficiency comes as a consequence of teachers' lack of familiarity, training and confidence in communicative language teaching (CLT) (Gorsuch, 2000; Nishino, 2008; Sakui, 2004) and an overemphasis on grammar-translation and audiolingual methods of instruction (Tahira, 2012), which are intended to prepare students for school and university entrance examinations that remain heavily weighted towards grammar and vocabulary (McVeigh, 2002). In addition, in Japan, a traditional belief still exists that the study of languages is first and foremost an intellectual pursuit as opposed to a tool to facilitate communication (Mynard, 2019).

On the surface then, social learning spaces, which prioritise learning through casual interaction in English, might seem like exactly what is needed for the context. However, there may be certain underlying contextual influences that are particular to Japan due to Japanese students' lack of English communicative proficiency and teachers' reticence to utilise CLT. In this chapter, we will examine these influences, discuss how they might affect students' identities and suggest what this might mean for social learning spaces.

Japan's Tempestuous Relationship with English

According to McVeigh (2004: 211), Japan has a 'love-hate relationship with English'. This tempestuous relationship is reflected in an undulating succession of fervour for and resistance to the English language and the foreign influence it contains (Bouchard, 2017). Some of the earliest engagement in English education following the Meiji Restoration (when Japan opened up to the outside world in 1868 after over two centuries of isolationist foreign policy) deliberately aimed to 'decode information from foreign sources' (Bouchard, 2017: 2) to facilitate modernisation and industrialisation based on a Western model. In contrast, the role of English as a means of intercultural communication was largely sidelined during this period. This strongly instrumental approach to language learning continued into the 20th century, manifesting itself in the *juken-eigo* (exam English) that appeared at the end of the Meiji period (around 1912). *Juken-eigo* emphasises sentence-level analysis of grammar and vocabulary memorisation for the purposes of test taking and has no communicative component (Fujimoto-Adamson, 2006; Hiramoto, 2013). Eventually, however, due to the growing awareness of a lack of English communicative ability among Japanese students, the government increasingly looked towards modern Western approaches to English education. As a consequence of the above, Japan has invited assistant language teachers (ALTs) – largely 'native speakers' from inner circle countries (Kachru, 1985) – to work in primary and secondary schools in order to fill the communicative gap of the past 50 years, starting in 1976 (Wada, 1987). More recently, MEXT's (2014) English Education Reform Plan Responding to the Rapid Globalization aims to put ALTs in all elementary schools by 2019 and to better promote their use in junior and senior high schools, so as to achieve more communicative ends. However, despite government-mandated attempts to change English language teaching (ELT) methodology via the Courses of Study implemented by MEXT, there remains a perceivable gap between these interventions and the realities of classroom teaching (Fujimoto-Adamson, 2006). This rift between exam English and communicative English represents a tension that Bouchard (2017: 3) claims is 'one of the most enduring characteristics of the Japanese EFL system', which will be discussed in greater detail in the sections that follow.

The English Dichotomy in Japan

Due to the divergence between *juken-eigo* and communicatively-focused English instruction and how this relates to the status and use of English in Japan, several researchers have claimed that an ideological dichotomy exists within Japanese ELT (Hiramoto, 2013; Hones & Law, 1989; McVeigh, 2004; Nagatomo, 2012, 2016). On one side of this division is *eigo*, an approach to English instruction based on *yakudoku* (direct sentence-level translation prevalent since the Meiji Restoration) (Law, 1995) and the aforementioned exam-oriented *juken-eigo*. *Eigo* generally regards English in the same way it was during the Meiji period, a code that can be deciphered and framed objectively and aimed predominantly at helping learners to pass standardised tests by developing knowledge of vocabulary and grammatical forms. As will be illustrated in later chapters, this was indeed the instructional approach that the majority of our participants experienced in their secondary English education. Furthermore, this experience appeared to have had a marked influence on their learner identities and their perceptions regarding the role of the English Lounge.

The flipside to *eigo* is *eikaiwa* or 'English conversation', which is largely based on developing oral proficiency. It draws on 'Western' methodologies such as CLT, and aims to foster communicative competence (Canale & Swain, 1980) in English. Stephens (2002: 89) describes *eigo* and *eikaiwa* as being 'indicative of how speaking the language is regarded as being separate from the language itself'. McVeigh (2004) and Nagatomo (2016) argue that *eigo* and *eikaiwa* represent, respectively, 'Japanese' and 'non-Japanese' versions of English and that this is reflected in socially ascribed roles for English teachers in Japan. These analysts observe that *eigo* is almost always taught by Japanese teachers, and *eikaiwa* by foreign teachers.

Nagatomo (2016) also raises the idea of the ideologically charged distinction between *eigo* and *eikaiwa* as competing sets of assumptions about language learning in Japan and a potential source of conflict. In interviews with foreign teachers in Japan, she found evidence that led her to state that *eikaiwa* was framed by some Japanese teachers as somehow inferior to the 'proper English' (Nagatomo, 2016: 134) that *eigo* represents. The slightly pejorative attitude reported to exist in Japan towards *eikaiwa* is embodied in accounts of team teaching between Japanese teachers of English (JTEs) and subordinate foreign ALTs in secondary education. Due to some JTEs' beliefs that *eigo*, rather than communicative proficiency in English, is useful for high-stakes entrance exams, *eikaiwa* has at times been relegated to something akin to a 'sideshow' to grammar-translation lessons (Sakui, 2004). Several scholars have also criticised *eikaiwa* and 'communicative' English in Japan for having an overwhelming focus on 'native speaker' teachers and 'Western-centric' methodologies such as CLT that may not gel with the contextual realities of Japanese classrooms due to factors such as students' and parents' expectations of classroom practice, or washback from high-stakes standardised tests (Bax, 2003; Holliday, 1994; Tanaka, 2009).

The distinction between *eigo* and *eikaiwa*, as well as the conflict and sociocultural baggage that comes with it, arguably lies at the core of many of the most enduring problems and debates in Japanese secondary language education. Over the last 30 years, MEXT has made efforts to put more emphasis on communication skills other than translation, including, in 1987, the introduction of the Japan Exchange and Teaching (JET) programme in order to achieve more communicative ends and promote internationalisation in schools (CLAIR, 2018). However, despite the JET programme and the call for English-only instruction in junior high and high schools in the 2013 Course of Study, progress has been described as sluggish (Humphries & Burns, 2015; Tahira, 2012). A perceived lack of progress in Japanese secondary education in terms of providing opportunities for communicative language learning may be reflected in the presence of the private English conversation school (*eikaiwa gakkou*) industry (Hiramoto, 2013; Seargeant, 2008). These institutions exist outside of the sphere of formal education and have, in a sense, been acting as a stopgap measure stimulated by negative public perceptions of MEXT's ongoing struggles with implementing communicative English instruction in schools (Hiramoto, 2013). Several studies have explored the gap between MEXT's communicative push and the realities faced by Japanese English teachers in secondary education (Bartlett, 2016; Cook, 2009, 2012; Nishino, 2008, 2011; Sato & Kleinsasser, 2004; Tahira, 2012; Tsukamoto, 2013; Underwood, 2012a). A great many of these studies highlight an incongruence between the top-down governmental reforms and the institutional constraints shaping teachers' practice. In several cases, JTEs had returned from overseas training programmes focusing on CLT or had expressed a desire to teach more communicative lessons but were often incapable of implementing them practically in their workplace. Table 3.1 provides a brief summary of some existing literature on English education in Japanese secondary schools and the perceived obstacles to MEXT's communicatively focused reforms.

As might be expected, the conflict between *eigo* and *eikaiwa* in Japanese schools has also had a significant impact on Japanese students, and a number of studies have examined students' voices on the content of their English classes. Although a study by Matsuura *et al.* (2001) revealed that some students preferred the more traditional *eigo* style of lesson commonplace in schools, other studies (Matsuda, 2011; Miyahara, 2015) have discovered a mismatch in terms of teacher and student expectations of the type of English practice that would serve them best in the future. Through interviewing teachers and students at a private high school, Matsuda (2011) discovered that both groups had significantly different conceptions of what constituted useful language study. While some of the teachers aimed to develop students' metalinguistic/grammatical knowledge in order to prepare them to read about different perspectives on world issues, students often placed value on other facets of English development. Many of the students desired a greater focus on developing English communication skills as they were perceived as 'practical' and important for their personal goal of being able to 'communicate with the

Table 3.1 Perceived obstacles to communicative English teaching in Japanese secondary education

Perceived obstacles to communicative approach	Studies
***Senpai-kohai* dynamic** The hierarchical *senpai-kohai* (senior-junior) dynamic can be found in a wide range of social settings in Japan including schools (Ishikawa, 2012), sports teams (Miller, 2013) and in the business world (Haghirian, 2010). Haghirian (2010: 19) describes the *senpai-kohai* relationship as 'a relay race in which information, experience, and skills are passed from generation to generation'. For an example specific to the educational context of Japan, in some studies it has been found that there is pressure on junior (*kohai*) teachers to teach using a grammar-translation/*yakudoku* approach from senior teachers (*senpai*).	Bartlett (2016); Cook (2009, 2012); Sakui (2004); Sato and Kleinsasser (2004); Underwood (2012a)
Teachers' language anxiety Many teachers have reported that they felt that their English proficiency, particularly in areas such as pronunciation, was insufficient to effectively teach English-medium or communicative lessons.	Glasgow (2013); Humphries and Burns (2015); Machida (2019); Nishino (2011); Suzuki and Roger (2014)
Concerns over testing oral skills Teachers have exhibited concerns over time and staffing demands stemming from large-scale assessment of speaking proficiency.	Bartlett (2016); Nishino (2008, 2011)
Concerns over classroom management Teachers have stated concerns that utilising more open, communicative activities could cause classroom management issues.	Sakui (2004); Underwood (2012a, 2012b)
Concerns over student passivity/proficiency Teachers perceive that Japanese students preferred to learn passively and did not have sufficient proficiency in English to learn using a communicative approach.	Cook (2009, 2012); Kurihara (2008); Matsuura et al. (2001); Suzuki and Roger (2014)
Student/parent expectations Teachers feel that they were pressured to acquiesce to students' or parents' expectations of preferred class content (especially regarding test preparation).	Cook (2009); Underwood (2012a, 2012b)
Lack of teacher training Teachers (both JTEs and ALTs) lack adequate training and information on what communicative language teaching is and how it could be implemented.	Cook (2012); Nishino (2008, 2011); Sakui (2004)
Exam washback Teachers have stated concerns that communicative language practice will not adequately prepare students for the high-stakes entrance exams they are required to take at the end of junior high and high school.	Cook (2009, 2012); Nishino (2008, 2011); Sakui (2004); Suzuki and Roger (2014); Underwood (2012a, 2012b)
Class duration Teachers believe that communicative activities are too time-consuming and not suitable for their 45–50 minute classes.	Nishino (2008, 2011)
Class sizes Teachers' perceive that communicative activities would not be easily implementable in large junior high and high school classes (sometimes 45–50 students per class).	Nishino (2008, 2011); Underwood (2012b)
Lack of preparation time Teachers in secondary schools often have substantial responsibilities outside of teaching, including running club activities and attending meetings. Therefore, some teachers stated that they did not have sufficient time to plan communicative activities for their classes.	Sakui (2004); Sato and Kleinsasser (2004)
Influence of state-mandated textbooks Teachers have reported that the state-mandated textbooks required to be used in classes are not conducive to communicative language teaching.	Cook (2009, 2012); Sato and Kleinsasser (2004); Underwood (2012a, 2012b)

world' (Matsuda, 2011: 47). The student perspectives from Matsuda's study were also observable in Miyahara's (2015) research into learner motivation and identity in university students. Several of the participants in this study (first-year English majors at a private university in Japan) expressed profound dissatisfaction with their junior high and high school English education due to a 'mismatch between [their] conceptualisation of English as a means of communication and the "hidden" school discourse of English as an object of academic study' (Miyahara, 2015: 94). As we will see in later chapters of this book, one participant in our study also specifically highlighted the *eikaiwa* approach of the English Lounge as representing 'practicality' (*jitsuyousei*). She too perceived the development of communicative English ability as being central to her desired future L2 self while also strongly questioning the value of her secondary English education. In total, we found evidence for the *eigo* versus *eikaiwa* dichotomy in all bar one of the case studies, that of Sachiko described in Chapter 9 of this book.

Interdependent Agency

Another approach to shedding light on some of the issues surrounding ELT in formal Japanese education is from a concept known in cross-cultural psychology as interdependent agency. Agency has been defined as the 'socioculturally mediated capacity to act' (Ahearn, 2001: 112) and is rooted in the judgements, intentions and decisions of an individual; however, how these factors develop might be very different from one context to the next (Sampson, 1985). How these judgements, intentions and decisions play out can be understood as 'cultural syndromes', which are subjective and intersubjective cultural themes that explain social and psychological processes (Triandis, 1995). For example, North American and British academic cultures tend to foreground the notions of independence, freedom, choice, ability, individual control and responsibility, personal expression, success, good self-esteem and happiness, and these are how judgements, intentions and decisions are framed in both those contexts (Moscovici, 1984). In the literature on cross-cultural psychology, this cultural syndrome is known as *independent* agency. As we will see in subsequent chapters, some of the regular users of the social learning space described in this book indicated they used the lounge in order to improve their English for self-gain, i.e. to improve their chances of getting a job after graduation. When individuals foreground this over other possible reasons, such as pleasing the other members of a social learning space community, they do so primarily with regard to their own independent self-interest. Pleasing their friends in the community might still be very important, of course, but it is subordinate in terms of how they rank their reasons for participating. Independent agency is widely regarded as the default for the North American and British contexts (Heine *et al.*, 1999; Kuwayama, 1992).

Understanding the Japanese context requires understanding that a different mode of agency is the default. Cross-cultural psychologists argue that agency in Japan is often constructed according to a framework wherein the needs of the wider social group are interwoven with one's own needs (Heine *et al.*, 1999; Kuwayama, 1992). For example, as will be shown in the case studies and discussed in Chapter 13, many of the core members of the social learning space foregrounded their desire to serve the interdependent needs of the wider community above their own needs. Of course, improving their English in order to pass a test and get a well-paying job is also very important, but as is common in the Japanese context, many of our students put strong emphasis on the needs of the wider community, and construct their identities in collaboration with its members. The interdependent agency model shows that it is expected that individuals living in Japan pay a great amount of attention to whether they are supporting the needs of the group, against their own individual needs (Heine *et al.*, 1999; Kuwayama, 1992). As is discussed in Chapter 13, we found evidence for this in our research; indeed, only one of the case studies included in this book, that of Sachiko (Chapter 4), offered no evidence for this cultural pattern of behaviour.

In general, Japanese students are more likely to be motivated to gain esteem by being seen to be working for interdependent interests, rather than their own needs (Hamaguchi, 1985; Kuwayama, 1992). In Chapter 13, we summarise how the drive towards interdependence seemed to incline our students to take ownership of the space so as to make it enjoyable, welcoming and useful for others. We found evidence for this behaviour throughout our research project, and can be seen in the case studies in Chapters 5, 6 and 8.

To conclude, English language education in Japan is mainly oriented towards vocabulary and grammar and has largely failed in instilling communicative ability. As will be explored in later chapters, learners' perceptions of the dichotomous manifestations of *eigo* (grammar/test-oriented English) and *eikaiwa* (English for communication) are influential in shaping their rationale for using the English Lounge and the way they see its role in moving them closer to their future ideal L2 selves. As we will see in later chapters, interdependence, or the tendency to support the needs of a wider community rather than one's own needs, was a recurring theme in our data, which had both positive and negative implications for our social learning space. For example, it encouraged students to take better ownership of the social learning space in order to make it more accessible and useful to others. However, those who saw themselves outside of the community that was already established there reported feeling uncomfortable joining as a consequence of not belonging.

4 Methodology

Michael Burke, Phoebe Lyon and Jo Mynard

In this chapter, we turn to the methodology and the procedures for researching the psychological phenomena in our social learning space. First, to reiterate the overall goal of the research project, we initiated the project with the aim of understanding why some students use the social learning space at our university more than others; how students might cause changes in that space; and how it might, in turn, cause changes in the way they see themselves. We then applied these findings to the wider learning ecology. The overall project is considered to be an ethnography situated within a constructivist paradigm which studies student participation in the English Lounge over several years. Our explorations were informed by (1) observations (Chapter 4); (2) an interpretative analysis (Chapter 4); (3) case studies (Chapters 5–10); (4) analyses using two theoretical models (Chapters 11 and 12); and (5) an examination of the presence of five key individual difference factors (Chapter 13). In this brief overview of the methods, we explain how we gained access to the participants, how we collected the data and how we analysed it. In Chapter 14, we reflect on these methods, examine the limitations and make suggestions for colleagues elsewhere interested in studying social language learning communities.

Our Approach to the Research

Our research is driven by the desire to make sense of the complex processes occurring in the micro-culture of the English Lounge and, in doing so, understand the role of social learning spaces more generally through our analysis. We attempt to understand how the students think, feel and act, and how this has an impact on their participation (or non-participation) in the space. We take the view that the ways in which people interact shape and define the space. In other words:

> Through our actions and discourses, we ascribe meaning to a space and transform it into a place. The product of everyday practices and discourses, places are dynamic and ever-changing. As we participate in

these processes, we appropriate spaces, embody them, impose our identities on them and at the same time have our identities shaped by the places we inhabit and the places we engage in. (Murray & Lamb, 2018: 2)

Our approach to the research was to draw upon multiple perspectives and interpretations from a diverse group of participating researchers and incorporate these views into the planning, data collection and data analysis. In addition to helping us to understand the nature of our social learning space, this kind of research has the educational benefit of enhancing the learning environment for our colleagues and students and, we hope, providing insights for other researchers wishing to do this kind of research. In disseminating our interpretations and involving colleagues and students in an extended and ongoing discussion, we are collectively shifting the focus of the English Lounge in subtle ways both intentionally (e.g. through the implementation of policy and movement of the furniture layout) and unintentionally (i.e. through shifts in thinking, leading to a developing rhetoric and as yet unknown actions).

Part 1: Initial Observation Study

We began the project by conducting systematic observations of the English Lounge in order to give us an initial impression of what was happening in the space. Our approach was a form of participant observation within a natural setting. The goal was to begin to construct a shared intersubjective reality (Hatch, 2002) with the other users of the space. Taking on the role of 'active participants' resulted in conditions that were ideal for providing us with insights into cultural, social and situational factors in the English Lounge (Dörnyei, 2007).

For this section of the research project, our question was:

- What characteristics and behaviours do students who frequent the English Lounge exhibit?

In order to investigate this, we formulated the following sub-questions, informed by Spradley (1980), Benson *et al.* (2013), Block (2007) and Norton (2000):

- How do students enter and leave the space?
- Where do they choose to situate themselves?
- What do they do while they are in the space?
- How do they interact with others?

The observations involved our research team members individually observing participants in the English Lounge in an attempt to learn more about who uses the space, how they use the space and what these insights might indicate about their identities. We were aware of an 'in-group' of very frequent users (subsequently renamed the 'Yellow Sofa (YS) Group' due to the colour of the furniture in the space), and wanted to better understand students' actions in the English Lounge and how the English Lounge might affect or be affected by individuals and groups using the space. We also wanted to learn more about how being part of one of these groups may impact or shape their identity. We conducted 10 observations over a two-week period. The observations were scheduled in advance at times convenient for each of us; however, we tried to cover a range of days and times throughout the week. To promote consistency among the observations, we developed guidelines, an observation form (Appendix 1) and a map of the space (Figure 4.1) for the observers to use. The observation lasted 90 minutes, during which we positioned ourselves in the English Lounge taking field notes, where possible, in real time. The observation form was based on Spradley's (1980) framework that describes '9 dimensions of descriptive observation'. Spradley's framework directs observers to consider space, actors, activities, objects, acts, events, time, goals and feelings. Further considerations came from the literature on communities of practice (CoP) (Lave & Wenger, 1991; Wenger, 1998) as well as the literature on identity (Benson *et al.*, 2013; Block, 2007; Norton, 2000). While we were not limited to nor bound by the items and descriptions listed, the form provided a framework for the observation, ensuring we were all collecting information pertinent to the research. Where possible, we noted what people were doing and what they were saying. In order to collect the data as naturalistically as possible, neither students nor lecturers present in the English Lounge were informed of the observations that were taking place. We referred to guidelines stated by the American Anthropological Association (2018) with regard to ethical research, and the project was approved by our research ethics committee.

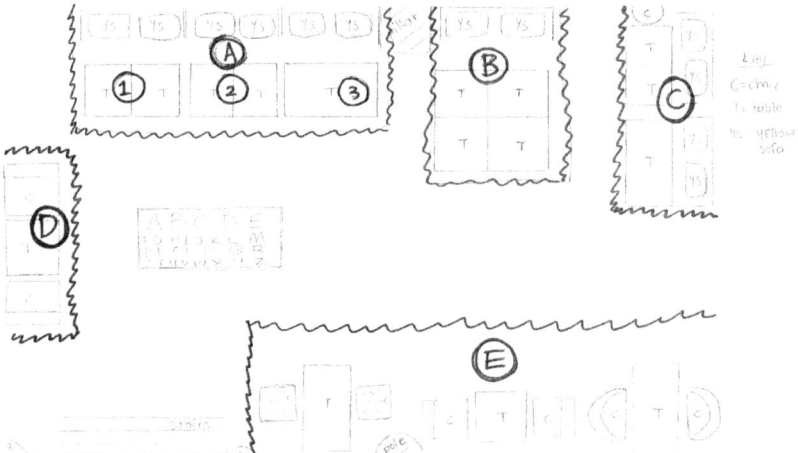

Figure 4.1 A map of the English Lounge for observers

Table 4.1 The most frequently observed behaviours

	Yellow Sofa (YS) Group	Other users
Entrances and exits	• Coming, going and freely moving around without asking permission • Leaving belongings unattended in the area, often for long stretches of time	• Approaching or hovering around the lounge • Waiting for a lecturer to initiate a conversation • Approaching a lecturer to ask for help with homework • Using exit strategies to leave politely
Interaction	• Being present without necessarily needing to interact with anyone	• Participating in a lecturer-led discussion
Activities	• Eating • Keeping occupied with various projects	• Keeping occupied with projects to hide their shyness or to allow them to observe without having to participate • Successful attempts to engage in conversation
Posture	• Relaxed and confident • Some lying down or sleeping	• Some appeared relaxed and confident • A few looked uncomfortable/like visitors to the space

Source: Adapted from Burke *et al.* (2018: 213–214).

After we had completed the 10 observations, three members of the research team (authors of this book) created a coding frame by examining the observation notes thematically together through a discursive process. We identified a total of 45 emergent codes (behaviours) from the observation analysis. Two of the researchers then manually coded the data separately, and the other researcher subsequently collated the two sets of analysis and used a qualitative software programme called HyperResearch to help us to examine the patterns. Through the analysis of the behaviours, we were able to easily identify two distinct groups of people present in the lounge: the YS Group and other users. We have summarised many of the behaviours that we observed in Table 4.1.

Part 2: Participants

In the observation study, we identified three kinds of participants we wanted to include in our study (YS Group members, and other users who might have been what we later termed 'Regular Users' and 'Non Users'). For the next part of the study, we gained access to potential participants in the following ways:

Regular Users and Yellow Sofa Group members

We created flyers asking for volunteers to participate in a study about the English Lounge and left them on the tables throughout the lounge for a two-week period around the midpoint of the first semester of the academic year. We encouraged students informally to consider applying to participate and told them that we were interested in finding out from students what they thought about the English Lounge. The flyer stated that participants would receive a small gift for participating in a 30-minute interview in either English or Japanese. The gift was a 500-yen voucher (approximately

£3.50). Interested students accessed the link to an online screening survey which ensured we knew something about the students before potentially contacting them. A total of 24 participants completed the questionnaire, and 21 indicated they were willing to be interviewed. We contacted all of the 15 students who had claimed to use the lounge every day or at least once a week and who had included their names and contact details on the form.

Non Users

In order to identify potential Non Users who would agree to be interviewed, we designed a second short questionnaire which we emailed to students in our classes and/or students we assumed did not use the English Lounge. The questionnaire did not make it clear that we were targeting non-lounge users and included a number of Self-Access Learning Centre (SALC) services among the items. However, this method of obtaining participation by Non Users was not effective and we received no interest. Instead, participants identifying as Non Users from their responses to a questionnaire on a separate but related study (not included in this ethnography) were contacted and agreed to be interviewed for this study. In all, the following participants were interviewed in this project:

YS Group members: 5
Regular Users: 6
Non Users: 4

Details of the 15 participants in the study are summarised in Table 4.2. Through the research process, we identified them as either being a member of the YS Group, a Regular User or a Non User. We explore the characteristics of members of these groups through the various chapters of the book. Membership of these groups was not always static or clear cut, but we assigned each participant to the category that best describes their identity and community membership.

Part 3: Data Collection

Interviews

The following research questions guided our interview preparation (see Appendix 2 for sample questions and Chapter 14 for some practical suggestions for preparing to conduct the interviews):

(1) How do participants view the role of the English Lounge?
(2) How do participants view themselves as English users? Specifically, how is identity conceptualised in the following facets (Benson et al., 2013; Harré, 2001):
   (a) reflexive identity (i.e. self-concept);
   (b) projected identity;

Table 4.2 Summary of participants

Assigned category	Name*	Gender	Major	Year at the university at the start of the study	Number of interviews	Notes
YS Group	Kyoji	M	Portuguese	2	2	Studying abroad in Brazil in Year 2
YS Group	Kokon	F	English	2	2	
YS Group	Sina	M	English	4	2	
YS Group	Suzuka	F	English	3	2	
YS Group	Tomoya	M	English	4	2	
Reg. User**	Kaede	F	Spanish	1	2	
Reg. User	Mei	F	Spanish	1	2	
Reg. User	Rintaro	M	Chinese	2	2	Studying abroad in Taiwan in Year 2
Reg. User	Ririka	F	Spanish	1	1	No response to interview request in Year 2
Reg. User	Ryunosuke	M	English	2	2	
Reg. User	Yuki	F	Spanish	1	2	
Non User***	Misa	F	English	2	2	
Non User	Sachiko	F	Chinese	2	2	
Non User	Sayaka	F	English	2	2	
Non User	Yukari	F	English	2	2	

*Some of the names are pseudonyms, others are the participants' real names retained at their request
**Regular Users have been abbreviated to Reg. Users or RU in this book
***Non Users have been abbreviated to NU in this book

    (c) recognised identity;
    (d) imagined identity (i.e. possible self/ideal self).
(3) How (if at all) do participants' identities influence ways in which they use the lounge?
(4) How (if at all) do participants' identities shift when using the English Lounge?
(5) What are the participants' beliefs about how languages are learnt?
(6) What are the main factors influencing these beliefs?
(7) What role do learner beliefs play in participants' use/non-use of the English Lounge?

We conducted the interviews (either in English, Japanese or a combination of both depending on the participant's choice) just after the midpoint of the first semester. The new building had been open less than three months, but we had observed that communities had started to form, and routines and behavioural patterns had started to emerge. We recorded all of the interviews, transcribed them as soon as possible after the event and shared the transcript with other team members. We also wrote notes about the interviews, either during the interview or shortly afterwards, to aid interpretation later. The researcher who conducted the initial interview would be responsible for sharing the interpretation with the participant, conducting any subsequent interviews with that participant, analysing the transcripts and writing the narrative case studies that are included in this book.

Using language learning histories (LLHs)

Prior to the second round of interviews, which were conducted approximately one year later, we also asked the participants to write and bring an LLH with them. LLHs are usually guided written narratives that students write to describe their own learning experiences in their own words. They have the advantage over other research methods such as questionnaires as they add more insights into 'meaningful aspects of learning from the perspective of the students themselves' (Murphey & Carpenter, 2008: 20). We sent some questions to guide the LLHs based on an instrument used with Japanese university students in a study by Murphey and Carpenter (2008), which was designed to investigate students' beliefs, attributions and agency in language learning (Appendix 3). This, and notes from the first interviews, were referred to in the second interviews.

Part 4: Data Analysis

We chose multiple approaches to analysing the data in order to get a full picture of the phenomena affecting interaction in the English Lounge. First, we chose a narrative approach as we wanted to ensure that we included an analysis of individual participants' cases in order to develop a deep understanding of their experiences. Secondly, we conducted typological analyses using pre-existing frameworks for identity (Chapter 11) and CoP (Chapter 12). In addition, we conducted an interpretative analysis as we could not identify a pre-existing framework that could easily be applied and also capture the complexity and interplay between various interacting factors. This was followed by the creation of our own analytic framework with which to analyse the data (Chapter 13). The various approaches to the analysis will be shared in this chapter, but the results of the analysis can be seen in subsequent relevant chapters.

(i) Case studies and narrative analysis

Case study research has a long history and has been used not only in education research, but also in other fields such as sociology, anthropology and psychology (Simons, 2009). Within this ethnography, we draw on data collected from the 15 participants whose collective stories span the period from their high school experiences prior to joining the university, to the year after graduation (in two cases). Interpretations of the term 'case' differ depending on the project, but for the purposes of this ethnography, one case is one student participant. Each of our participants shared their story through interviews with one of the researchers and through LLHs. Although all of the cases are unique and interesting, for the sake of space we chose six stories to include as complete case studies in this book. Two of the cases, Sina and Kokon, are participants who were core members of the Yellow Sofa Group. Two participants, Kaede and Rintaro, were Regular Users of the English Lounge, but did not consider themselves to be core members of the community that had formed in the space. Finally, two participants, Sachiko and Sayaka, had never used the space and were considered to be Non Users. Chapters 5–10 contain the narratives of these six participants, and the aim of this section is to capture the 'lived experience' (Clandinin & Connelly, 1994) or 'story' of each of them that helped us to have a greater understanding of our students, their engagement with the English Lounge and the impact the English Lounge had on the learners' beliefs and identities. The research team members who wrote the case study chapters had access to the original recordings, an LLH written by the participant, the interview transcripts and the typological and interpretative analyses done by different members of the team (see Chapters 11–13 for the results of this process).

Narrative inquiry (NI)

NI is often associated with case study research in many fields and stems from work by Dewey (1997). Within an NI framework, stories are reconstructed in light of new events and are shaped by a community (Canagarajah, 1996). NI assumes that human beings 'make sense of random experience by the imposition of story structures' (Bell, 2002: 207), but it goes beyond just telling stories and always involves a close examination of assumptions and insights in the analytic process (Bell, 2002). The interpretations shared in these narratives draw on the dialogue generated by all of the researchers, which represents the social and relational nature of a narrative (Johnson & Golombek, 2002). As we engaged in NI, we kept in mind some potential features of NI, i.e. that the process may uncover unconscious information and beliefs from our participants and researchers, and also that the process would illuminate the temporal notion of an experience. Chapter 14 discusses the limitations of taking a case-study approach and provides suggestions for conducting this kind of research.

(ii) Typological analysis

The purpose of the typological analysis was to ensure that we analysed the data according to two of the key research questions we were exploring (related to identity and community). According to Ayres and Knafi (2008: 901), a typological analysis is 'a strategy for descriptive qualitative (or quantitative) data analysis whose goal is the development of a set of related but distinct categories within a phenomenon that discriminate across the phenomenon'. In other words, this kind of analysis would allow us to explore our data from different perspectives within frameworks we had identified. We used the Facets of Identity framework (Benson *et al.*, 2013) to investigate identity (Chapter 11) and the CoP framework (Lave & Wenger, 1991) to investigate the nature of the communities in the lounge (Chapter 12).

(iii) Interpretative analysis

The English Lounge is made up of a host of factors that affect use and interaction with the space. Each user of the space brings with them beliefs, experiences, personal histories and other factors that will influence the people around them in unpredictable ways. The space could be seen to be a kind of dynamic system evolving over time with other dynamic systems nested within it. Although students may come together at certain times to form a community, there are other influencing factors not constrained to the temporal and physical space (Van Lier, 2004); as human beings, users engage in dynamic interrelationships with others (Sampson, 2016). It is difficult to capture the dynamics and motivations of the users in the lounge, and we agree with Ushioda (2014: 48) that 'learners are not simply located in particular contexts, but inseparably constitute part of these contexts. Learners shape and are shaped by context'. One way to begin to understand the roles of the key factors affecting the use and views of the English Lounge is to conduct an interpretative analysis. Interpretative analysis is a way of working with qualitative data in order to transform it into meaning (Hatch, 2002). This interpretation can be done through a guided process which includes: thoroughly reading (and rereading) the data; consulting data sources, notes and other artefacts; recording and studying memos; coding and recoding; summarising; and sharing interpretations with participants. We conducted an interpretative analysis in order to explore emergent themes and connections that we had not pre-defined, allowing for a holistic interpretation of phenomena (Hatch, 2002). We used the findings from the interpretative analysis as a departure point for exploring the presence of learner beliefs and other individual difference factors and the relationships between these factors (Chapter 13). We began by conducting an interpretative analysis of the first-year data in order to identify the most influential factors. From there, we created an analytic framework which we then applied to the remaining data. Later, we visually represented our data to examine the presence and interaction of influential factors over time.

The creation of an analytic framework

Creating a framework is a practical approach to guiding the interpretative coding for large amounts of data (Miles & Huberman, 1984, 1994) and for finding patterns in the entire data, in this case, the existence of beliefs about learning and other factors affecting the use of the lounge. For this portion of the analysis, we drew upon methods associated with Framework Analysis (Ritchie & Spencer, 1994), which uses a combination of *a priori* interests and initial observations within the data and is a flexible approach to analysing data thematically (Brooks *et al.*, 2015).

Through the interpretative analysis process described in the previous section, categories and codes emerged, which were collapsed or split until the research team established the full list of categories and codes. From discussions following the coding process, it became apparent that learner beliefs, the L2 motivational self system, previous learning experiences/*eigo-eikaiwa*, language anxiety and interdependent agency in particular were affecting the ways in which learners viewed the lounge and their participation within it. We created an analytic framework (Table 4.3) based on these five categories and subsequently used this as a template to analyse both the first and the second round of interviews. For the initial analysis, we combined all of the data from both years to look at how beliefs and other factors affected participants' perceptions and use of the lounge. For practical purposes, at this stage we focused on two core codes associated with each factor. Later, these were expanded to 14 core beliefs (described in Chapter 13). Codes and data excerpts associated with each key factor are presented in Table 4.3.

Table 4.3 Analytic framework for understanding the role of key factors

Factor	Codes	Excerpts from the data
Beliefs about language learning The ways in which individuals view the learning process and how it affects approaches to language learning.	(1) Participant believes that using the target language(s) is important for the learning process.	'It's important to like make a space, make a situation to use English in Japan'. (Misa, Non User, Interview 2)
	(2) Participant believes that learning grammar and vocabulary is necessary before you are ready to speak the target language(s).	'I think my English skill is not enough to speak fluently'. (Sayaka, Non User, Interview 1)
L2 motivational self system The views individuals have about the roles of the target languages(s) in visions of their future selves, or external pressure that is felt.	(1) Participant has a vision of their future self using the target language(s).	'Yeah so hopefully I can come back here in Brazil and use my language skill, international communication skills in Brazil like that's my dream, yeah that's my dream right now'. (Kyoji, YS Group, Interview 2)
	(2) Participant feels pressure to study languages for external reasons.	'I sometimes get some pressure to get like TOEFL score or something. It's kind of like external pressure'. (Sina, YS Group, Interview 1)
Eigo-eikaiwa **distinction** How in Japanese English education 'speaking the language is regarded as being separate from the language itself' (Stephens, 2002).	(1) Participant can reconcile the study of language and the use of language as part of the same process.	'Sometime you need to improve grammar and also sometime when I have a conversation I am not conscious of the grammar'. (Rintaro, RU, Interview 1)
	(2) Participant feels that 'speaking the language is regarded as being separate from the language itself' (Stephens, 2002).	'Like, is it okay if I ignore grammar and just speak?' (Kaede, RU, Interview 1)
Language anxiety A feeling of apprehension when using a second language.	(1) Participant may have initially felt anxious, but this passed.	'At first I was nervous, but now I'm used to it so I enjoy going'. (Mei, RU, Interview 1)
	(2) Participant continues to feel anxious about using the English Lounge.	'I'm nervous, always nervous because yeah, I'm lack of grammar skill, so maybe I can't talk with correct English'. (Misa, Non User, Interview 1)
Agency and interdependence Awareness of the agency and actions of the group as well as the individual.	(1) Participant takes joint ownership of the space and hopes to improve it for the benefit of the wider community of students.	'To begin with, like my seniors did, I create a welcoming atmosphere and try to make friends'. (Mei, RU, Interview 1)
	(2) Participant recognises that another group, of which they are not a member, is in operation and so feels unable or unwilling to join as a consequence.	'I often come to SALC and see Yellow Sofas, but always same students are there, so I don't feel comfortable to join them'. (Yukari, Non User, Interview 1)

Visual presentation of data

Visual representations can be useful for looking at patterns and interconnections between factors and we used three methods of presenting our interpretative data: (1) we used a method known as 'threading' (Davis & Sumara, 2006) where interpretations of aspects of data are plotted on a grid so that it can be visualised, and patterns and connections (if any) can be identified. (2) In another round of analysis, we colour-coded data for each participant in order to identify the connections between the five key factors. (3) We created diagrams that show the relationships between the five key factors for three of the participants (one participant from each group) in a process known as 'nesting' (Davis & Sumara, 2006). The threading and nesting are described in more detail in the results section of Chapter 13.

In this chapter, we have given a brief overview of all of the methods that we applied to the data in the course of the ethnography. As we will see in the following chapters, the findings from each of these detailed and focused investigations shed light on different aspects of the space. In Chapter 14, we return to the topic of research methods and offer a reflective account that could serve as a toolkit for researchers wishing to carry out similar work. In Chapter 15, we summarise the main findings and provide some detailed implications for our context and social learning spaces more generally.

Part 2
Case Studies

5 'If some freshman come to us, I said like, "Please join us"': Kokon's Story

Phoebe Lyon

At the start of the project in 2017, Kokon was a second-year English major who self-identified as a core member of the community of practice (CoP) we were studying. She was outgoing and very eager to share her experiences of using the Self-Access Learning Centre (SALC) and the English Lounge, relaying how her experiences using the lounge and her role within it had changed as she moved from her first year to her second year.

Before University

In junior high school, Kokon mostly learnt English through the grammar-translation method, where grammar is explicitly taught through translation exercises (Lightbown & Spada, 2010). Kokon felt that studying English at school required immense memorisation; in order to pass university entrance exams, there was a focus on grammar and vocabulary rather than communication (Hosoki, 2011). Kokon admitted that she did not enjoy learning English at junior high school, largely due to there being, for her, no meaningful learning. It was not until she was given a summer homework task that required her to read a children's book that she realised that she could enjoy learning English. Upon reaching high school, Kokon was relieved to find that the textbooks had become content based, marking the point at which she could see a clear purpose to reading in English, which she now identifies as reading to understand the content. A recommendation from a friend to listen to English songs further increased her joy of English language learning, and she found this to be an effective way to connect with fellow high school students with similar interests.

First Impressions of the University

Upon entering university, Kokon expected to read books and speak English. However, she was surprised by the high level of English produced by her classmates. She also became aware of the SALC, but initially didn't fully realise its purpose or what it could be used for. One area within the SALC that she soon discovered was the English Lounge, an area where one could come and go as one pleased to practice English conversation. Kokon began to attend the English Lounge from her first week at university. She joined fellow class members the first time she visited and was immediately impressed by the level of English she heard used by other students. Although she had initially felt nervous and awkward about attending, she was happy to find that the senior students and lecturers were very welcoming, and she quickly became a frequent visitor.

During the first interview, Kokon talked about the English Lounge or the 'Yellow Sofa'; she felt very comfortable with the area and with the people she met there. In fact, she spent a lot of her free time there, often visiting multiple times on any given day. This was a trend that had started in her first year and continued throughout her time at the university.

K: I have classes and almost every lunch time I come to the Yellow Sofa and I ate lunch and after classes and if I have a time after school I just sitting around.

(Interview 1)

One of the reasons Kokon gave for frequenting the English Lounge was that she had a lot of friends with whom she liked to socialise in the lounge. In addition to meeting old friends from her days as a first-year student, she was interested in making new friends and found the lounge an ideal place. She viewed the English Lounge users as motivated and therefore believed the area was a place to meet 'good' friends. Having self-identified as a motivated learner, she wanted to be around likeminded people. She also said that she found the English Lounge to be a comfortable space where she could eat and drink, study and just generally relax without worrying about anything. To her, it was a meeting place, much like a cafe.

K: So, I think I feel like the Yellow Sofa is where I supposed to be (laughs) by far.

(Interview 1)

Beliefs about Language Learning

The English Lounge clearly played a fundamental role in her language learning. Kokon believed that she learnt language best through conversation; that listening and speaking were essential. One year later during the second interview, it was apparent that she still thought that listening and using English were important; however, she specifically added that she also valued listening to people she perceived to be 'native speakers'. In order to improve her speaking, Kokon clarified two modes of study that incorporated follow-up participation in the English Lounge: (1) listening to English through classroom-based study and (2) watching movies and TV dramas on YouTube. Through these two methods, she was able to learn a lot of new vocabulary and expressions which she would write down with the purpose of using them the next time she was in the English Lounge. In addition, she would attempt to use any new vocabulary and expressions that she learnt in the English Lounge in her next classroom lesson.

The Shifting Role of the English Lounge

Although Kokon had been a constant user of the English Lounge for several years, the way that she used the area changed over time. Kokon talked to lecturers more in her first year than she did in her second. Her focus in her second year was just to talk to people, regardless of who they were. By her third year, she talked mostly with one good friend, but she also talked to lecturers she had met in her second year, to new first-year students she had met through attending Freshman English Camp (an orientation for first-year students) as a helper and to foreign exchange students. The role of the English Lounge had changed for Kokon since she first started frequenting it. In her initial visits with her classmates in her first year, her impression of other students using the area was that they were cool and could speak English well. On the other hand, she felt that she was not able to say much at all, and was grateful to both the older students and the lecturers for making her experience enjoyable by being encouraging and providing support. In her first year, her main purpose for attending the English Lounge was simply to practice English. As a second-year student, however, she saw her role as one of encouraging other students to use the area. She adopted a role of being a mentor to first-year students, encouraging them to participate actively in the English Lounge.

K: Like, um, well like just not just sit there or like, um, if some freshman [first-year students] come to us, I said like, 'Please join us' and I just start conversation and they can't run away. (laughs)

(Interview 1)

Possibly due to her outgoing personality, Kokon had adopted a mentor role in her second year (which was the first year that the lounge was in the new building). However, she mentioned that from that year, the atmosphere in the English Lounge area was not always perceived by newcomers as welcoming. Kokon recognised that she was part of a group or community composed of many of the students she had met during her first year and with whom she had become good friends. She was equally aware that her group members dominated the lounge space since they were there so often. When asked how she thought her group might be perceived, Kokon said that she had learnt that first-year students were intimidated by her group; they were intimidated by the group members' familiarity with each other and their confidence and proficiency. In fact, she confessed that some first-year students had told her that they did not feel that they could easily join the existing community.

Supporting Other Learners

Knowing how new visitors to the area felt when approaching the English Lounge, Kokon explained that she was not comfortable with the situation. She felt strongly that it was important for members of her group to help these students feel comfortable joining the space. Since not all of the members of her group agreed with her sentiments, she said that it was necessary for her to leave her group at times in order to interact with other students. However, she did not seem to mind since one of her goals for using the area was to make new friends. Her desire to help and mentor younger students stemmed, in part, from her not so distant memories of her own nervous and awkward first attempts to go to the English Lounge as a first-year student.

During the first interview, Kokon admitted that she went to the English Lounge less frequently in her second year than she did in her first. After initial contemplation, her response was that she had less time in her second year, mostly due to having a busy class schedule. Upon further prompting about how she felt about the move of the English Lounge from the old location (in another building) to the new one in Kanda University of International Studies (KUIS) 8, she admitted to being disappointed by the atmosphere in the new building. With the larger size and new layout, she felt that there was less 'policing' of the English-only language policy by lecturers and SALC staff. She said she felt compelled to use Japanese with very low-level students while also admitting that she found the use of Japanese annoying. Even though Kokon saw herself as part of the core group in the English Lounge and took on a leadership role, she did not feel it was her role to enforce an English-only environment.

Diminishing Role in the English Lounge

As a third-year student at the time of the second interview, Kokon said that although she still encouraged new students to use the space, her role as a mentor had diminished. Her change in focus seemed to be the result of several factors. Kokon mentioned that although she still felt like she was part of the core Yellow Sofa Group, more groups had formed. For example, another student, now in their second year, had taken over the role of managing the study group in which she used to have a lead role. She described how the student led the study group and encouraged newcomers to use the English Lounge. She admitted that she was no longer as active in encouraging new students to enter the space.

K: I don't want to feel like, feel that but I feel like I've got lazy
Interviewer: OK
K: a bit because it's a little tir, tiring to you know, to speak to new friends and they can't speak English that much.
(Interview 2)

She also mentioned that her old community had weakened because there were fewer members in it that spoke English well. She elaborated, saying that she was the only third-year student from the previous year's core group who still went to the English Lounge. In the first interview, she had mentioned that many of the friends she socialised with that year were fourth-year students. They were the older students she had met at the original English Lounge when she had been in her first year. At the time of the second interview, those students had since graduated. It appears that the dissolving of the 2017 core group was another element that influenced how Kokon interacted in the English Lounge in her third year. Although Kokon occasionally met some of the old first-year students with whom she had become good friends during her second year, she saw less of them as a result of them coming less often. Her impression was that this was due to their second-year schedules being busier.

A third factor seems to be that Kokon started to interact with another group of students who often used the spaces in and around the English Lounge, the foreign exchange students. In the first interview, Kokon stated that she would describe the English Lounge as a place where students could practice English with lecturers and friends, and that it was also a good place to meet new friends. In the second interview, although she still felt that it was a very comfortable place in which she felt safe, she added to her description of who one could talk to there.

K: Um, Yellow Sofa is the area who where you like you can practise speaking English with native English speakers and exchange students, including students, and your friends, teachers, like everyone.
(Interview 2)

When talking about the addition of 'exchange students', Kokon mentioned that while in her first year she had associated with some exchange students, in her second year she had felt that they sat clustered in one area (away from the English Lounge) and were thus difficult to approach. Kokon believed that since a change in the layout of the English Lounge that occurred mid-2017, which saw the yellow sofas being spread out, the exchange students began to use some of the area. This, she felt, made it easier to associate with them. She also got acquainted with some of them through one of her friends who was an EPal (a student volunteer who helps the exchange students upon their arrival). The following statement, however, really highlights how confident in the space she had become and how this possibly contributed to her forming relationships with the exchange students.

K: Yeah, and plus Yellow Sofa I think it affects um because y.., like this year exchange students use Yellow Sofa area and I feel, OK this place is my place, then I, I'm not hesitate to speak to exchange students
Interviewer: Ahhh
K: They come to my place I feel.

(Interview 2)

Use of English Outside the English Lounge

Kokon's use of English in the English Lounge continued to affect her life in her third year as a student. In the second interview, Kokon said that she once again visited the English Lounge every day, frequenting it at lunchtime to eat with friends, and also often going during first period to do homework. She also continued to go after school to 'hang out'. She said that her increased time in the SALC correlated to an increased amount of free time. However, she stressed that she did not find herself limited to the English Lounge. She said she felt comfortable speaking English anywhere; in fact, she explained that she had begun to sit at an area called the Informal Gathering Spot, another space on the upper floor of the SALC, located just outside the lounge area, as well as the areas downstairs where the language policy is not restricted to English.

It was clear from the first interview not only that Kokon loved to speak English, but also that the act of using English had influenced her personality. During that first interview, she explained how since becoming more fluent in English she had come to feel that she was more outgoing, not just in English but also when she spoke Japanese. It seemed her daily use of English at the English Lounge had increased her confidence in general. Even though she admitted to being quite talkative in both Japanese and English, she felt she was even more so when she spoke in English. Furthermore, her use of English in her second year was not restricted to the English Lounge or the classroom. She said that she sometimes spoke in English to her friends on the way home from school, showing how her confidence had increased. As mentioned above, this confidence continued to increase into her third year.

K: But, so the Yellow Sofa gave me the confidence and opportunity and ability to speak English.

(Interview 1)

In the second interview during her third year, it was apparent that her English identity was continuing to evolve. Although Kokon *projected* a sense of confidence throughout the project period, her actual confidence using English had further developed and she was now using English outside of the English Lounge.

K: Outside of the SALC we tend to use English, not Japanese, so it's kind of weird from you know other people.

(Interview 2)

After having used the SALC, and in particular the English Lounge, for so many hours a day over two years, Kokon was using English even more frequently outside of the university campus. She was aware that this was not usual for many students, and as such this was something of which she seemed proud.

Kokon said that she had started using English more than Japanese, and as a result of her increased use of English, she said she was sometimes having trouble communicating her ideas in Japanese. This suggested that her social identity was changing, and that her Japanese linguistic ability was being affected by her increased use and confidence in her English ability.

K: Yeah, but it's a little bit hard because when I want to talk about my worries or problems to my family, I can't explain it in Japanese because I already talked about it with [my friend] in English.

(Interview 2)

English has clearly had a huge impact on Kokon's life. The English Lounge, which allows students to be surrounded by English, and in which students can connect with a diverse range of people, has been particularly instrumental in her language learning journey. Kokon's frequent participation in the English Lounge has allowed her to become more sociable and confident, to develop mentoring skills and to define her multilingual identity.

6 'We see the same people like every day so I feel like yeah it's kind of like a community, Yellow Sofa community kind of thing': Sina's Story

Ross Sampson

At the start of the research project in June 2017, Sina was a fourth-year student majoring in English. He often visited the English Lounge and could identify other members of the Yellow Sofa Group with whom he had formed a community. In the first interview in 2017, Sina was the oldest member of the Yellow Sofa Group, and was well placed to be able to provide valuable insights about the English Lounge as well as his identity as a language learner. Sina was generally interested in the Self-Access Learning Centre (SALC) and the English Lounge, which had influenced his original choice to enrol at the university. In his language learning history (LLH), he wrote that 'communicative competence' was the biggest thing he thought about before beginning university. He also found the English Lounge to be 'relaxing'.

First Introduction to the English Lounge

Sina first visited the lounge when he was in his first year at the university. He had suggested to two or three of his friends to go – which they did. However, these friends eventually lost interest. He remembered talking to a Brazilian exchange student the first time he went to have a conversation. He described how his impressions of people using the lounge changed after he started getting to know them:

S: Yeah, the first time I went there alone I remember I talked to somebody and it was one of friend, an exchange student from Brazil, and he was alone in the Yellow Sofa and I was kind of afraid, but I know like those people in Yellow Sofa is so open to talk.

(Interview 1)

Beliefs about Language Learning: Motivation and Fun

During the interviews, Sina drew particular attention to the concept of motivation. It was clear this was an important factor in learning for him. He mentioned that the number of students who spend time in the lounge at the start of an academic year is high, but decreases as the year progresses. He attributed this to fading motivation:

S: It is easy to have a fantastic motivation at the beginning, but actually keep doing that and keep being motivated and keep coming here [the English Lounge] is kind of much more difficult thing to do.

(Interview 1)

Sina explained how many students are 'motivated' and 'push themselves' at the start of the year, but after the summer break they become 'lazy', just like his friends did. Despite being 'afraid' the first time he went to the lounge, and even though his friends ceased going, he continued undeterred. Another recurring theme throughout the interviews was 'fun'. Sina emphasised this in relation to his use of the English Lounge and his reasons for English language learning as a whole. According to him, the best way to learn a language 'first is to have fun'. He described the lounge as 'somewhere you can talk' and elaborated by saying:

S: I think in my case it's more for like fun, and of course I want to keep like using English. Yeah, it's a good opportunity to keep, keep using English there.

(Interview 1)

Persistence

Sina saw himself as a driven, disciplined and motivated person, and also someone who liked to talk. He suggested that in order to really develop confidence and fluency in English at the lounge, students must make a habit of going and 'keep doing it'. He argued that there were students who stopped going and made excuses for doing so. However, it should be said that it is difficult to know the extent to which 'excuses' were a factor in other students' lack of participation; certainly other factors may have contributed. In addition to being sure of the importance of motivation and fun, Sina was also sure of his approach to English learning, which he described as 'less effort and more gain', which could be interpreted to mean that he did not feel forced by anyone, likely leading to his enjoyment in his pursuit of acquiring English. Furthermore, he said he very rarely experienced problems when communicating in English. He explained how, since his first year at Kanda University of International Studies (KUIS), he was driven to achieve language success, and when he said he did not use English elsewhere on campus, the value and purpose of the English Lounge for him seemed to resonate.

Sina described his routine relating to the English Lounge. He visited it about four times a week, mostly in the afternoons and for the purpose of meeting his friends. He said his motivation was just to be able to 'use English', and believed this to be the same for most students who frequented the lounge. The English Lounge had enabled him to become more fluent in English by increasing the time he had to use the language:

S: The more I use English the more I feel easy to use English, and kind of like more fluent I become.

(Interview 1)

The English Lounge made him feel 'free' and 'able to talk to anybody'. He revealed that even if there were challenges in communication, 'we [whoever he was talking with] can handle it'. He said it excited him when his English improved just by using it. Of course, he could potentially use English elsewhere, but it was apparent that the English Lounge provided the kind of platform he had been seeking.

Community Membership

Sina was aware that he was part of a group of English Lounge users who tried to be there often:

S: We see like the same people like every day so I feel like yeah it's kind of like a community, Yellow Sofa community kind of thing.

(Interview 1)

The members of the group became friends over time, and as their English level improved, they were unintentionally viewed as intimidating by other students. However, the group's actual aim was to be welcoming to other lounge users and to create an English language community:

S: Yeah, we are not intending to do it, but I kind of understand because there are several people always there, it might seem yeah, it might seem to be a group, you kind of like cannot really get in easily... We never make an atmosphere that is like kind of like closed and we are like group and keep out or something.

(Interview 1)

Sina appeared to recognise that due to his group's confidence and high English proficiency, going to the English Lounge could be rather daunting for students who do not yet possess similar English language skills and abilities. During Interview 1, it seemed evident that Sina was aware of this situation and was actively countering it with the kind of identity he intended to project outwardly. Speaking on behalf of the group, he insisted:

S: Like actually we not intending it to be a group but just like somebody you know and you can feel free to, I mean feel free to talk to somebody, just be yourself.... Like we are trying to talk to newcomers who seem to be alone and kind of not engaging doing something, so we try to be open to them.

(Interview 1)

Having a sense of community where people could 'get to know each other' in the space was the most important thing to Sina, as opposed to what test scores students may have achieved, and also continuing to be motivated from within to build friendships through language. In the second interview, Sina continued to describe the space as 'a place to talk and improve speaking English'. He still felt 'more open' when he communicated in English versus Japanese. He felt that there was a societal expectation to adjust the level of formality in Japanese, depending on the interlocutor. He stressed this by saying:

S: If I don't know the age of the person I'm talking to, I have to like, yeah in most of the case I will use honorifics, which makes a distance between us, but I feel like using English is more friendly to anybody, like even older or younger.

(Interview 2)

Sina expressed empathy with first-year students and how they must feel in relation to their anxiety about using English in the lounge. He actively made efforts to be a welcoming and friendly face to anyone who wanted to talk, projecting himself as an approachable *senpai* (senior) and role model to more junior students.

Developing Confidence and Competence

The qualities Sina embodied as a learner may be linked to his time spent at the lounge. He provided details of his experiences and feelings towards the English Lounge, indicating that it had had an influence on his competence and confidence using English. He had made consistent use of the social space as a language resource since his first university year, saying he 'feels free' to talk to anyone in the lounge area and saying he was able to develop his fluency. The more English that Sina used, the easier it became; in fact, he felt it was actually easier to communicate in English than in his first language, Japanese:

S: Sometimes I feel more like easier to talk in English, yeah depending on the context.

(Interview 1)

It seems clear that the English Lounge positively affected Sina as a language learner. He appeared intrinsically motivated to improve his English language fluency and overall abilities.

Shifting Role of the English Lounge

In the second interview in June 2018, Sina had graduated from the university. This meant he no longer spent the same amount of time at the English Lounge as he had done previously. However, as he had recently enrolled as an MA student at the university but on a different campus, he still attended the lounge about twice a month, mostly to tutor other students. This tutoring provided him with practical opportunities to develop his teaching skills which would help his English language teaching career. He still interacted with the same group of friends he regularly met with before; he also talked with students whom he tutored and with some exchange students. In short, he still felt like he was part of a community: 'I don't feel like I'm totally a stranger here'. However, he said he did not make as much effort to talk with new people in the lounge as he had done prior to graduating, despite being very sociable and not having any problems meeting new people through English.

Shifting Goals, but Continued Persistence

Sina's motivation for learning English hadn't waned over the year; in fact, it was still growing. Yet, his learning goals had shifted from speaking to reading and writing in a bid to gain more 'academic English', as he phrased it. Sina was aware he made mistakes, which he said were mainly grammatical. He said that some days words just 'don't come out', regardless of the language. In regard to his mistakes, he didn't think people would care about his errors or even notice them. However, he himself cared about his own mistakes. This appeared to indicate the self-reflective and critical stance he took towards himself. Sina recognised that 'native speakers' of English also made mistakes, although he stated his 'ultimate goal' was to be like a 'native speaker' of English. This statement could be understood to mean that his intention was to have the identity of someone indistinguishable from a 'native English speaker', thus his potential interlocutors would not identify him as a 'non-native' speaker of English. He suggested that the difference between himself as a learner and 'native speakers' was that he was consciously processing language as he spoke it much more than he believed 'native speakers' did:

S: I don't think a lot of native speakers have to care about I am talking about like one person, so I have to put 's' after the verb.
(Interview 2)

He demonstrated his autonomy through his understanding of the benefits of taking charge of his own learning, by making decisions about what resources best suited him and by constantly evaluating himself. He used language learning resources such as online videos and talk shows. In the learning histories paper he wrote prior to the second interview, Sina mentioned that he originally found motivation to learn English through board games. He explained that when he was able to choose to do or learn something without anything external forcing him to do so, he became motivated. Furthermore, because of his drive to understand the board games, he felt a sense of achievement. He said his attitude was 'not to quit something in the middle' and to 'keep going until the end'.

When explaining how he had changed over his four years at the university, he used the analogy of a 'host' and a 'guest'. He said in his fourth year he felt like a 'host', whereas when he was a first-year student, he felt like a 'guest'. This metaphor made how he viewed the English Lounge and the students who attended it clearer and allowed for a deeper understanding of how he situated himself within the space. He expressed empathy when he spoke about his desire to help first-year students, whom he identified as being in the same position that he once was when he was a first year. This pointed to the role model/mentor role he was actively trying to adopt, even after graduating. This role had possibly led him to start tutoring students, which he had been doing to aid his pursuit of becoming an English language teacher. When asked about the best way to teach a language, he answered:

S: The best way is to see the difference between learners and try to figure out what might match to their own kind of goal or character.
(Interview 2)

Throughout the interviews, it was noticeable that Sina was very engaged with his future career aspirations. It seemed that he was thinking out loud at times as to the direction he should go in and what kind of English teacher he should become. When asked about his use of English in the coming years, he said:

S: Yeah I think, I'll be using English to teach English. Yeah my future vision is to be an English teacher like you. Yeah, I haven't decided what kind of teacher I am, whether I'm teaching at cram school or *eikaiwa* or like university like here or Advisor. Whichever the way that is, I must be somebody who use English to teach English or at least help somebody else English learning. I think that's maybe the way.

(Interview 2)

Sina appeared to understand learning as a lifelong journey. He presented himself as a very autonomous learner and viewed the English Lounge as a key language learning resource in his developmental language gains throughout his university years. As a place to 'talk' and 'have fun', the lounge had enabled him to make friends through English and at the same time build his identity as an English language user who became a role model for younger, less-confident students. While it was apparent that Sina had been driven about his future before he came to KUIS, it appears that the English Lounge provided a space and opportunity for him to further develop his identity as an English language user.

7 'Is it okay if I ignore grammar and just speak?': Kaede's Story

Daniel Hooper

In the summer of 2017, Kaede was a first-year Spanish major who was using the English Lounge once a week. Kaede's shyness and lack of confidence in her English proficiency was a consistent theme present in her interviews, underlying her manner of participation, her perceived role in the English Lounge and her broader relationship with English in general. On a number of occasions, she made it clear that her shyness did not purely stem from her lack of confidence in English and that she was fundamentally *hitomishiri* (not comfortable around people).

Kaede's Use of the English Lounge

Kaede invariably chose to attend the English Lounge as part of a group of friends from her Spanish course, and this reliance on affective support from her peers did not change even as she became a second-year student. Kaede felt that attending the English Lounge in a group was comfortable because it meant that she wouldn't be forced into a high-pressure situation wherein she would be required to engage in one-on-one interaction in English. Her friends provided a level of scaffolding and security that were essential to her continued participation in the English Lounge.

A year later in June 2018, Kaede had been going to the English Lounge less, and she attributed this development to changes in her class scheduling, her starting a part-time job, as well as her persistent lack of self-confidence. Kaede also stated that she only felt comfortable with a limited number of on-duty lecturers whom she had got to know well, or lecturers who were able to scaffold her in Spanish when she experienced communication breakdowns in English. This recurring issue, which she alluded to in her first interview, reinforced her need for support from friends when she went to the English Lounge as a consequence of her lack of confidence in her English proficiency.

K: *Dakara, nanka... hanasenakute, kowai... chotto hanasenai no ga iya dakara, hanaseru tomodachi to ikanai to, ikitakunai.* [So, I'm afraid that I can't speak fluently, so I don't want to go unless I've got friends with me who can speak English well.]

(Interview 2)

The Role of Other Students in the English Lounge

Apart from the support that her friends provided her when attending the English Lounge, she was also able to gain motivation from some of the more established members of the larger English Lounge community who acted as role models and conversational facilitators for her. Kaede talked about how one *senpai* (older student) in particular had impressed her due to her attitude, personal situation and English proficiency.

K: *Perapera da shi...* [She speaks fluently and...]
Interviewer: *Un, ganbatta kara?* [Because she tried hard?]
K: *Nanka,* [Like,] she go to Yellow Sofa every day. *Ryuugaku shita koto ga nai no ni sugoi perapera kara...* [Because even though she's never studied abroad, she speaks so fluently...]

(Interview 1)

Kaede also respected this senior member because of her friendliness and her ability to come to the English Lounge alone. Furthermore, she claimed that, rather than being intimidated by older English Lounge users who were confident and fluent English speakers, her motivation would actually increase when she spent time with them in the English Lounge. The fact that the older student Kaede mentioned was Japanese and had achieved an advanced level of English without having studied abroad suggests that she could have been acting as a near peer role model (NPRM) for her. Murphey (1998: 201) describes NPRMs as 'peers who are close to our social, professional and/or age level who for some reason we may respect and admire'. The concept of NPRMs has foundations in Bandura's (1977) research into self-efficacy, in which he describes vicarious achievement – the idea of seeing those similar to us succeeding in tasks – as a powerful influence on our own potential to succeed in any given endeavour. Seeing her *senpai* as a figure similar to her in terms of age, cultural background and study opportunities could therefore have offered Kaede a view of a potentially attainable ideal second language (L2) self (Dörnyei, 2005).

In her second interview, Kaede revealed that due to differences in her class schedule and the fact that the aforementioned *senpai* was going to study abroad, she had been unable to talk with her at all during her second year. That being said, the impact that her *senpai* had had on her continued as Kaede claimed that because of her fluency and confidence, 'sometimes I think her... because she is role model for me'.

Anxiety and Lack of Confidence in a Senior Role

Unfortunately, in her new position as a second-year student and now herself a *senpai*, Kaede claimed that her greater seniority in the English Lounge had actually exacerbated her anxiety and self-confidence issues as she had become more self-conscious of her perceived lack of English proficiency. When asked how she felt about being a *senpai*, she stated that she didn't feel her English had improved from her first year. This heightened stress meant that she had found it more difficult to go to the English Lounge as a second-year student. Rather than her enhanced status and greater familiarity with the English Lounge area increasing her confidence, it appeared that the social weight that she perceived to be attached to her current role had actually served to negatively affect the way she perceived herself.

K: *Sagatta. Biginaa dakara, kyonen made wa, mada oome ni… yurusareru. Kedo, kotoshi wa Sophomore de, ichinen Kanda ni iru kara, bunpou wakaranai to ka itteru baai ja nai.* [I feel less confident. Last year, as a beginner, it was okay that my English wasn't so good. But this year, I cannot make excuses that I don't understand the grammar. I had a full year studying at KUIS.]

(Interview 2)

Kaede's perceptions of herself as 'not positive' or 'passive', as well as her self-definition as a deficient English user were, therefore, recurring factors that shaped both her self-defined role in the English Lounge and her evolving pattern of English Lounge usage. Through Kaede's language learning history and the nature of her antecedent interactions with English learning, she revealed the possible experiential foundations of some of her enduring self-confidence issues as well as signs of her evolving learner beliefs.

Previous Experiences with Learning English

Kaede had a rather mixed and tempestuous relationship with English during compulsory education. Overall, she 'hated English in high school'. She had been moved into a class of '*eigo ga dekinai hito*' [students who can't do English], but thanks to one of her English teachers, who taught in a way that suited her, her interest in the language was revived in her final year of high school.

In summer 2018, Kaede wrote a language learning history in which she described her English studies in junior high and high school. She stated that she studied 'according to the textbook' and that in high school she 'learnt words and answered questions accordingly'. However, in the previous year, she discussed how she actually 'really hate[d] studying with a textbook' and that she wasn't able to learn effectively using the primary methods espoused in her high school education.

K: *Nanka, eigo benkyou suru no wa suki datta kara jukensei no toki to ka ni, daigakujuken to ka no toki ni yarou to omotteitan desu kedo amari dekinai kara atteinai. Yarikata ga henna no kana to omotte…* [Like, I liked studying English so when I was taking exams, trying to pass entrance exams for university, I tried but I couldn't really do it and I didn't do well. I thought my study methods were maybe strange…]

(Interview 1)

The apparent disconnect between the prevalent language learning approaches from her experiences in high school and what Kaede perceived to be effective for her English development also appeared to have permeated her learning experiences in university. Kaede described what she regarded as a dichotomous relationship in which what she does and feels in her classes starkly contrasts with her interpretation of the English Lounge. This could arguably be tied into the prevailing distinction within Japanese English education between *eigo* (focusing on exam preparation and linguistic knowledge) and *eikaiwa* (based on developing oral communication skills) (Hiramoto, 2013; Chapter 3, this volume). Whereas Kaede's experiences as a high school English learner can be seen as being situated very much in the sphere of *eigo*, the English Lounge provided her with opportunities to focus solely on *eikaiwa*. In her language learning history, Kaede emphasised the value of oral proficiency, and as one of the goals of the English Lounge is to provide a space for English conversation, this was compatible with Kaede's long-term goals.

The Role of the English Lounge

In addition to the practical opportunities to use English that the English Lounge provided, it also represented a venue in which she could construct a new and more confident identity. This offered an alternative to some of the more negative classroom learning experiences, as the following excerpt indicates.

Interviewer: Okay, so, Yellow Sofa *ni iku toki ni, nanka, dou iu Kaede ga….* [When you go to the Yellow Sofas, like, what kind of Kaede is….]
K: *Ah… uh… eigo ga shabereru (laughs) Kaede.* [Kaede that can speak English.]
Interviewer: *Ja, jyugyou wa?* [So, how about in class?]
K: *Jyugyou wa eigo ga dekinai! (laughs) 'Eigo dekinai yo!' tte natte.* [I can't do English in class! It turns into 'I can't do English!']

(Interview 1)

In her 2018 interview, however, the formerly dichotomised identities in the classroom and the English Lounge had begun to blur somewhat over time. In her second year, Kaede felt significantly more comfortable in her classes than she had as a first-year student. After receiving a test score which was higher than she had expected, she started to realise that her English was actually improving. Furthermore, she suggested that she no longer perceived a significant shift in her learner identity between the two settings. Kaede's evolving understanding of the combined value of both *eigo* and *eikaiwa* approaches to her development may have led to a reconciliation related to the complementary benefits of classroom and English Lounge environments.

K: *Ima no kurasu wa amari kowagarazuni shabereru kara, sonnani kawaranakunatta.* [I feel more comfortable speaking in my current class, so my personality doesn't change much now.]

(Interview 2)

Beliefs About Language Learning

Another conflict in Kaede's language learning beliefs that appeared to have resolved itself over time was the role of grammar in her studies. In 2017, she repeatedly referred to grammar in negative terms as a point of stress for her and an exemplification of her self-defined linguistic deficiency. She stated that when she first went to the English Lounge, she was always worried about her grammar and, perhaps as a coping mechanism, began to de-emphasise its importance in English communication. Grammar was also something that she linked with her high school English studies and, by extension, her status as a 'student who can't do English'. In fact, at the very end of her first interview, she asked whether she could ignore grammar altogether and just focus on English as a means of communication.

Interviewer: *Kikitai koto arimasuka?* [Is there anything you'd like to ask?]

K: *Kikitai koto... eh... nanka, bunpou mushi shite, shabecchatte mo daijoubu na no?* [Something I'd like to ask... eh... like, is it okay if I ignore grammar and just speak?]

(Interview 1)

The following year, however, Kaede's experiences of living in Spain seemingly brought about a transformation in her views on the contribution of grammar study to her language development. While she still asserted that her lack of grammatical knowledge was at the heart of her perceived deficiency as an English user, Kaede appeared to have somewhat renegotiated her relationship with grammar study. She confidently stated that she had changed her mind about the prospect of ignoring a grammar component in her studies. She asserted that this had come about as a result of her time in Spain, where she had studied Spanish grammar in the morning and then applied what she had studied in conversations with her Spanish host family in the afternoon. Kaede found this merging of language-focused and communicative engagement with Spanish to be very useful, and this had, in turn, affected her views on the role of grammar in learning English.

As a consequence of her experiences in Spain, Kaede had perhaps resolved a conflict between the grammar-focused *eigo* approach from high school, which led her to frame herself as someone who 'can't do English', and the communicative *eikaiwa* style of the English Lounge as a haven from grammar dogmatism. It is possible that she had come to view these not as incompatible entities, but instead as distinct but complementary facets of language learning.

One final perceived role of the English Lounge that Kaede discussed was her view of it as an international area that she could use in lieu of actually going abroad. Even though her main language of study was Spanish, during her time in Spain she found that English was an important communication tool. She believed that, rather than developing her English ability in a country where English is the dominant language, the English Lounge was a good substitute for her. She therefore appeared to have a more instrumental/functional perspective towards her use of the English Lounge, as opposed to a bond with any specific English target culture like the US or the UK.

K: *Sou ne. Eigoken ha nai. Tokuni nai kedo, demo, eigo mo juuyou datte, supein ni itta toki ni omotta kara, eigo wa benkyou shitai. Chotto, ima, ryuugaku wa dekinai kara… eigoken ni. Dakara Yellow Sofa de.* [Yes. I'm not so interested in English speaking countries, but, when I went to Spain, I felt English was important too, so I want to learn it. I can't go to English speaking countries to study, so I go to the Yellow Sofas instead.]

(Interview 2)

Future Plans

Regarding her plans after graduation, Kaede did not really change over the year that separated her two interviews. She stated that she wished to go overseas and speak with foreign people but elaborated a little more on this desire in her second year. She claimed that she was interested in getting a job related to overseas travel in some way, such as in the tourism industry. This was connected to a desire to work in a profession that facilitated travel to many different countries. One common trait related to Kaede's perceptions of the international nature of the English Lounge and her imagined future L2 self was the fact that Kaede's desire to go abroad did not seem to be tied to specific L2 target cultures and was instead oriented towards a more general sense of an international world/community (Yashima, 2009).

Kaede's two interviews provided a glimpse into some of the elements contributing to her language learner identity construction. These elements were also often intertwined with her view of the English Lounge: the perceived opportunities as well as the constraints that influenced her usage of the area. Some of the themes that emerged from Kaede's year-long participation in the English Lounge painted an evolving and sometimes contradictory picture of her self-image, along with her views on language learning. Despite describing feelings of empowerment provided by the communicative nature of the English Lounge, she also expressed an unrelenting sense of self-doubt in which she cast herself as a deficient learner. Furthermore, rather than mitigating the anxiety that initially stemmed from her newcomer status in the English Lounge, her transition from first-year student to *senpai* had, in fact, exacerbated her anxiousness, which she attributed to performance pressure and feelings of responsibility towards her juniors. Her time in Spain seems to have been key for beginning to reconcile the formerly dichotomous relationship between studying grammar in the classroom and speaking English in the English Lounge. Kaede has begun to appreciate how the former can help with the latter as a result of several critical language learning experiences. She has apparently managed to strike a balance between the communicative *eikaiwa* of the English Lounge and the grammar-centric *eigo* that she had struggled with so much in high school. This has also played into a decreased distance between her identity in the English Lounge as 'Kaede who can speak English' and her deficient identity in the classroom. As time went on, she described an increasingly coherent learner identity more comfortable in either setting.

8 'Don't be afraid of making mistakes': Rintaro's Story

Phillip Taw

At the time of the first interview, Rintaro was a second-year student who was majoring in Chinese with a minor in English. He had been a regular user of the English Lounge since his first year at the university, frequenting it nearly every day when his schedule permitted. The first interview with Rintaro took place in July 2017 in the lounge, but a subsequent interview could not be done in person due to his studying abroad in Taiwan. As an alternative, the second interview took place in June 2018 via Skype.

Routines and Goal Pursuit

Rintaro maintained a fairly regimented routine for his studies at the time of the first interview. His approach to his studies seemed to be a result of his personal assessment of the skills he would need for his career and how he perceived that he could best obtain those skills. He chose to study Chinese as his major because he was interested in trade as his future career path and saw China as an important player in the field, so he decided that learning the language would be integral to his career. Rintaro explained that although the Chinese language is not considered as important as English, he believed that it would grow in importance as China's influence on global economics continued to grow.

Busy with his studies, Rintaro emphasised the importance of routines and the efficient use of time in his personal life. He woke up at approximately the same time every school day and began his day by watching the BBC or CNN to practice his English listening skills while keeping up to date on world news. Then, on his hour-long commute to school, he practiced his listening skills further by using an application on his phone designed for studying the test of English for international communication (TOEIC). Looking at how Rintaro strategically used his time and resources to achieve his desired learning outcomes, it is possible to imagine how the English Lounge could fit into his approach to studying, using it to practice other facets of his English skills he could not address by other means. For example, television and applications are not able to provide the opportunity for genuine language output that interacting with real people in a social learning space can provide.

Role of the English Lounge

In addition to Chinese, Rintaro believed that English would play a large role as a medium of communication in his future career in trade, so he focused on improving his communication abilities in both Chinese and English. He regularly visited the English Lounge as part of his study routine in order to practice and improve his English abilities. In contrast to other student users of the English Lounge who stayed for full periods of 90 minutes or even longer, Rintaro often used the spare time between his classes or activities to stop by the English Lounge and partake in just a few minutes of conversation practice. In addition, the English Lounge provided Rintaro with a place not only for practicing his English conversational skills, but also for socialising by sharing some of his interests, such as performing magic and playing *Go*, a strategy board game utilising black and white stones.

At the English Lounge, Rintaro met fellow students who would invariably ask him about his hobbies, a common question when meeting someone in Japan. When he replied with 'performing magic', the response would normally be pleasant surprise followed by a request to see a trick. This was a good way for Rintaro to combine making new friends and practicing English in one space. Even though his interactions at the English Lounge enabled him both to practice speaking English and to socialise, he seemed to view the purpose of the English Lounge as a pragmatic tool to aid in his ultimate goal of English language improvement, which he clearly identified as a need in his future career.

R: I think the purpose is to practice for conversation and to improve, of course, conversation. And then at the same time I think we can improve in English.

(Interview 1)

There was further evidence of his pragmatic view of the English Lounge, i.e. he considered it to be a place for English practice. While he did not place any importance on the change of location and layout in the English Lounge from his first year to his second year, this contrasted with some students who stated a preference for the former English Lounge. During Rintaro's first year at the university, the English Lounge had been located in a different building with a different type of seating in a different arrangement from the English Lounge at the time of the interview. He noted the physical difference with the previous English Lounge, which was much more spacious than the current English Lounge, but stated that was not a factor in his use of the English Lounge: 'I feel I want to use in English. Even if it is Yellow Sofa is wide and narrow, it doesn't matter'.

Supporting Other Learners

Rintaro recognised that there were many different kinds of people in the English Lounge; some were afraid of participating, others were more confident. He realised that people come for different reasons. In regard to the English Lounge and his fellow Chinese majors, he expressed a desire to encourage them to also use the English Lounge. He appeared to have a deep, empathetic understanding of how people similar to him, such as Chinese majors, feel and think. Rintaro attempted to be a good role model/*senpai* to people who were his *kohai* because he knew that what they were experiencing was similar to what he had experienced. This could possibly stem from his own personal experiences of difficulties and triumphs in his language learning journey. He recounted an experience attempting to speak English at the freshman (first-year) orientation trip at the start of his university studies. During the orientation trip, students can join various themed lessons using English with topics ranging from cooking and snooker to practical English lessons. He joined a workshop focusing on creating goals for the TOEIC. He recounted that he was very nervous and sometimes could not talk due to his nervousness. He described it as a bad experience, but also a good experience because it was ultimately a learning experience. Realising that something that feels like a bad experience can actually be good in the larger perspective of improving, Rintaro consistently tried to encourage his fellow Chinese major students to overcome feelings of fear and shyness, noting that they hesitated to go to the English Lounge because they were afraid of making mistakes. He suggested that Chinese majors were possibly even more shy and afraid of making errors using English than English majors and International Communication majors at the university. Rintaro seemed to understand his classmates' possible reticence because he admitted that during his first visit to the English Lounge in his first year, he felt extremely shy and nervous. He proposed to help them by suggesting the Self-Access Learning Centre (SALC) create a large sign to put on display.

R: As I said, I think we have to make a poster that is written 'Don't be afraid of making the mistakes'.

(Interview 1)

Studying Abroad in Taiwan

In Year 2 of the study, Rintaro was studying abroad in Taipei where he attended a prestigious university and was happy to meet many other people, such as Chinese students from mainland China and other international students, in addition to the local Taiwanese students. Having studied there for little more than three months at the time of the second interview, Rintaro had developed his routine for his university life in Taipei. Similar to his routine in Japan, Rintaro seemed to develop his routine in Taipei based on his ultimate goals. Being in a Chinese-speaking country, he decided to focus entirely on his Chinese studies rather than splitting his efforts between Chinese and English as he had done in Japan. He still felt English to be of importance, but it made more sense to him to make the most of his opportunity to study Chinese in Taipei.

At the start of his studies in Taiwan, Rintaro felt that he was not good at speaking Chinese. He expressed frustration during this period of his study-abroad experience due to difficulties in understanding his teachers. The classes were conducted entirely in Chinese and the instructors spoke very quickly, so he had difficulty catching anything the professors said during the lectures.

R: Yeah. I didn't catch the teacher says. What teacher said. So I was really... how can I say... I feel like I want to cry.

(Interview 2)

Despite his difficulties and resulting emotions, he persevered by continuing to practice conversation with his new Taiwanese friends, and he came up with a strategy that helped him improve in the classroom.

R: I improve Chinese better, I think, because sometimes I saw a lot of news that is written in Chinese, especially BBC and also CNN... so when I conversation with people and I talk about the news.

(Interview 2)

This was similar to Rintaro's strategy for practicing his listening skills in English the previous year when he listened to BBC and CNN. Fortunately, BBC and CNN are offered in Chinese as well. Although the learning curve at first was steep in Taipei, by the time of the interview he felt he had made enough improvements to feel more confident in understanding his classes.

The Influence of Other Learners

Different cultural attitudes were also very apparent to Rintaro, and this was another area that required adaptation and personal adjustments as he encountered many Chinese students in addition to the local Taiwanese students. He described the Chinese students as more assertive than typical Japanese students, or even typical Taiwanese students. According to Rintaro, Japanese students were still the most 'conservative' and least assertive which meant that he had some challenges in navigating social cues, requiring him to become more assertive himself.

Despite this frustrating beginning to his study-abroad experience, Rintaro wanted to give future study-abroad students advice similar to the advice he wanted to give his *kohai* students majoring in Chinese. His advice to students who may pursue studying abroad is to 'not be afraid'. This attitude stemmed in part from his own experiences with difficult circumstances. Even when he didn't understand the instructors in his classes, which was a demoralising experience for him personally as a study-abroad student, he remained diligent and persistent. Remembering his initial nervousness upon visiting the English Lounge for the first time, Rintaro wished to offer the advice of 'Don't be afraid of making mistakes' to his juniors who may have similar experiences. His study-abroad experience seems to have enriched his learning experience and his plans for the future. He knows he wants to work for a trade company, and is taking all the necessary steps towards realising his plans. In addition to his conscious efforts at improving his language skills, he also incidentally gained important social skills. Rintaro used performing magic at the English Lounge to make casual social connections, and then built upon those skills in Taipei by learning to become more assertive.

Identity and Language Use

Rintaro considered himself to be shy and inadequate at expressing himself in English. However, the identity he projected was of someone not afraid of making mistakes, who could talk without worrying and who could be a mentor to others. He displayed several aspects of a typical Regular User of the English Lounge. He primarily viewed the English Lounge as a tool to improve his language skills. He fit his visits to the lounge into his schedule, even if he only had 10 minutes, with the purpose of practicing conversation. Even though he used magic as a means of breaking the ice with new people and directing the topic to an area he felt familiar with, he did not state that the English Lounge was a place to hang out with friends. Rather, he was happy to practice conversation with anyone who was there, and use magic as it offered a quick means to initiate an engaging interaction upon meeting someone new. Furthermore, he did not place any weight on the appearance and layout of the space, as long as it was a space designated for English-only speaking. This clearly showed his priority of motives in using the English Lounge. Whether he would continue to use the English Lounge in the future 'depends on the situation'. These characteristics distinguish Rintaro from students who fit into the Yellow Sofa Group. Members of this group describe using the space as a regular social gathering spot and a place that has contributed not only to their English language growth but also to their personal growth. Rintaro did not attribute his increase in assertiveness to his use of the English Lounge. He credited other experiences, specifically his study-abroad experiences in Taipei, with these positive changes. It was most likely that overcoming obstacles, such as his experience of nervousness at the first-year student orientation camp and his inability to understand his professors at the beginning of his study abroad, that helped him develop. In contrast, he viewed the English Lounge, where he may have felt nervous upon his initial visit but did not face a challenging obstacle, as a tool similar to the TOEIC app on his phone or watching the BBC or CNN.

Rintaro's use of the English Lounge and his study-abroad experience appeared to have had an impact on his identity. Firstly, the view he had of himself was of someone who wasn't 'afraid of making mistakes' and, later on, someone who simply was 'not afraid'. Despite difficulties and obstacles, he persisted and overcame challenges.

R: Because I'm in Taiwan, I make the effort to study Chinese. And also, when I come to Taiwan, but I felt it-I felt that I was no good at speaking Chinese. But then I improve.

(Interview 2)

Rintaro also talked about his future dreams as a form of 'imagined identity' (see Chapter 11). He still wanted to work for a trading company to be able to communicate well with people from different countries, and to be more proactive at using English. Because he envisioned himself as a person working in trade, he chose to major in Chinese as he saw the language as necessary for his future career path. Although his ideal future self was left open in some ways, such as where and exactly what kind of career he would pursue, he had wisely narrowed down the parameters in order to focus on his skill sets. He saw himself as someone who would work internationally, in Asia in particular. In addition to Chinese, he focused on English for the same reason, and thus frequented the English Lounge to that end.

Rintaro saw himself using Chinese and English as part of his career because he saw himself as someone who could communicate with people from different countries. The English Lounge provided Rintaro with not only a tool to improve his English language skills, but also benefits of which he may not have been aware. His future plans involved conversing with people from various nations and cultures, and the English Lounge provided Rintaro with a chance to experience talking with international students and teachers along with the opportunity to develop critical social skills.

9 'I should be more confident in talking with people': Sachiko's Story

Ross Sampson

At the start of the research in June 2017, Sachiko was a second-year student of Chinese who was a Non User of the English Lounge. In the first interview, she was quite shy and nervous in general, particularly about being interviewed in English, but she was more relaxed in the second interview as a third-year student.

Impressions of the English Lounge

Sachiko had never been to the English Lounge during the two-year research period, and in the first interview she confessed that she did not know what happened there:

S: I don't know what they are doing... I don't know how the Yellow Sofa is used.

(Interview 1)

She assumed that the purpose of the space was 'to improve English speaking' and believed that only students who specialised in English went there. However, in the second interview, her understanding expanded somewhat and she explained: 'I've heard any students can go there and talk about anything'. Nevertheless, in the first interview she claimed to have 'no confidence' in speaking English, along with a dislike for talking with people in general, which explained why she had not visited the lounge. In fact, she reiterated her dislike for talking with people throughout the interview, for example,

Interviewer: And what would you say is the reason that you've never been?
S: Reason? Hmmm, because I still have no confidence for speaking English, and I don't like talking with people.

(Interview 1)

In both interviews, however, she did express an interest in going to the lounge (possibly to seem agreeable to the interviewer), but her lack of confidence and self-professed introverted personality rendered it difficult for her to do so. One of the underlying features of Sachiko's narrative in general was the evidence of contradiction. For example, she mentioned that she might be interested in visiting the lounge, but simultaneously stated reasons why she would be unlikely to do so:

Interviewer: Umm if we talk about the future, Sachiko do you think you will go to the Yellow Sofa area next semester or next year?
S: Ehhh I, maybe no I won't go.
Interviewer: Ok, and what do you think is the main reason that you won't go?
S: I think, hmmm, I still don't have confidence.
Interviewer: Do you have any friends that go to the Yellow Sofa area?
S: Umm, maybe no.

(Interview 1)

Attitudes Towards Communicating in English

Even if she did not ultimately visit the English Lounge, Sachiko mentioned that communication skills were something she wanted to develop. However, in both interviews she tended to use the word 'should' when talking about qualities she felt she lacked, in essence being critical of herself:

> I should be more confident in talking with people. I think I have learnt writing and reading so much, so I should speak, practise speaking from now on.
>
> (Interview 1)

In Interview 2, there was a clear shift in that she began to see the value of speaking in English. She even started to enjoy speaking with friends and the Self-Access Learning Centre (SALC) staff on occasion in English and had more opportunities to do so as there were fewer mandatory classes to attend.

Identity and Language Use

In terms of the relationship between language use and identity, when it came to acquiring and communicating in languages, Sachiko felt that it was important to take on characteristics that she judged to exemplify speakers of her target language cultures. She said that she felt she needed to be 'like a Chinese person' when speaking Chinese. In the case of communicating in English, she expressed a desire to be 'like an American'. This was because of the American English which she said she had learnt. Even though her attitude towards using languages became more positive in the second year of the study, confidence was still an issue: 'I still don't have enough confidence, but I became to like using languages'.

Sachiko's English communication ability was that of an intermediate speaker, and she was diligent in studying languages and using resources – mainly books and computers. Furthermore, as a student in the Chinese department and a self-identified 'introvert', she did not relate to or identify with the English Lounge or its users. However, she did think it necessary to become more outgoing, and that she should engage in more oral communicative interactions.

Views on Using English with Others

In the first interview, Sachiko explained that she liked being alone and that her dislike for talking to people was not limited only to English. This was dissonant given that she was learning Chinese and English and learning languages normally involves communicating with people. Around the time of the second interview, she was in her third year at the university and had more free time. This enabled her to use that time to go to the SALC about two or three times a week and use English with the SALC staff. She had come to see the benefit of interacting with people in order to improve her English-speaking skills. The SALC staff are generally Japanese people who use English at work, which makes them approachable role models for many students. She also saw her friends as a positive influence: 'all of my friends are so talkative ... they like contact with students and teachers'.

Another contradiction in Sachiko's narrative was the role of those who she perceived to be 'native speakers' of English. On the one hand, she was more comfortable speaking to friends and the SALC staff in English than lecturers, as speaking to 'native speakers' was more of a challenge. She perceived that speaking to 'native speakers' required the need to *behave* in a different way, but that was something that she aspired to do: 'I like behaving, because I like when I speak English to behave like American people do... how to reply just like natives'.

A further contradiction in Sachiko's narrative related to her plans after graduation. In both interviews, she claimed not to talk to people much, but despite this, she divulged in Interview 1 that she had a boyfriend, with whom she spoke to in English every day. He was from and lived in New Zealand, where she planned to move after graduating. She also revealed her lack of confidence in communicating with her boyfriend, but realised that she needed to overcome her reluctance to be with people: 'It is a pretty big problem for me, but I should overcome being with people'.

English Improvement

A year after the first interview, Sachiko had come to like using languages because her friends were so 'talkative'. She was still in a relationship with her English-speaking boyfriend from New Zealand and thus still used English every day. A year before, she talked about her struggles with her boyfriend's vocabulary use. However, she felt she had only improved her writing:

Interviewer: Last time you said you had some difficulty with your boyfriend's vocabulary. Do you think that's improved?
S: Yes, I'm sure I've improved a lot, but just for writing or texting.

(Interview 2)

Sachiko's overall language competency had improved over the year and she used English every day, although she still claimed to lack self-confidence (although this had improved a little). In between interviews, she had been to New Zealand, and had become used to interacting in English.

In the second year of the project, Sachiko maintained that her weakest skill in English was still speaking, although she thought her speaking and communication skills had improved since the first interview. Explaining that, she had realised that being shy and not interacting with anyone was not fruitful for language learning. She also explained that she had had more opportunities to communicate.

Even though Sachiko detailed many things to indicate a lack of confidence in herself and an overly modest attitude, when talking about high school, she explained she wasn't challenged enough:

S: Actually the level of high school wasn't high enough, wasn't high compared to my level.

(Interview 2)

This was the first time she talked positively about herself and her perceived abilities. Additionally, she said that even though she felt happy when she got good scores, she wondered why she had received a good score and what she should do to maintain or improve it. She revealed that she believed learning should be challenging and difficult.

Beliefs

Sachiko believed that the best way to learn English is by 'talking'; however, another contradiction emerged in her response when asked about this:

S: I think only reading or writing the computers in the SALC can improve my English.

(Interview 2)

When asked about advice for language learning, she would recommend 'movies' or 'to read' to other students as a means to improve their English if they don't like 'talking' like herself. She talked about how she came to the SALC to make use of books in an effort to improve conversation. This suggested that she preferred to work alone, even for something such as improving conversational ability. Therefore, it was not surprising that she had not been to the English Lounge even once.

Shortly before the second interview, she had begun a part-time job at a nearby international airport, which she claimed to enjoy. Her comments suggest a change in beliefs about talking to others:

S: There are lots of foreigners. I enjoy talking and smiling with them.
(Interview 2)

However, after previously explaining that she didn't like speaking, stating a lack of confidence to speak, it was quite surprising that she enjoyed talking to strangers in a job that required a lot of interaction with people. The job didn't appear to connect with the kind of person Sachiko had described herself to be. Perhaps she was just projecting an alternate identity, or maybe she had actually come to enjoy interacting with people, particularly in English. Nevertheless, she said she was enjoying her part-time job and using English for work.

In both interviews, it was not completely clear why Sachiko was studying languages at university, what her motivations were or if she truly enjoyed the language learning process. The two biggest reasons she gave for learning English and Chinese were 'for getting my job' and 'fun'. During both interviews, she expressed her thoughts in a number of ways which were somewhat contradictory. It could be that she was unsure of herself, or that different environments of English language use may have rendered different feelings for her. The challenge of language learning may not have been a comfortable one for her, but one she did see benefit from, although, as she previously stated, in her opinion, learning shouldn't be an easy process.

Sachiko was modest in the interviews about her overall ability and assessment of herself. It might be that by having a perpetual feeling of dissatisfaction, she was able to continue to strive for improvement. Of course, there are many areas of English in which Sachiko could improve, but it didn't seem like she was willing to look at herself in a positive light in regard to her language learning.

10 'Just try is I think the most important thing': Sayaka's Story

Bethan Kushida

At the time of the first interview in July 2017, Sayaka was a second-year student majoring in English. She was very interested in using the English Lounge and understood how it could help her achieve her learning goals. Still, there were certain factors that held her back from visiting and she was yet to try it out. However, by the time of the second interview in June 2018, Sayaka had overcome her reservations about using the lounge and had visited a few times, with mostly positive experiences.

Before University

Two people had a big influence on Sayaka during her early English education. One was her father, who was a high school English teacher, and as a child Sayaka would often watch what he was doing. Sayaka credits him as being one of the biggest reasons why she wanted to study English and why she chose to come to Kanda University of International Studies (KUIS). The other was her third-grade junior high school teacher, who was a graduate from KUIS and had a very good level of English. This teacher's classes were fun and comfortable, and the students had a lot of opportunity to speak English and raise their hands to volunteer answers. Although her future plans later changed, Sayaka's dream when she was in junior high school was to become an English teacher like her third-grade teacher.

The style of classes in junior high school was mixed, depending on the teacher, but in addition to the use of a textbook to learn grammar and vocabulary, there were many games and activities to help the students get used to English. During this time, the foundations of Sayaka's English skills were built. Like most students in Japan, things changed in high school when the focus switched to preparing for university entrance examinations. The games and activities stopped, and all the class time was spent on studying from a textbook and practicing how to answer the type of questions that would be asked in the exams, such as multiple choice, filling in the blanks or writing short sentences in English.

Since there was no speaking component to the entrance exams, there was no emphasis on putting the language they had been learning into practical use. High school English was not an entirely negative experience for Sayaka since she was grateful that she could get used to reading long articles in English before entering university. However, she regretted that she didn't have time in class to practice speaking English.

Classes at University

When Sayaka entered KUIS, she was surprised that the style of classes was so different from what she had been used to in high school. She found it very hard to go from classes where the emphasis was on reading, grammar and vocabulary to classes in which the students were expected to discuss and share their opinions. Nevertheless, she enjoyed the fact that there were about half the number of students per class than there were in high school (around 20 as opposed to 40 students), and she appreciated how the smaller class sizes facilitated communication among the students and the lecturers.

In her second year, the focus in her compulsory classes moved away from speaking and more towards reading and writing. She missed having the opportunity to speak much English in her compulsory classes, but an elective class called 'Ways of Learning English' gave her a chance to talk to third- and fourth-year students with a passion for speaking English. These students had a big impact on her, and she is still in touch with one particularly motivated friend who continues to give her advice.

Moving into her third year, the number of classes dropped, but the workload increased. Sayaka found herself spending a lot of time doing assignments and preparing for her translation class. She enjoyed being in classes together with fourth-year students because she could find out from them what it was like to go through the job-hunting process, which she would have to do in her fourth year, although she missed the stability of her second-year classes as many of the third- and fourth-year students were regularly absent from class for interviews and other job hunting-related activities. She also liked the fact that she could now choose which classes to take and had the freedom to select the lecturers and what to learn.

Goals

There was no specific job that Sayaka expressed an interest in doing in the future, but she hoped for a job that would allow her to use English some of the time, such as a hotel receptionist or other job in which she could help non-Japanese people in Japan. Her preference was to work in Japan or close by in Asia so that she could be near her aging parents. Before looking for a job, she was thinking of taking a gap year to study abroad. She had never been to another country and wanted to travel overseas in order to gain a new perspective, broaden her ways of thinking and learn new things. In Japan, she felt her way of thinking was very narrow. She was considering Australia, where one of her classmates had had a great time, and one of her high school teachers had also recommended New Zealand as a good place for Japanese students to learn English.

As for her language learning goals, in addition to improving her speaking, her short-term goal at the time of the first interview was to improve her reading speed in order to get the institutionally required number of points in the Test of English as a Foreign Language (TOEFL) exam. She achieved this, and at the time of the second interview, her goal was to be able to read novels in the original English rather than in the Japanese translation. She also stated a short-term goal of using the Self-Access Learning Centre (SALC) more.

She expressed a desire to be able to use English outside of KUIS, for example at her part-time job in a video rental shop, where she sometimes wasn't able to explain something in English as well as she would have liked to a non-Japanese customer. She also wanted to be able to use more formal English with customers.

Her ideal self as an English user was to become 'a very sociable person by using English', not afraid to talk to new people, and she hoped that a gap year would help her get a new perspective and become a sociable, open-minded person.

Beliefs about Language Learning

For her, the most important thing was to try. Even if one makes a mistake or has a bad result, it's better than never trying.

S: …the result is good or not, […] I think it doesn't matter, so maybe the first try is very important, to speak or learning something.
(Interview 1)

More than taking classes or reading books a lot, she recommended that new students go to the upper floor of the SALC and just enjoy speaking English. If they can have fun learning English, they will get the motivation to study more. In the second interview, she repeated her advice to not be afraid of speaking English. She said that it was not helpful that she was so worried about making mistakes when she was a first-year student and that mistakes can actually help you learn. She didn't want students to waste their time and their school fees.

Identity and Language Use

One of the reasons Sayaka enjoyed speaking English was that it made her feel like a different person. She found it hard to explain, but she called it a 'fresh feeling'. When she listened to recordings of herself speaking, she felt that the person wasn't her. When asked which she preferred, she said it was hard to choose because English was difficult for her, but she would say the *English Sayaka* because she was more positive and brave. The *Japanese Sayaka* had a fear of speaking English and was hesitant to go to the English Lounge, but once she started trying to speak English, she gained confidence and a belief that she was capable.

> S: It's kind of strange but when I'm Japanese me, I feel I'm afraid to speak English, so I can't go Yellow Sofa or SALC so much, but when I turn to speak English, like switch, yeah, I don't know, it's strange but I feel confidence. Maybe 'I can speak English!', or like that.
>
> (Interview 1)

She mentioned that this effect was occurring during the interview too. Before the interview, she worried that she wouldn't be able to explain herself well or sustain the conversation for 30 minutes, thinking 'It's impossible', but once the conversation started, she realised she could do it and even enjoy it.

Use of the SALC

Sayaka started to use the SALC regularly in her first year and continued in her second year. She went there two or three times a week, mostly to study vocabulary and grammar, but sometimes to listen to English using the audiovisual media resources. At the time of the first interview, the most useful area of the SALC for her was the writing support area, where she could get one-to-one advice on how to improve her essays and become a better writer. However, she wasn't using any of the areas or attending any of the events for practicing spoken English in the SALC, and she had never visited the English Lounge. She had once made an appointment with a lecturer in the one-to-one conversation practice area, but that was only because her first-year English lecturer had set an assignment to have a conversation in English outside of class. At the time of the second interview, her usage of the SALC had dropped because she had less free time and found the SALC a little too noisy to do her assignments, preferring instead to use the quiet library. She had, however, by that time visited the English Lounge a few times.

Use of the English Lounge

At the time of the first interview, Sayaka didn't have any experience of visiting the English Lounge. Nevertheless, she had a well-formed image of what she thought the lounge was like, and from what she said during the interview, it can be assumed that she had imagined herself going to the area. She described the area as a place where you can speak English with strangers, with Japanese and with people from other countries. Her image was that it's a place where you can talk about anything you like, and you don't have to worry about your level of English. When asked what she thought the purpose of the area was, she replied that maybe it's good for 'decreasing the fear of speaking'. She imagined that if she went there two or three times a week, she would get 'confidence to speak English', maybe 'make more friends' and become the kind of person who isn't 'afraid to speak to strangers'.

Her image of a student who goes to the English Lounge was someone who is a 'very active person'. They are 'people [who] really like to speak English or really want to improve their skills'. In her 'Ways of Learning English' class in her second year, Sayaka met many students who loved to speak English and go to the English Lounge or the one-to-one Practice Centre. She described them as not being afraid of making grammar or vocabulary mistakes. Sayaka was impressed by one girl in her class with whom she partnered. This student cared more about the quantity of language rather than the quality. She spoke a lot and used different vocabulary and gestures to explain what she was trying to communicate, and even though she made mistakes, Sayaka could understand what she wanted to say. These students had a big impact on Sayaka and her motivation to go to the English Lounge.

S: They are very kind, and their passion made me to be like her or him. [...] Because of them now [...] I became the person who want go there. They have very big influence on me.

(Interview 1)

This feeling of wanting to go to the English Lounge was strengthened by the fact that second-year classes are more focused on reading and writing than first-year classes, and she had less opportunity to speak English in class in her second year. However, despite being aware of the benefits of going to the English Lounge and having a strong motivation to go, taking the step of making the first visit proved difficult for Sayaka. At the time of the first interview, she gave two main reasons why she had never been.

The first reason was that she was afraid to go because she didn't think she had a high enough level of English to speak fluently in the lounge, and she was worried about making mistakes. This became even more of a block when she became a second-year student because she worried that people would expect her level to be higher having already completed a year of university.

S: I'm sophomore, so everyone think my English skill is maybe improved than freshman, so I'm worried about that.

(Interview 1)

She imagined that if she were ever to go to the lounge, she would feel more comfortable speaking to 'non-native' speakers rather than non-Japanese

English speakers. She presumed that those who she saw as 'non-native' speakers would have the same worries about making mistakes and lack of confidence about speaking English as her, and she could empathise with their feelings.

S: Maybe I think they have same feeling with me, [...] so maybe they worry about making mistake, or they don't have confidence to speak English or something, so I want to speak the person who is close to me.

(Interview 1)

Nevertheless, she didn't care whether the person she would talk to was younger or older than her, and she saw talking to older students with a high level of speaking skills as a good opportunity to learn and improve her English.

S: When I [...] talked with junior or senior [third- or fourth-year students] they have great English speaking skill so they lead to me to speak English, so it's great, I think.

(Interview 1)

When discussing the difference between *English Sayaka* and *Japanese Sayaka*, she conjectured that she might find it easier to go to the English Lounge if she spoke in English a little bit with someone before entering the lounge. Flipping the switch from *Japanese Sayaka* to *English Sayaka* in this way would build up her confidence and her belief in her abilities, she imagined, enabling her to take the first step of approaching the area.

The second reason that she hadn't been to the English Lounge was that she was reluctant to visit alone.

S: I've never been to there because I [...] think I can't go there alone. So, yes. I didn't have enough opportunity to go there with my friend.

(Interview 1)

However, she said that if her friends agreed to go with her, she would be willing to visit the lounge and mentioned that an invitation from someone close to her would have a stronger effect than a recommendation by a lecturer. She thought that holding events at the English Lounge to which the regular users could invite their friends would be a good way to bring in non users such as herself. Over the course of the interview, perhaps as a result of the switch being flipped to confident *English Sayaka* through the use of English, or perhaps as a result of her vocalising her imagined visits to the lounge, her confidence about taking the step of making a first visit to the space seemed to be growing. She even finished the interview by suggesting that perhaps she herself would ask a friend to go with her rather than wait to be invited. (It should be acknowledged that taking part in the interview probably had an influence in this decision by providing Sayaka with the opportunity to reflect on the reasons why she chose not to use the English Lounge.)

One year later, during the second interview, Sakaya revealed that she did eventually ask some friends to go with her. Her visits to the lounge with her friends, one of whom was a regular user, were mostly positive experiences. She had a fun time, and she enjoyed the chance to speak English. She also spoke to an older student and asked him how to improve her speaking. She subsequently returned three or four times. One of those times was by herself, when she talked to a third-year student, although she was more nervous at that time and couldn't talk much. For her, it was easier to talk with friends because she could ask them how to say something if she didn't know how, and she could feel more relaxed. At the time of the second interview, she hadn't been back since starting her third year due to lack of time, but she felt that she should go.

Since using the English Lounge, her image of the area had changed. Before going, she had thought everyone there would be good at speaking English, but she had since realised that there are students of all different levels.

S: Of course yeah some of the student are very good at it, but on the other hand, some of the student are just like me. They want to improve their speaking skill, so they go there.

(Interview 2)

She felt that the experience of going to the English Lounge had changed her as a language learner and that she was now more positive and open to learning. She had realised that there was nothing to be afraid of.

S: I think that I became open to, yeah, or positive to learn, and yes, before, before I go there or before I use SALC a lot, um, I'm, I was afraid to go or I was afraid to use kind of the booth, but after that I realised it's there there is nothing to I have to concern.

(Interview 2)

Her time at the English Lounge made her feel 'brave and positive and kind of optimistic' about talking with strangers. She still worried before speaking about making mistakes, but once she began to talk and became *English Sayaka*, she stopped caring. She also still felt an expectation to have a better level of English than she did, and felt even more pressure now that she was a third-year student and supposedly more proficient and more capable of giving learning advice to younger students, but she said this would not stop her from using the English Lounge again in the future if she had time.

Without knowing her story in detail, Sayaka would appear to be the kind of student that one might expect to make use of the English Lounge. She enjoyed talking in English and wished she had more opportunities to practice; around her were some influential near peer role models (NPRMs) (Murphey, 1998) who were users of the English Lounge; her stated advice for learning was just to try and to not worry about making mistakes; and her ideal second language (L2) self (Dörnyei, 2005) was someone who is 'a very sociable person' in English and is not afraid to talk to new people. She was capable of imagining herself using the English Lounge, she recognised how she could benefit from it and she was motivated to use the space. Nevertheless, she was held back for over a year and a half by anxiety over her level of English and a fear of going to the space alone. This is the same fear that many KUIS students describe when they explain why they are reluctant to use the English Lounge. However, in Sayaka's case, she had a very high awareness of herself as a learner and was eventually able to devise suitable strategies (flipping the switch from *Japanese Sayaka* to *English Sayaka*; asking a friend to accompany her) that enabled her to control her anxiety and gain the confidence necessary to break through that fear. In her third year, a new obstacle had presented itself in the form of a lack of free time, but Sayaka would no longer hesitate to visit the English Lounge if she had the opportunity. Thanks to even just the short time that she had spent in the lounge, she now had a more open and positive attitude to learning and had narrowed the gap between her current self and her ideal L2 self as a sociable person who is not afraid of talking to new people.

Part 3
Exploring Concepts Through the Research

11 Exploring Identity in a Social Learning Space

Jo Mynard

The purpose of this chapter is to explore the role of learner identity in relation to the English Lounge. Our research has approached this in three ways: (1) by understanding the identities of our participants, i.e. the students who use the English Lounge and also those who actively chose *not* to use it; (2) by exploring whether the participants' identities have affected the ways in which they perceive and use the English Lounge; and (3) by understanding the roles that the English Lounge and the dynamics evident within it have played in shifting the learners' identities. This chapter starts with a brief literature review in order to situate the study. It then outlines the chosen framework and finally presents the findings, paying particular attention to the dynamic processes and shifts.

Background

Why focus on identity?

Although the overall study described in this book covers a lot of theoretical constructs, identity was the one that we began with which inspired us to initiate this project. From our observations of social language learning spaces at our own institution and elsewhere (i.e. at other centres in Japan, and also in Mexico, the UK, Thailand, Turkey, Ireland and Cambodia), it was evident that learner identity must have a role to play in how such spaces operate and has an effect on users in those spaces. This project gave us an opportunity to examine the literature in greater depth and consider how we might research and understand phenomena occurring in the English Lounge, and by extension, in other micro areas of the Self-Access Learning Centre (SALC).

What do we mean by identity?

Identity research has frequently been used to frame studies into human behaviour and is useful for exploring phenomena within a given context. Identity has been defined as 'the ways in which individuals and groups regard themselves as similar to, or different from, each other'

(Sherry, 2008: 414). Identity is said to be fluid rather than static, i.e. perceptions can change over time. Like many applied linguists writing in this area (e.g. Block, 2007; Norton, 2000), we take a poststructuralist approach which originally comes from the field of sociology. This is a rather complicated framing of the world, but it allows for a nuanced and multi-levelled interpretation of social conditions influencing a person's identity. This approach to identity research is defined as 'socially constructed, self-conscious, ongoing narratives that individuals perform, interpret and project in dress, bodily movements, actions and language' (Block, 2007: 32). Someone's sense of identity is determined by membership of social categories, and this is something that we have been able to explore within the social structure of the English Lounge. In addition to social categories and social conditions, a poststructuralist approach also takes into account participants' personal constructions of their individual identities.

How can we research identity?

There are several ways in which to explore important phenomena when studying identity. Firstly, we considered a discursive interpretation (e.g. Miller, 2014; Weedon, 1997). Given that the context under investigation was a language conversation lounge, a discursive interpretation was particularly appropriate, and this was approached in two ways: (1) we considered the content of the semi-structured interviews and the language learning histories; and (2) to a degree, the actual *choice of words* used by the participants was taken into account, although we did not undertake a thorough micro-analysis of linguistic features. Secondly, we were able to interpret non-linguistic features (Block, 2007; Gee, 1996) to incorporate into the observation study (see Chapter 4) and in the interviewer observation notes. Finally, we drew on performativity theory (e.g. Butler, 1997; Goffman, 1959/1990) which looked at the actions and roles that our participants displayed in the English Lounge. As Japan has certain social roles and hierarchies running through all aspects of society (see Chapter 3), the degree to which these roles were evident in the English Lounge was also important to document. In fact, identity can be seen as a kind of *acting* where participants are performing particular roles (Goffman, 1959/1990), and these give hints to their identities. This research aimed to investigate these three important aspects of identity by taking an ethnographic approach.

One final factor that we need to be aware of is the researchers' roles in the English Lounge and in the research project. Taking an ethnographic approach allowed us to observe behaviours in the English Lounge over an extended period of time, but we recognise that as researchers we were inevitably contributing to changes taking place. We were therefore considered to be one of the environmental factors that affected the 'society' of the English Lounge which may have influenced the participants with whom we were working. An example of this can be seen in Sayaka's narrative (Chapter 10), where she shifted from being a Non User of the English Lounge to an occasional user, potentially partially because of the interviews she participated in for this project.

Research Framework

Keeping in mind the various aspects of identity that we were interested in capturing, the complex nature of identity research and the nature of the context, we decided to use an established framework to guide our research. The framework we chose was devised by Benson *et al.* (2013), who investigated identity construction in a study-abroad context according to six facets (summarised in Table 11.1).

The fact that there were six facets in this framework appealed to us as it allows for a multi-levelled, systematic analysis. The first three facets in Table 11.1 draw on earlier work by Harré (2001) and are concerned with conceptions of the 'self'. *Embodied identity* can be defined as the self that exists as part of our physical selves. All of the participants in this study were Japanese university students aged 18–21, but we did not explore other embodied identity facets specifically.

Reflexive identity is one's own view of the self. These views are shaped throughout our lives through experiences, our interactions with others and through our inner dialogues. These experiences occurring within a second or other language add an extra layer to these views, and individuals may have different conceptions of themselves depending on where they are, who they are talking to and which languages they are using.

Projected identity is when someone consciously and intentionally constructs the identities that they want others to see as a form of self-presentation (Goffman, 1959/1990). These constructions may have the effect of influencing others or in creating a public identity.

Table 11.1 Facets of identity

Facet 1	Embodied identity	The self as a mobile point of perception located in a particular body
Facet 2	Reflexive identity	The self's view of the self, incorporating self-concept and attributes and capabilities
Facet 3	Projected identity	The self as it is semiotically represented to others in interaction
Facet 4	Recognised identity	The self as it is preconceived and recognised by others in the course of interaction
Facet 5	Imagined identity	The self's view of its future possibilities
Facet 6	Identity categories and resources	The self as it is represented (by self or others) using established social categories and semiotic resources

Source: From Benson *et al.* (2013: 19).

Recognised identity is how we are perceived by others. This facet might be difficult to ascertain from interviews with the participants themselves, but may be combined with insights from observations, reports of incidents, correspondence exchanges and through interviews with peers and associates.

Imagined identity is a facet stemming from original work by Markus and Nurius (1986), who developed the possible selves theory. This conceptualisation may incorporate views of our past and possible future selves. In this kind of research, *imagined identity* refers to the groups or roles to which a person aspires to belong. This might relate to current ideas about community membership, or about possible future situations that will require language skills. Yashima (2009) makes a distinction between someone identifying with a target language (TL) group and having a more international posture. Incidentally, the English Lounge is deliberately presented as an international space where English is a tool for communication and does not represent any particular TL community.

Finally, *identity categories and resources* are the labels given to possible selves after considering the various social categories and experiences that define a person.

The facets of identity that can be seen in Table 11.1 were explored by Benson *et al.* (2013) in a study-abroad context by using a narrative inquiry approach. Data was analysed from interviews before study abroad; blogs, emails, MSN and Facebook posts kept during a study-abroad period; and interviews after returning home from the study-abroad experience. As the English Lounge at our university is unlike a traditional Japanese university learning space, students often liken it to a study-abroad experience, so we felt that the framework would suit our purposes well.

Research Questions

This portion of the research was guided by the following questions using the methods described in Chapter 4.

- How do participants view themselves as English users? Specifically, how is identity conceptualised in the following facets:
  - reflexive identity;
  - projected identity;
  - recognised identity;
  - imagined identity;
  - identity categories.
- How (if at all) do participants' identities influence ways in which they use the lounge?
- How (if at all) do participants' identities shift when using the English Lounge?

Findings

As we had already identified three groups of participants, they could be assigned identity categories according to facets included in Benson *et al.*'s (2013) framework. The groups/categories were:

Group 1
Identity category: Yellow Sofa Group members (five participants): These students were extremely frequent users and formed part of the community of practice (CoP) (see Chapter 12).
Group 2
Identity category: Regular Users (six participants): These students used the lounge several times per week, but were not core members of a CoP.
Group 3
Identity category: Non Users (four participants): At the start of the project, these students had never used the English Lounge.

We analysed the narratives for identity facets and these were labelled:

Reflexive: (R), Projected: (P), Recognised: (Rec), Imagined: (I)

In order to show how the analysis was done, we provide summaries of some of the participants' narratives (i.e. those that were not presented in Chapters 5–10) by group.

Group 1: Yellow Sofa Group

Views of the English Lounge

Overall, the students in Group 1 considered the English Lounge to have three main roles: (1) leisure, (2) social and (3) improving English. Firstly, all of the participants in Group 1 considered the English Lounge to be a relaxing place where they could meet friends and have fun. In one case, a participant implied that there was no pressure to use high-level academic English as might be the case elsewhere. One of the main reasons that the students in this group frequented the lounge was for social purposes. As we will see in Chapter 12, they are participants of a CoP, and this is one of the indicators of membership of a community. However, they mentioned that they liked to talk to anyone in that environment, not just other members of their group. Finally, the participants valued the opportunities to be in an English environment and to improve their English through speaking. In some cases, this increased their confidence; in others, there was a feeling that they could speak more freely in English than in Japanese. Identity facets for each participant will be explored below.

Kyoji

Kyoji is a Portuguese major and was in his second year at the university at the start of the project. In his interview in Year 1 of the study, he recalled how he initially felt nervous when approaching the English Lounge for the first time, but soon relaxed as he felt confident that his English was better than other students (R/Rec). In addition, he felt he was more outgoing and comfortable when he used English than when he spoke Japanese (R). He wanted to be seen by others not only as a competent speaker of English, but also as supportive, friendly and approachable (P). Kyoji found the English Lounge easy to access, but it did not challenge him. He seemed to have already outgrown it, but was nevertheless part of a community of motivated friends who helped each other to develop. He perceived users of the English Lounge to be hard-working, persistent and motivated learners (Rec). He planned to move to Brazil in the future (I). Kyoji was interviewed again in Year 2 while studying abroad in Brazil, but little was gleaned with regard to identity in relation to the English Lounge in the second interview as he was not at the university at the time.

Suzuka

In Year 1 of the study (her third year at the university), Suzuka considered herself to be nervous and shy in general when speaking English (R). However, at the English Lounge she felt free to talk about personally meaningful things and did not feel nervous (R). The English Lounge helped her to increase her confidence (R). Her initial impressions of the English Lounge were that it was an intimidating space full of very fluent English speakers (Rec); however, after visiting several times with a friend, she saw the place as somewhere fun and relaxing (Rec). She also brought a *kohai* to the English Lounge in order to share the positive experience (Rec). She did not claim to project a different identity in the English Lounge and said that her personalities in English and Japanese were the same (P). She planned to use English in the future, either by becoming a teacher or perhaps working for a company in another useful role (I). In Year 2, Suzuka's perceptions of the English Lounge remained the same; however, as a consequence of her commitment to finding a job upon graduation, and the time commitment she felt that required, she drifted away from using it and found herself associating less and less with the people she had enjoyed spending time with the previous year.

Tomoya

In Year 1 of the study (his fourth year at the university), Tomoya felt a sense of responsibility to help others (R). In the English Lounge, he highlighted his role as a mentor and role model for other students in a friendly way in order to help them feel comfortable. Although he wanted to be seen as a good role model and respected by others, he did not actively encourage other students to perceive him as a *senpai* (P). In Year 2, as Tomoya was only a part-time student taking a few teacher's licence courses, he had a sense of detachment from the English Lounge, although he still went regularly to meet friends and use English. Even though he said 'I kind of retired' from being the leader of a study group, he still felt he had a role to play in mentoring younger students (R, Rec), although the focus had changed. In the second interview, Tomoya reflected on his attempts to socialise students into the English Lounge: 'Last year... we dragged people to upstairs or have conversations ... we, uh, always try to use English. We kind of created a chance for, you know, using English upstairs', but acknowledged the new leader of the study group that year had the role of creating opportunities for younger students. His role was to provide leadership opportunities for the new generation of leaders (R).

Other members of Group 1
    Kokon (see Chapter 5 for Kokon's full case study)
    Sina (see Chapter 6 for Sina's full case study)

Summary of Group 1 identities

Using the framework of Benson *et al.* (2013), our analysis of the identities (reflexive, projected, recognised and imagined) of participants in Group 1 showed that although each participant had a unique experience, we could make some observations about identity shifts from Year 1 to Year 2. To summarise, for *reflexive identity* in Year 1, all five participants told us that they remembered lacking confidence or feeling shy or nervous when they first used the English Lounge. However, directly because of using the English Lounge regularly, the participants developed their confidence in using English through community membership. This experience influenced how they developed their perceptions and roles in the English Lounge over time. Related to *projected identity*, the growing confidence in using English in the lounge resulted in feelings of responsibility to welcome new students to the space and to be seen to be role models. The *recognised identities* of other English Lounge users were that they were nervous or insecure about their English skills and needed help in participating in the community and using English. Several participants in this group also recognised how their group might seem to others – perhaps intimidating and part of an already established group – which was not their intention. In the second half of the first year of the project, we made some improvements to the layout of the furniture based on suggestions by members of this group in an attempt to make the space less intimidating (Chen & Mynard, 2018). In terms of *imagined identities*, there was little specific data, but a general sense that English was already a big part of these students' lives and would continue to play an integral role in their future plans.

Group 2: Regular Users

Views of the English Lounge

In general, there were three overarching reasons why the participants in Group 2 chose to frequent the lounge: (1) being able to practice and improve their English, (2) being able to relax and have fun and (3) being able to meet other people and express themselves. However, through analysing the data in more depth, it became apparent that all six Regular Users particularly valued the *functional* nature of the English Lounge. For them, the English Lounge was a place where they could interact with 'native speakers'. In addition, analysing the data from the perspective of the identity facets revealed that participants in Group 2 varied and this variation will be summarised below.

Mei

Mei, a first-year student in the Spanish department, considered herself to be nervous and shy when she first started going to the English Lounge, but gradually became more comfortable (R). She considered other users of the lounge to be very 'active' and have a high level of English. In addition, she claimed that other users tried to create a friendly and welcoming atmosphere (Rec). She said that she would also like to create such a welcoming environment for other students (P). Her future goals involved being able to communicate well in English. She wanted to live in North America (I). In Year 2, comparing herself with others, she considered herself lazy and someone who could not speak English well (R). However, she had overcome her shyness and could go to the English Lounge by herself (R). She wanted to project a friendly image to first-year students (P) and had dreams of speaking multiple languages in the future (I).

Ririka

Ririka, a first-year student of Spanish, only participated in one interview (Year 1), and considered herself to be confident, motivated and diligent (R). She likened the English Lounge to a foreign country (Rec). She wanted to be seen as friendly (P) and dreamt of being a flight attendant in the future (I).

Ryunosuke

In Year 1, Ryunosuke, a second-year student in the Department of English, felt that other people using the English Lounge had better language skills than he did (R) and felt that he needed to become a different person in order to be there (P). He recognised that regular users of the space were active and had good English skills, which motivated him (Rec). He expressed a desire to use English in his future and planned to work in the UK or the US (I). In Year 2, he no longer felt the need to project a different personality in the English Lounge as his English and Japanese selves had merged (P). Comparing himself to others, he considered himself lazy and not proactive (R). He made an observation that the relationships in the English Lounge could be superficial and people were cold and reluctant to speak to other users outside the English Lounge (Rec). He still planned to work overseas in the future, but considered Asian countries as places where he could use English at work (I).

Yuki

In Year 1, Yuki, a first-year student of Spanish, felt shy using the English Lounge, but also 'cool' and 'excited' (R). She considered herself to be more outgoing and fluent when speaking English in the English Lounge than when in a classroom (R). In addition, when she used English (rather than Japanese), she felt that she was more positive about her abilities (R) as she could be around supportive friends. She felt that her English skills and confidence improved in the first year because of her regular interactions in the English Lounge. Yuki recognised two types of people in the English Lounge: older students with good English skills and first-year students (like her) with poor English skills (Rec). In the future, Yuki said that she would like to live overseas (I) and use English and Spanish. In Year 2, Yuki started to feel insecure about her English because she couldn't speak as fluently as she perceived some of the new first-year students could, even though she was now a second-year student. However, she felt that the English Lounge had helped her to improve her English skills and give her confidence (R). She imagined speaking English smoothly like a 'native' in the future and wanted to travel to places where English is spoken and continue to use the English Lounge (I).

Other members of Group 2
    Kaede (see Chapter 7 for Kaede's full case study)
    Rintaro (see Chapter 8 for Rintaro's full case study)

Summary of Group 2 identities

Using the framework of Benson *et al.* (2013), our analysis of the identities (reflexive, projected, recognised and imagined) of participants in Group 2 showed that although each participant had a unique experience, we could make some observations about identity as an influence and also about identity shifts from Year 1 to Year 2. To summarise, for *reflexive identity* in Year 1, the majority of the participants indicated that they lacked confidence or felt shy or nervous. In Year 2, many participants had developed their confidence, but simultaneously still held reflexive views of themselves that were quite critical.

In terms of *projected identity*, some participants stated that they wished to be viewed as someone who could speak English or, in one case, felt they needed to be like a different person in the English Lounge in order to participate. In Year 2, the Regular Users were aware of their projected identities and the impact they would have on others as this extract indicates:

> I'm a *senpai*, so I've got to speak fluently (Kaede, Interview 2)

From the perspective of *imagined identity*, participants mentioned the desire to be international, to work overseas or to use English in some capacity in the future. By Year 2, there were more references to *imagined identities*, and participants were more specific about their career aims and had clearer images of their future selves using English. With regard to *recognised identity*, in Year 1, the Regular Users tended to view members of the Yellow Sofa Group with something akin to awe, and were surprised that Japanese students could be so confident and fluent in English as these extracts from the interviews indicate:

> she go to Yellow Sofa every day... even though she's never studied abroad, she speaks so fluently... (Kaede, Interview 1)

> the person who stay at the Yellow Sofa, the people is really active and they're really have a good skill of, of English, so then I am motivated by them, yeah, so that's why I went to there. And I go there. (Ryunosuke, Interview 1)

In Year 2, the sense of surprise was less apparent, but the Yellow Sofa Group students continued to be seen as a source of motivation and inspiration for Regular Users because of their perceived confidence.

There were also shifts in the ways that the participants in Group 2 viewed the role of the English Lounge which tied in with their imagined identities. In Year 1, participants viewed the English Lounge as a place that had practical associations, for example, to 'improve English communication', 'make/meet friends' or 'use English only'. In Year 2, views varied. However, likening the English Lounge to a 'study-abroad' experience was a recurring theme suggesting that their imagined identities were shifting and the lounge was becoming a space that could potentially support their imagined future selves. Students consistently referred to the English Lounge in Year 2 as a comfortable/familiar place, where they felt at ease going by themselves. Participants also indicated that they had begun to feel part of the community which contrasted with the indications of anxiety they experienced in using the English Lounge in Year 1.

One participant began to see a negative aspect to the English Lounge in Year 2 and felt that it supported only superficial relationships. Another participant felt more pressure in Year 2 to be a more competent English speaker than the new students coming in. Two of the Regular Users noted that the space allowed them to be more autonomous and they felt a sense of agency over their participation which they contrasted with the passive behaviours they engaged in during classes. See Hooper *et al.* (2019) for a deeper analysis of the following themes within the data participants in Group 2: (1) confidence development, (2) social interaction, (3) group identification and roles and (4) the views of the lounge (for some of the participants) as an international space.

Group 3: Non Users

Views of the English Lounge

Although the participants in Group 3 did not use the English Lounge, their non-use of the space was at least partly due to matters of identity. In addition, the space impacted these identities as we will see in the analysis of their narratives below.

Misa

In Year 1, Misa was a second-year student in the English department. She had used the previous English Lounge in the older building and found it useful, but had not used the lounge in the new building. The main reason was that she assumed that the English Lounge was full of fluent speakers and international students (Rec). Misa was also reluctant to join established groups (Rec). However, she did see the potential benefits of the space. Misa was self-conscious about what people thought of her (P/R). In addition, she was more comfortable talking to others in a one-to-one situation (R). She considered herself to be nervous when speaking English and insecure about her grammar (R). Misa used other SALC services such as the one-to-one conversation practice desk and the learning advisor service. She imagined working with foreigners in the future either at an airport or teaching Japanese (I). She also planned to go to the English Lounge in the future and wanted to be able to communicate easily with foreigners (I). In Year 2, Misa had returned from studying abroad in the United States, and this experience had had a profound effect on her. She explained that although she was actively engaged in many different kinds of opportunities to use English, she still did not use the English Lounge. Although she still preferred one-to-one conversations to group discussions, she indicated an interest in joining a group discussion in the English Lounge at some point. However, she still perceived it to be a closed space containing established groups (Rec), despite one positive experience of being invited to join by a learning advisor and realising that lecturers there are friendly and supportive (Rec). She still considered her level of English to be too low (R). She felt she could express a different side of her personality through English (P). In the future, she imagined herself using English at work and maybe living overseas (I).

Yukari

In Year 1, Yukari (an English major in her second year) considered herself to be a confident English user and an effective language learner with established and successful weekly routines (R). As a regular user of the SALC spaces and of other SALC services such as the conversation practice desk and the advising service, she often observed the English Lounge. She projected the image of a 'good student' who knew how to use the SALC services to study effectively (P). She considered this to be in contrast to the students who used the English Lounge and often used Japanese and did not study seriously (Rec). She admitted that this was just her perception of the space; being reluctant to break into what she perceived to be established groups (Rec) prevented her from actually joining any of the conversations, but she was curious to try it one day. In the future, Yukari planned to work overseas (I). In Year 2, Yukari was still engaging in regular use of the SALC services as a confident English user and learner (R). She had tried the English Lounge a few times in the intervening time, and had had a fairly positive experience, but did not make it part of her usual study routine. It appeared that using the other services was deemed more fitting to Yukari's identity as a serious and dedicated student (R). Yukari was now learning Spanish independently in the SALC and projected an image of someone really dedicated to learning languages (P) with the intention of emigrating to Australia after graduation (I).

Other members of Group 3
Sachiko (see Chapter 9 for Sachiko's full case study)
Sayaka (see Chapter 10 for Sayaka's full case study)

Summary of Group 3 identities

The data from the Non Users suggests that beliefs play a big role (see Chapter 13), but identity is also a factor. In terms of *reflexive identity*, the students indicated an understanding of the kinds of students they were and how such students should behave. For example, if someone perceives themself to be an effective, efficient and motivated learner of English, then there are certain activities that are appropriate for them. Examples were making individual appointments with teachers and learning advisors (in the cases of Misa and Yukari), joining optional extra classes (in Sachiko's case) or learning through individual study. The

Non Users often perceived users of the English Lounge to be a different type of student, for example not serious or already part of an established group in which they did not want to be included. In Year 2, some of the participants were curious about the English Lounge and even started to use it (Sayaka and Yukari). This may have been partly prompted by their involvement in this research project, but possibly for other reasons too, such as the influence of peers, more free time and a shift in beliefs, i.e. that speaking practice is needed when learning a language (see Chapter 13). As a result of experiencing the English Lounge, the students' *recognised identities* of others was challenged. In Year 1, the Non Users perceived English Lounge users to be confident, proficient and extroverted or – in Yukari's view – not very serious. By Year 2, there was a general understanding that the English Lounge could be for people like them who wanted to practice their English-speaking skills in a comfortable environment. With regard to *projected identity*, whereas the participants in Groups 1 and 2 often intentionally projected an identity when using the English Lounge, there was little evidence of Non Users projecting an identity. As the English Lounge is a space unlike others in Japan, Regular Users need to be willing to take a risk and go there. Also, in order to sustain their engagement or manage their lack of confidence, the Regular Users and YS Group members often projected a different identity, for example by intentionally being role models to others. Interestingly, most were aware that they were projecting a different identity, which is an indication of their autonomy as learners (Benson & Cooker, 2013b). Identity projection is considered an effective strategy in language learning and one that students can be made more aware of in order to overcome their fear of taking risks. To the Non Users, however, although they were aware of their reflexive identities, they did not intentionally project identities in order to engage in different kinds of activities in the SALC. In other words, their reflective and their projected identities were the same, and consequently they were likely to engage in certain activities consistent with their established self-image. In terms of imagined identity, the Non Users were as likely to have an international posture, a desire to use English or an interest in using English in their future as the participants in other groups.

Trajectories

Having interviewed students in all four university years and (in two cases) after graduation, a tentative trajectory begins to emerge. Of course, the specific details will vary from learner to learner, but the general development can be summarised in Table 11.2. This trajectory draws on similar trajectories that map the development of learner autonomy and metacognition in learners, e.g. Kato and Mynard (2016), Everhard (2013), Nunan (1997) and Sinclair (1999).

Table 11.2 Trajectory of English Lounge use

	0. Before using the English Lounge	1. Becoming a user of the English Lounge	2. Reflecting on the role of the English Lounge	3. Influencing and supporting others	4. Mentoring others
Behaviours	Student avoids using the English Lounge for a variety of reasons. Student has noticed the English Lounge, but makes assumptions about the kinds of students who go there. Student finds other ways to meet language learning needs.	Student initially feels awkward, shy or afraid to use the English Lounge. Student may only be interested in talking to lecturers/'native speakers'. Through repeated visits and encouragement, student starts to feel comfortable using the English Lounge (even by themselves without their friends).	Student uses the English Lounge regularly. Student reflects on how the English Lounge benefits them. Student may develop a different opinion about the purpose of the English Lounge. Student is keenly aware of their own language skills compared with those of other students. Student notices the limitations of the English Lounge. Student may stop using the English Lounge at this point if they no longer see benefits.	Student feels a sense of belonging to the space. Student takes a role in welcoming others to the English Lounge and supporting them. Student becomes a member of a community in the English Lounge.	Student feels comfortable in the space, but is also detached from the majority of students who use the space for language learning purposes only, rather than for mainly social purposes. Student looks for a new generation of students who can welcome and support others, and mentors those new leaders.
Reflexive identity	Student has a well-formed reflexive identity as a language learner. Student assumes that their reflexive identity does not match that of people who use the English Lounge.	Student focuses on their limited English or other negative points.	Student focuses on their own language abilities and confidence levels.	Student feels a sense of responsibility to help others feel comfortable in the space.	Student feels a sense of responsibility to contribute to the long-term growth of the English Lounge.
Projected identity	Student may actively project an identity of someone who does not use the English Lounge.	Student may not be aware of projected identities. Student notices recognised identities of role models/sempais.	Student may compensate for language fluency insecurities by projecting a sense of confidence.	Student intentionally projects confidence in order to inspire other users. Student wants to be seen as friendly and approachable.	Student intentionally projects confidence in order to inspire other users. Student wants to be seen as friendly and approachable.

Conclusions: How Do Different Students Perceive and Use the Lounge?

Returning to the research questions for this portion of the project, we were able to explore facets of identity for each individual participant according to the model (Benson *et al.*, 2013). In addition, we were able to see some patterns which allowed us to propose a trajectory of English Lounge use in terms of exhibited behaviours and shifts in reflexive and projected identities. Over time, it appears that Regular Users of the English Lounge overcame their anxiety about using the space, developed confidence in their language abilities, reflected on their language learning processes in the English Lounge and may have eventually invested in a CoP. In addition, the English Lounge is likely to be a space where they can intentionally project an identity that helps mitigate insecurities they may feel about their English abilities. Non Users were initially avoiding the lounge for three main reasons: (1) the perception that users were not like them; either they were perceived to be fluent English speakers, extroverted and confident, or they were not very serious students; (2) the assumption that the English Lounge contained established groups that would be difficult to break into; (3) a strong self-awareness and reflexive identity of being a particular kind of person who should engage in appropriate language learning activities. Year 2 of the study saw identity shifts for participants in each of the three groups due to English Lounge use. Being a special space unlike any other in Japan served the purpose of challenging established beliefs (see Chapter 13) and identities in unfamiliar ways.

In Chapter 15, we explore the implications that these findings have for practice and in Chapter 16 we discuss ways in which students can be made more aware of the role of identity in their learning and be helped to challenge it and project identities that might help them to benefit from becoming more active users of a social learning space in ways which are appropriate, meaningful and effective for learning.

12 Understanding Communities of Practice in a Social Language Learning Space

Daniel Hooper

The purpose of this chapter is to explore the social learning space and the relationships of the learners within it through a community of practice (CoP) framework. We begin with an overview of CoP, some key definitions and a review of how some other researchers have applied CoP to similar learning contexts. We then explain why a CoP framework was one way in which the research team examined the social learning space. Finally, we describe the ways in which the research team collected and analysed our data, along with some findings that shed light on the English Lounge.

CoPs are 'groups of people who share a concern or a passion for something they do and learn how to do it better as they interact regularly' (Wenger-Trayner & Wenger-Trayner, 2015: 1). Lave and Wenger's (1991) ubiquitous theoretical framework has been applied over the last 28 years to a plethora of varied settings in sociology, education and business (Wenger-Trayner & Wenger-Trayner, 2015), where it has been used to explore conceptions of identity, learning and how we interact with the world at large. The CoP model, it could be argued, is well suited to the field of language learning due to its relatedness with well-established Vygotskian and Deweyian theories of learning (Wenger, 1998). Furthermore, a number of influential studies in the areas of academic socialisation in English as a second language (ESL) contexts (Morita, 2004), non-participation in language classrooms (Norton, 2001) and learner identity (Toohey, 1998) were conducted with the CoP literature as a key theoretical underpinning.

Due to its focus on issues of identity, accessibility, interdependence and self-sustainability among members of a learning community (Wenger, 1998; Wenger et al., 2002), it was not surprising to us that studies on learning within self-access centres had often turned to the CoP model as a viable theoretical framework (Gillies, 2010; Noguchi, 2015). More specifically, we noticed that social learning spaces within self-access centres were defined by some researchers as CoPs. A common feature of a social learning space that we felt was compatible with the CoP literature was the voluntary 'self-organizing and volunteering to lead conversations' by learners (Acuña González *et al.*, 2015: 316). Other studies have noted that learners embraced a community member identity distinct from that of a classroom learner (Noguchi, 2015), and that a gradual movement of learners often occurred from the periphery of the group towards more active participatory roles through the support of their fellow members (Bibby *et al.*, 2016). These findings reinforced our case for the adoption of the CoP framework as one theoretical 'roadmap' for interview data analysis.

In this project, we were concerned with student use of the English Lounge – an example of a social learning space – within a university self-access centre. We gradually became aware of a number of distinct patterns of behaviour among different groups of users from our initial observation study (Chapter 4) and noted several points of congruity with the CoP model. We interviewed English Lounge users with the intention of understanding different learners' participation in the English Lounge in relation to the central CoP components: *domain, community* and *practice* (Wenger *et al.*, 2002; Wenger-Trayner & Wenger-Trayner, 2015). In short, through this study we hoped to identify what traits, if any, marked the English Lounge as a CoP and what influence this space had on how the CoP was defined. In this chapter, we explore cases where learner engagement, development and identity were closely linked with learners' position in a CoP, their individual investment in its practice and their stake in its future. We first position our study in relation to the existing literature on CoPs by setting out what they are, what constituent elements they are composed of and their place in language learning within social learning spaces. After these theoretical foundations have been established, we analyse the community of the English Lounge in terms of Wenger *et al.*'s (2002) criteria of *domain, community* and *practice*. In this way, we hope to provide a detailed description of the workings of the English Lounge CoP and investigate its influence on regular and core users' language learning and second language (L2) selves.

What are Communities of Practice?

One important characteristic of a CoP is its allowance for varying levels of member participation (Wenger, 1998; Wenger *et al.*, 2002). The notion of 'legitimate peripheral participation' lies at the foundation of Lave and Wenger's (1991) original theory as they highlight the varied and ever-changing roles that members of a CoP can inhabit:

> Peripheral participation is about being located in the social world. Changing locations and perspectives are part of actors' learning trajectories, developing identities, and forms of membership. (Lave & Wenger, 1991: 36)

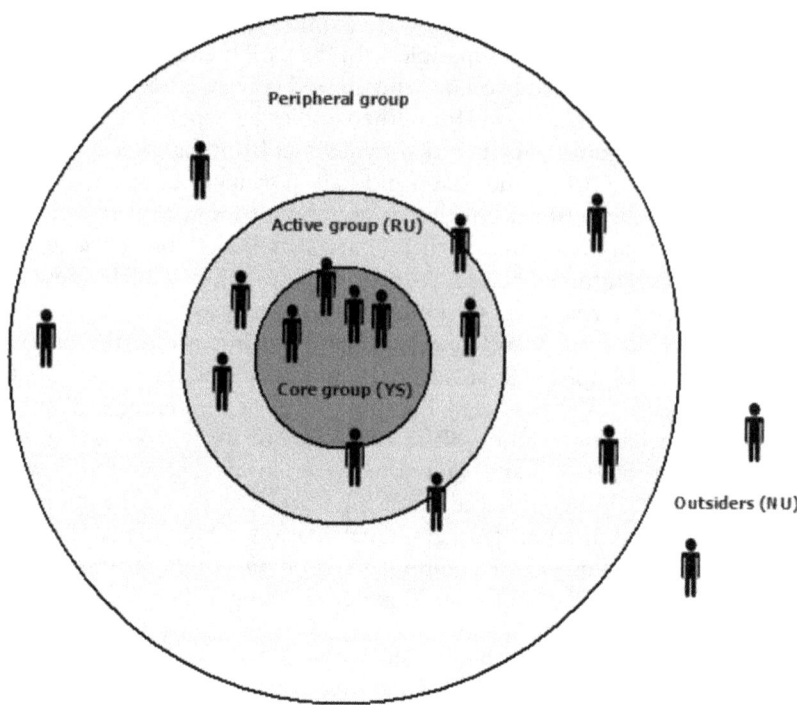

Figure 12.1 Levels of community participation (Adapted from Wenger et al., 2002)

The structure of a CoP is explained in clearer terms by Wenger *et al.* (2002) as they highlight several distinct levels of community participation (see Figure 12.1). The first is a small *core group* who act as the heart of the community and essentially ensure the CoP stays on course to succeed in their chosen endeavour by providing 'intellectual and social leadership' (Wenger & Snyder, 2000). Next is a slightly larger *active group* who maintain regular attendance in group activities and sometimes share ideas regarding the community's endeavours, albeit with less zeal than the core members. Finally, the largest group, making up approximately 75% of the community, are *peripheral* members who remain largely as passive participants for a number of reasons such as limited time, perceived lack of authority in the CoP or due to a choice based on their individual identity (Wenger, 1998; Wenger *et al.*, 2002). However, as stated previously, the roles of CoP members are often in flux. Due to the fluid nature of these groups, peripheral members, assuming their legitimacy is recognised in the community, can move closer towards the centre of the community. In the same way, core members are also able to step back into a less prominent position in the CoP if they so desire (Wenger *et al.*, 2002). Following the results of the observation study, we were confident that these levels of participation by different groups of students were present in the English Lounge.

According to newer conceptions of the model, a CoP is said to consist of three fundamental elements: *domain*, *community* and *practice* (Wenger *et al*., 2002; Wenger-Trayner & Wenger-Trayner, 2015). The *domain* can be viewed as the 'common ground' that members share based on the competences that separate members and non-members (Li *et al*., 2009). Furthermore, it guides members on what ideas and activities are worthwhile, in line with the goals of the community. The *community* refers to the way 'members engage in joint activities and discussions, help each other, and share information' (Wenger-Trayner & Wenger-Trayner, 2015: 2). This element is also concerned with how members are aware of and are guided by their standing in relation to each other in the CoP. The *practice* is 'the specific knowledge the community shares, develops, and maintains' (Wenger *et al*., 2002: 29). This can be in the form of resources such as experiences and stories (Wenger-Trayner & Wenger-Trayner, 2015). This can also be reified as artefacts or approaches created by members in order to address commonly occurring problems that may affect the effectiveness or sustainability of the CoP (Wenger *et al*., 2002). We decided that these three elements created a helpful guide for us in developing interview schedules and interpreting meaningful patterns from our data.

Learning Communities in Social Learning Spaces

Murray (2017a: 117) defines a social learning space as 'a place where learners can come together in order to learn with and from each other'. Social learning spaces are key components of a number of self-access centres both in Japan (Bibby *et al*., 2016; Murray *et al*., 2014; Thornton & Noguchi, 2016) and internationally (Acuña González *et al*., 2015). At our university, the definition of the English Lounge is simple and broad in scope: 'You can have a free conversation in English with teachers and other students here. You can also come with your friends and chat in English' (Kanda University of International Studies, 2016).

Due to the foundations of self access and social learning spaces being in sociocultural theories of language development (Bibby *et al*., 2016; Murray, 2017a) and being based on the claim that learner autonomy develops 'through interdependence rather than independence' (Benson & Cooker, 2013b: 8), it is perhaps no surprise that the CoP framework regularly features in social learning spaces research. In a paper examining reasons behind greatly increased usage of a conversation lounge area in a Japanese university's self-access centre, Bibby *et al*. (2016) noted the importance of several features of the lounge that are compatible with certain characteristics of a CoP. The researchers stated that lounge staff or lecturers should be aware of the need to provide newcomers with opportunities for 'legitimate peripheral participation' (Lave & Wenger, 1991: 36). By not forcing newcomers to actively participate, the researchers argue that they are allowing these learners on the periphery of the group to 'move centrally within a situation, offering heightened participation' (Bibby *et al.*, 2016: 307).

Acuña González *et al.* (2015) conducted a study focusing on a social learning space at the Universidad del Caribe in Mexico. This research found that 'conversation sessions', a programme implemented to provide students with increased opportunities for English spoken interaction, led to the creation of a CoP in which both students and staff shared a 'repertoire of resources and conventions created over time in order to form, transmit and advance knowledge' (Acuña González *et al.*, 2015: 313). A key feature of the conversation sessions that supports its status as a CoP is the nature of student participation. Students voluntarily lead conversations, help develop innovative ways of using materials and offer suggestions for developing the space. Furthermore, senior students sometimes inhabit the role of 'old-timers' (Lave & Wenger, 1991), taking a leadership role and managing the session without staff assistance. This concept of 'old-timers' from the first conception of the CoP framework describes the presence of exemplars within the CoP that may socialise new members into the practices of the community. In language learning terms, these exemplars in the community may take on a role akin to near peer role models (NPRMs) (Murphey, 1998), who are higher proficiency learners that are relatable in some way to the newcomers starting their learning journey. This relatability has been theorised to motivate language learners by increasing their sense of self-efficacy through vicarious modelling (Bandura, 1977). The concept of NPRMs also connects with Dörnyei's (2005, 2014) motivational self system as NPRMs provide learners with real-life examples of possible future 'ideal L2 selves'. The examples illustrated above show several ways in which 'conversation sessions' were compatible with the original CoP model (Lave & Wenger, 1991) and its features of (a) mutual engagement, (b) a joint enterprise and (c) shared mutual knowledge. The research team at Universidad del Caribe stated that although originally they were not guided by Lave and Wenger's model, as the approaches adopted in running the lounge were gradually refined, a CoP eventually formed (Acuña González *et al.*, 2015).

The English Lounge as a Community of Practice

Domain

To recap on previous points made in this chapter, we consider a domain to be a shared sphere of interest which features 'shared competence that distinguishes members from other people' (Wenger-Trayner & Wenger-Trayner, 2015). In order to determine whether the English Lounge represented a shared domain of interest, we felt that we needed to answer two key questions:

(1) Did English Lounge users perceive that the English Lounge represented a domain of interest and, if so, what distinct traits did they feel its members possessed?
(2) What shared beliefs existed regarding English Lounge users' views on the desired approach to, and motivation for, language learning?

Is there a domain of interest?

Concerning the first question, we identified ways in which English Lounge users, and in particular YS Group members, were regarded by the students we interviewed.

Core members

It was clear that for many of our participants, there was a well-defined 'type' in terms of who they perceived the core members of the English Lounge to be. These students were often described as active, motivated, good at English and sociable by many of the RU members that we spoke to.

> *Uh, sugoi eigo ga jouzu na imeeji.* [Uh, that their English is really good.] (Mei, RU, Interview 1)

> Active, for example the person who studies abroad, study abroad, or he or she participates in the National interpreter, yeah, like, they're really, how can I say, yeah, really high motivated. (Ryunosuke, RU, Interview 1)

Active members

Aside from the markedly positive image that many English Lounge users ascribed to the YS Group, we specifically asked participants about their perceptions of the characteristics of 'Regular Users' of the area. While high English proficiency did not generally feature in these descriptions as it did for the YS Group members, perhaps as expected a desire to improve speaking skills was a common theme. In terms of perceived personality traits of frequent English Lounge users, there was a mixed picture ranging from 'shy' and 'lonely' to 'passionate' and 'outgoing'.

> Typical student? Outgoing people. Uh, and typical, like, who likes talking to someone is typical people. (Yuki, RU, Interview 1)

> The identity is different but the like how can I say the atmosphere or the vision or something is enthusiastic yeah the mind the mind is really enthusiastic really strong. (Ryunosuke, RU, Interview 1)

> Some people hesitate to talk. Just adapt the atmosphere. But some people are talkative in English. It depends on the people I think. (Rintaro, RU, Interview 1)

One YS Group member raised the idea that another defining trait of all English Lounge users is that they are perhaps motivated by a higher purpose other than simply wanting to graduate from university.

> For example, like in order to, like, graduate this university you don't really have to use Yellow Sofa and be better at English, like, at least you're getting, like, minimum credit and somehow managed to, like, getting credit. So but those people coming here is maybe aiming at something different than just graduating here, so they have their own like motivations. (Sina, YS Group, Interview 1)

These excerpts reflect the impressions of almost all of the YS Group and RU members we spoke to and make a strong case for the idea of the English Lounge users perceiving active and core members as inhabiting a shared domain of interest distinguishable from other students in the university.

What shared beliefs exist in this domain?

In many ways, the most salient example of a shared belief among the English Lounge users could be said to reflect a tension that exists within English education in Japan at a macro-level. Having all progressed through the Japanese compulsory education system, there was often a sense of dissatisfaction among many of the participants towards the way that English had been taught in their junior high school and high school classes. Other research into L2 learner identity has also raised the sometimes problematic nature of classroom settings due to purely academic concerns stifling opportunities for the construction of L2 identities (Block, 2007). There have also been many cases reported where extremely motivated learners have resisted the CoP of the classroom due to it being teacher led, grammar heavy or overly test focused, while simultaneously embracing a wider global CoP of English users (Lamb, 2013; Miyahara, 2015).

> *Sore made ha sugoi kirai datta kara, ima mo zenzen bunpou ga dekinakute...* [Until then (university), I really hated English, also even now I can't use grammar at all.] (Kaede, RU, Interview 1)

> to learn language you have to to output, so ah, communication is quite important for me. Ahh, well, you know normally Japanese students seem to study on the desk. (Tomoya, YS Group, Interview 1)

> You can learn language not only with those like serious material like because language is not really like subject of study, it's more like how you use and like tool of communication. (Sina, YS Group, Interview 1)

This tension can be traced back to what has been theorised to be a dichotomy running through English language teaching in Japan between *eigo* – the language treated as a subject of study with a focus on grammar and test-focused exercises, and *eikaiwa* – the language being viewed as a communicative tool with more time spent on developing communicative strategies and opportunities for free production of language (Hiramoto, 2013; Nagatomo, 2016). Frequent English Lounge users appeared to share the belief that it was through an *eikaiwa* approach, i.e. using language as a communicative tool, that their proficiency would increase. By 'aligning [their] practice with those who are experts' (Miyahara, 2015: 19) – in this case the communicative English use of the YS Group members – new active members of the English Lounge sometimes experienced a shift in identity. Through participation in the English Lounge and its *eikaiwa* orientation, one RU, Kaede, found she was able to renegotiate her identity from high school, where she felt she was labelled as a '*eigo ga dekinai hito*' [person who can't do English]. By observing the 'experts' in the English Lounge and by seeing English as a communication tool rather than a test of grammatical minutiae, Kaede was able to construct a possible future L2 self that was not characterised by deficit.

Interviewer: Okay, so, Yellow Sofa *ni iku toki ni, nanka dou iu Kaede ga....* [When you go to the Yellow Sofas, like, what kind of Kaede is....]
K: Ah..... uh... *eigo ga shabereru (laughs) Kaede (pseudonym).* [Kaede that can speak English.]

(Kaede, RU, Interview 1)

The focus on *eikaiwa* rather than *eigo* also corresponded with the sense of instrumentality that existed in the domain – students were studying at the English Lounge for practical reasons beyond simply graduating university. One word that Mei (an RU) used frequently during her interview was *jitsuyouteki* (practical). She saw the *eigo* classes she experienced in high school as being impractical and ineffective. Due to having a desire to live and work overseas after graduation, she saw the English Lounge as a way of meeting her needs. Yashima (2013) supports this perspective as she describes English in Japan being positioned merely as a school subject with few opportunities for students to engage with other L2 communities and develop their possible L2 selves.

> Um, high school English class, um, I don't like it. It's, I'm... *amari jitsuyouteki de wa nai.* [It's not very practical.] (Mei, RU, Interview 1)
>
> *Jitsuyoutekini, speaking to ka, listening to ka, jissai ni shabette mita hou ga ii to omoimashita.* [Practically, speaking, and listening... actually trying to speak is better, I think.] (Mei, RU, Interview 1)

This learner's belief in the practicality that the English Lounge represents and other members' perceptions of what is required for the development of communicative competence in English all contribute to a shared commitment to the domain. Communicative *use* of English, rather than *knowledge* of English as a subject, could also be considered an example of a 'regime of competence' (Lave & Wenger, 1991: 6) existing within the domain, that members are accountable to and that influences the extent to which they identify with the CoP.

An additional potential shared belief of English Lounge users can be tied to Wenger's (1998) concept of 'imagination' in a CoP and Norton's (2000) notion of 'imagined communities' being influential in language learning motivation. Many of the active users spoke about the English Lounge as an international area. The learners we spoke to often exhibited a marked international mindset (Yashima, 2009), had sometimes already studied abroad and frequently stated a desire to work and live overseas.

> *Honkakutekini kaigai ni sumitai to omotta no wa chuugakusei no koro de... de hontouni youchien no toki gurai kara ironna kaigai ni kyoumi ga motteimashita.* [On a serious level, I wanted to live overseas from when I was a junior high school student... when I was in kindergarten, I was interested in different foreign countries.] (Mei, RU, Interview 1)

> *Shourai, kaigai ni itta toki to ka, nihon de gaikokujin no hito to tomo ni shaberu you ni naritai.* [In the future, if I went overseas or, in Japan I want to be able to speak with foreign people.] (Kaede, RU, Interview 1)

In Mei's case, her past experiences (as shown in the previous excerpt) and her future desire to become a flight attendant are both important as Dörnyei (2005: 98) argues that an imagined community comes from 'a combination of personal experiences and knowledge (derived from the past) with imagined elements related to the future'. An additional shared trait within this CoP, therefore, may also have been the English Lounge serving as a site where learners could participate in a target community of global English users. Yashima (2013: 48) states that for a large number of learners, a target community 'refers to a country or region where the target language is used or to a group of people who use the language'. Following this definition, we can see that the English Lounge provided access to a target community for CoP members as it afforded contact with both foreign (lecturers and exchange students) and Japanese English users. Due to CoP members sometimes referring to the English Lounge as a different country and learners with study-abroad experience actively participating in the area, it could be argued that the CoP also functioned as an environment where learners could continue to develop their L2 selves in a target community.

The potential function of the English Lounge as a connection with users' imagined communities can also be linked to Miyahara's (2015: 22) concept of 'discursive space' – 'the spatial and temporal space formed as individuals explore their imagined ties with the future'. The notion of discursive space builds on Dörnyei's (2014) motivational self system, in which he theorised language learning motivation in terms of learners' ought-to and ideal L2 selves and the L2 learning experience. The ideal L2 self is a learner's image of the person they would ideally like to become as an L2 user, whereas the ought-to L2 self is based on the 'L2 attributes that one believes one *ought to* possess to avoid possible negative outcomes' (emphasis original) (Dörnyei, 2014: 8). In addition to the internal factors of ideal and ought-to L2 selves, the L2 learning experience focuses on external elements in the immediate learning environment that may serve to enhance motivation such as teacher–student rapport or experiences of success. Miyahara ties Dörnyei's interpretation of the L2 learning experience with Dewey's (1997) conceptualisation of experience by highlighting the significance of connecting not only present, but also past experiences in influencing future motivational drive. Miyahara conceptualises this interconnection between previous and current learning experiences in 'the experiential profile'. This refers to 'a rich bank of domain-specific resources that interacts with one's past, present and future to create, maintain or develop one's Ideal L2 self' (Miyahara, 2015: 26). We believe that the stories told by many of the members connect with the concept of the experiential profile. We observed that their past positive and negative experiences appeared to play a significant part in how they viewed the value of the English Lounge, their motivations for continued participation in the CoP and the evolution of their future L2 selves.

> My orientation is like I just want to have fun at the same time want to be better at English and in my case, like I gained my English mostly through like having fun, first of all I like to speak, I mean I like talking. (Sina, YS Group, Interview 1)
>
> *Chuugakkou kara roku nenkan kakawarazu yomeru kedo mattaku hanasenai de no ga chotto yokunai na to omoimashita.* [In spite of studying for six years from junior high school, I could read but I couldn't speak at all. I thought that was not very good.] (Mei, RU, Interview 1)

The English Lounge CoP was, therefore, a domain where members, driven by their experiential profiles, had come to embrace a number of shared beliefs and values that they felt would positively contribute to their evolving L2 selves and their participation in their target imagined communities.

Community

The concept of community is defined as one in which 'members engage in joint activities and discussions, help each other, and share information. They build relationships that enable them to learn from each other; they care about their standing with each other' (Wenger-Trayner & Wenger-Trayner, 2015). To determine whether Wenger-Trayner and Wenger-Trayner's version of community existed, we felt that we needed to address the following questions:

(1) What roles, if any, are members assigned within the community, and how do they situate these roles in relation to other members?
(2) In what ways do members perceive their identities to change over time?

What roles are members assigned within the English Lounge?

Just as in the 'conversation sessions' at the Universidad del Caribe (Acuña González *et al.*, 2015), we soon became aware of the feeling among several RUs that the YS Group members were perceived as 'exemplars' (Lave & Wenger, 1991: 95) or role models.

> Yeah, Japanese friends, and I think, how can I say, the person who stay at the Yellow Sofa, the people is really active and they're really have a good skill of of English, so then I am motivated by them, yeah, so that's why I went to there. (Ryunosuke, RU, Interview 1)

When talking about why she respected one YS Group member, another student stated that it was because of her high proficiency in English despite never having studied outside of Japan.

> **K:** *Uh... pera da shi...* [Uh, she speaks fluently and...]
> **Interviewer:** Uh, *gambatta kara*? [Because she tried hard?]
> **K:** *Nanka, (Like,) she go to Yellow Sofa every day. Ryuugaku shita koto ga nai no ni sugoi pera kara* [Because even though she's never studied abroad, she speaks so fluently]
> (Kaede, RU, Interview 1)

This may be an example of the YS Group member acting as an NPRM (Murphey, 1998) as she provided a living example of vicarious, potentially attainable success rather than the comparably distant figures of the 'native-speaker' lecturer or exchange student. Murphey has described NPRMs as offering learners a vivid image of a possible ideal L2 self (Dörnyei, 2005) that is both relatable and attainable. The literature on NPRMs also has ties to Bandura's (1977) research on self-efficacy due to the notion that NPRMs engage in vicarious modelling where others observe them making gains through 'effortful coping behaviour' (Bandura, 1977: 197). Witnessing the high proficiency achieved by NPRMs therefore stimulates other learners' belief that success is possible for them in a given endeavour (Murphey & Arao, 2001).

How do members perceive their roles to change over time?

A central component of the CoP model since Lave and Wenger's original conception of it is the notion of 'old-timers' existing within the core group who guide and socialise newcomers into the practices of the CoP. We saw in one senior YS Group member an indication that he had come to accept his old-timer role in the English Lounge.

T: So, it's, actually, it's true that it takes time to get used to be in the Yellow Sofa be in the SALC. But someone has to help them to you know, stay there (laughs).
Interviewer: Yes.
T: And, I'm trying to do that kind of you know role.
(Tomoya, YS Group, Interview 1)

It was perhaps because this 'old-timer' remembered the struggles that he experienced during his time as a newcomer to the English Lounge that he later recognised the need for support for new students on the periphery.

Interviewer: Can you remember your first time coming to the Yellow Sofa?
T: I was scared too.
(Tomoya, YS Group, Interview 1)

Reflecting on their own historical trajectories in this community was something that appeared to influence several participants from both the YS Group and RU group in embracing a facilitator or socialiser role within the lounge. Students would often clearly remember the feelings of anxiety or isolation they had felt as they made their first tentative steps into the English Lounge and often hinted at a sense of duty to ease the transition for other newer members presently or in the future. Lave and Wenger (1991: 57) refer to these important members as 'journeyfolk' – relative 'old-timers' who may act as a bridge between newcomers and the core.

Interviewer: OK, and what does that mean for you? Being a senior?
K: Like, um, well like just not just sit there or like, um, if some freshman come to us, I said like, 'Please join us' and I just start conversation and they can't run away. (laughs)
(Kokon, YS Group, Interview 1)

Interviewer: Eh, nani, nan no tsumori ga arimasuka? [Um, what's your plan?]
M: *Toriaezu, senpai ni shite moratta yori, ano welcome na funiki wo tsukutte, tomodachi ni narou to omoimasu.* [To begin with, like my seniors did, create a welcoming atmosphere and try to make friends.]
(Mei, RU, Interview 1)

Here, we also saw another example of Murphey's (1998) NPRMs, this time not solely as a possible ideal L2 self (Dörnyei, 2005) but also as a socialising agent encouraging greater participation in the community.

We had certainly noticed signs of community roles existing in the English Lounge before we carried out our interviews, and it was one of the reasons for our initial interest in the CoP framework. However, it wasn't until we analysed each member's interview and their perceptions of the other lounge users along with their own role in the lounge that we came to realise the extent to which a sense of interdependence ran through this community. Many of the YS Group members we spoke to were aware of their relative position to other users and had, in some cases, assigned themselves responsibilities that they felt came with that status. The old-timers we spoke to reflected on the struggles they experienced as they first entered the English Lounge years before and had often taken steps to ease the same rite of passage for newcomers. In turn, the RUs often saw their YS Group counterparts as relatable role models who they could respect and aspire to become.

We also observed signs that these relative newcomers had begun to accept their responsibility to act as guides for the next intake of first-year students. Here, we see these 'journeyfolk' moving along their own trajectories in the English Lounge and ensuring the cycle of the CoP continues. Their trajectories within the English Lounge CoP may have also been influenced by the *senpai/kohai* system that runs through organisational structures in Japanese culture such as schools, companies and sports clubs (Johnston & Ochitani, 2008; Takeuchi, 2015; Thomson & Mori, 2015). *Senpai* and *kohai* are, respectively, senior and junior members of a group with each title coming with certain responsibilities to the other.

> I'm joined this group when I was a first year student and so, in my second year, kohai came in this group, so that made really happy for me.
>
> (Suzuka, YS Group, Interview 1)

In exchange for the respect that *senpai* receive from the neophyte *kohai*, they are expected to guide and mentor these new members into the practices of the group. This cultural influence may strengthen learners' commitment to the CoP and its other members while also stimulating fuller participation in the CoP over time (Murray, 2008; Thomson & Mori, 2015). However, it is important to note that in other studies of peer-oriented language learning (Ishikawa, 2012; Takeuchi, 2015), the *senpai/kohai* dynamic has sometimes been found to have a constraining effect on interpersonal relations as a result of the culturally embodied power differential it creates. We see this in one of the YS Group 'old-timers' who states that he wants newer users of the English Lounge to forego the formality that comes with them seeing him as a *senpai* and instead desires more friendly and casual interactions with them.

Interviewer: So even though you're a bit older you still like to have that casual, relaxed feeling?

T: Yeah, yeah... I don't want them to see me as *senpai*... you know, as friends.

(Tomoya, YS Group, Interview 1)

Practice

Practice is defined as: 'a shared repertoire of resources: experiences, stories, tools, ways of addressing recurring problems' (Wenger-Trayner & Wenger-Trayner, 2015). We sought to discover the existence of such a practice in the English Lounge by answering the following questions.

(1) What recurring problems within the English Lounge are members aware of and trying to address?
(2) What artefacts and practices have been created within the community and what purpose do they serve?

What recurring problems exist within the English Lounge?

No community is perfect, and the English Lounge is no exception. Both as lecturers and researchers, we became aware of claims that the lounge area was hard to enter and one reason for this was the presence of the YS Group members. In our interviews, we found that the YS Group was often aware of the fact that some students found them to be intimidating and that this was a potential barrier to new members entering the community.

> And then the other students um they are, I heard they are scared of us. (Tomoya, YS Group, Interview 1)

> Some students say that because of the group including me that is one of the reason why they don't come to the Yellow Sofa. (Kyoji, YS Group, Interview 1)

As mentioned in the previous section on community, many of the YS Group members remembered the anxiety they felt when they entered the English Lounge as newcomers. This sense of empathy towards new members' feelings of insecurity, as well as the recognition that they might in fact be unintentionally contributing to this situation, meant that many of the YS Group seemed to be concerned with ways that they could resolve, or at least mitigate, this recurring problem. Here, we have another example of YS Group members taking on the responsibilities of the CoP's core in order to reinvigorate its membership and bolster the chances of its future survival.

> Ah, um, we ask, we should ask, um you know, freshmans to bring their friends to Yellow Sofa and talk to us and then make our community bigger. (Tomoya, YS Group, Interview 1)

> I think, yeah. I, I think we should change the situation because I think we are the core member of Yellow Sofa. (Kokon, YS Group, Interview 1)

What artefacts and practices have the community created and for what purpose?

A further way in which the practice of a CoP is manifested is through the construction of artefacts or 'tools' that can be used to deal with recurring problems or issues. From our interview data, we encountered some examples of such tools, formed by YS Group members to attract new members to the English Lounge. A test of English as a foreign language (TOEFL) study group was set up by the YS Group members to prepare students for mandatory test requirements, but this also may have served as a way to socialise new first-year students into the group and direct them towards the English Lounge community.

> Interviewer: So you said there's a lot of new freshman students. How did they join the group?
> K: Um, actually we have, um, do you know study group?
> Interviewer: Ah, yes, like the SALC thing?
> K: Yeah, yeah, like. And it is not official one. But we made it actually. We made it.
> (Kokon, YS Group, Interview 1)

> I love it (the study group). Now I think it is important because, um, my feeling is that freshmans are a little bit scared. (Tomoya, YS Group, Interview 1)

Other YS Group members also suggested new ideas that they felt could benefit the English Lounge and help it to more effectively meet the needs of its different members. These included posters being put up to remind students that they did not need to worry about making mistakes, and the establishment of a discussion circle for advanced students who want to debate complex social or political issues. Additionally, a rearrangement of the furniture in the English Lounge stemmed, in part, from suggestions made by a core CoP member who wished to stimulate future use of the area by students who previously felt intimidated to enter (see Chen & Mynard [2018] for details).

A final example of the CoP's practice is the way in which various members were invested in monitoring the 'English-only' language policy. Although this language policy was based on research involving user input (see Imamura [2018] for details), it was a form of 'vertical administration' (Lave & Wenger, 1991: 13) in that it was implemented by the university.

As it was impractical for the institution to enforce the language used in the English Lounge, responsibility for adhering to this policy was assumed by the CoP members exemplifying what Lave and Wenger (1991) refer to as 'horizontal accountability'. However, while recognising the need for English use in fulfilling the purpose of the domain, many users took a pragmatic approach to this policy, choosing to use their first language if they saw it necessary to maintain communication or facilitate learning.

R: I think we must speak English, not Japanese. But sometime I use little bit Japanese explain a word.
Interviewer: Oh, when you explain you'll use a little.
R: Yes a little bit. But basically we must speak English.
(Rintaro, RU, Interview 1)

This is an example of the CoP reflecting meanings reached by its members despite external effort attempting to 'shape, dictate, or mandate practice' (Wenger, 2010). Even when the members comply with external mandates, they are still creating their own practice, reflecting their engagement with their situation. 'A practice has a life of its own' (Wenger, 2010: 2).

Despite the English Lounge existing within a formal academic institution and receiving educational support from the SALC staff and English Language Institute (ELI) lecturers, a great many problems threatening the continuation and effectiveness of the community were identified and tackled by the members themselves. Several ideas that led to the evolution of the English Lounge space emerged from a collaboration between the SALC staff and core English Lounge users. Many YS Group members reflected on their trajectories within the community, from starting out as nervous outsiders to becoming central participants, and it was these experiences that provided them with insights into the issues new members faced. We observed many ways in which the YS Group attempted to negotiate and mitigate these issues independently through peer discussion and the creation of community artefacts designed to attract and socialise new members to the CoP. Furthermore, we became aware of a sense of investment in the CoP's domain (a place for English communication) that manifested itself in a level of horizontal accountability where members co-constructed, refined and subsequently policed rules of use that they felt supported a shared goal.

What we learnt

Through our interviews with the active and core members of the English Lounge, we uncovered several ways in which this community of language learners had formed a CoP. By using Wenger-Trayner and Wenger-Trayner's (2015) framework, we were able to identify and analyse the beliefs and evolving identities of users within the community, as well as the developing sense of investment that came with their increased participation in the group. Members of the YS Group expressed a desire to build relationships with each other, provide mutual support for members' engagement in the English Lounge and construct community artefacts to increase the efficacy of both of these endeavours. Furthermore, we became aware of a sense of interdependence within the community, where members relied on each other to address problems that came up in their daily practice and proactively worked together to ensure the lounge met the needs of the CoP.

In Chapter 15 (Summary of the Findings) and Chapter 16 (Implications and Practical Interventions), we examine some implications relating to learners' beliefs about the role of social learning spaces, as well as the impact of learners' interpersonal relationships within areas like the English Lounge. We discuss how factors such as learners' past learning experiences, cultural conventions such as *senpai/kohai* relationships and the presence of NPRMs may come together to facilitate the emergence of a CoP within a social learning space. Additionally, we propose ways in which a CoP can stimulate autonomous language learning and the development of learners' future L2 selves.

13 Understanding Learner Beliefs and Other Individual Differences in a Social Learning Space

Jo Mynard, Michael Burke,
Daniel Hooper and Ross Sampson

The purpose of this chapter is to examine how learner beliefs interact with other individual differences in order to understand some of the reasons why learners use, or choose not to use, the English Lounge. Whereas in the preceding two research chapters we isolated the two areas of *identity* and *communities of practice*, in this chapter we take an interpretative approach (described in Chapter 4) to analysing our data and highlight some of the key factors that influence the ways in which our learners use, or choose not to use, the English Lounge. We begin by reviewing the literature on the five key factors which emerged from the interpretative analysis (Chapter 4) which are pertinent to our data and context, starting with learner beliefs, which has played a significant role. We will then outline factors that emerged in our initial data that enabled us to create an analytic framework for understanding our social learning space. We then apply the framework to subsequent data in order to understand our participants' individual differences and how these differences affected their engagement with the English Lounge. In addition, we look at the connections between the five key factors over time and visually explore these through the techniques of *threading* and *nesting*.

Approaches to Understanding Individual Differences in Our Space

From the coding process (see Chapter 4), we identified five key factors (including learner beliefs) that influenced participants' use of the English Lounge. We chose these five factors because either they featured prominently in our interpretative coding of the first-year interview transcripts or they were context specific and would allow us to understand our learners and their interactions with the learning space in more depth. The five key factors (learner beliefs; second language [L2] motivational self system; previous learning experiences/*eigo* and *eikaiwa*; learning anxiety; and agency and interdependence) will be explained briefly below.

(1) Learner beliefs

Learner beliefs can be defined as the ways in which individuals view the learning process which can have an impact on how they approach language learning. Early work on beliefs (cf. Horwitz, 1988; Sakui & Gaies, 1999; Victori & Lockhart, 1995) operated under the assumption that learner beliefs were fixed. However, contemporary views taking a sociocultural theory perspective assume that learner beliefs are socially constructed and can shift over time (Tanaka & Ellis, 2003). In addition, there is believed to be a dynamic relationship between belief and action (Navarro & Thornton, 2011). It is notable, however, that few studies have investigated the relationship between learners' reported beliefs and action, particularly in a self-directed learning context (Navarro & Thornton, 2011).

Early studies have suggested various ways of categorising types of learner beliefs. For example, the Beliefs About Language Learning Inventory (BALLI) (Horwitz, 1987) highlighted five factors related to the difficulty of learning a language, language aptitude, the unique nature of language learning, the use of strategies and psychological dimensions, i.e. motivation and expectations. In another approach, Wenden (1999) identified three dimensions: the ways in which the language is used, beliefs about how languages are learnt and personal factors including self-concept and aptitude. Another approach to interpreting learner beliefs by Benson and Lor (1999) focused on the sense that learners made of the concepts of *language* and of *language learning* and categorised them into higher-order and lower-order conceptions of beliefs. Examining *sources* of beliefs has also been an approach to understanding how learners view language and learning (Little & Singleton, 1990), and research shows that students' beliefs are often shaped by previous learning experiences.

One final area to include related to beliefs is personality. Personality refers to 'individual differences in characteristic patterns of thinking, feeling and behaving' (American Psychological Association, 2019). Although many people assume that certain personality types such as extroversion might be helpful for language learning, actual research on the relationship between personality and language learning is mixed. The personality trait of extroversion does not necessarily mean that a student is better at learning languages in general, but it might be beneficial for speaking tasks (Verhoeven & Vermeer, 2002). However, research by Dewaele and colleagues (e.g. Dewaele, 2002; Dewaele & Furnham, 2000) has shown that extroverts have better short-term memory than introverts, are less affected by stress and anxiety, and speak more fluently, although results may be affected by moods, emotions, external factors and strategic action (Liyanage & Bartlett, 2013). In the context of the English Lounge, an extrovert might create more opportunities to practice English and may appear to be more competent and confident to others.

In this chapter, we focus in particular on general beliefs about how language should be learnt, looking at (1) how they relate to the ways in which our participants made use of (or avoided) the English Lounge and (2) how the other factors dynamically interact with their beliefs.

(2) L2 motivational self system

Theories of motivation have influenced our understanding of the ways in which learners have engaged with the English Lounge. These have included Gardner and Lambert's (1959) concept of integrative motivation, Deci and Ryan's (1985) self-determination theory (including intrinsic and extrinsic motivation) and Dörnyei's (2005, 2009, 2014) L2 motivational self system. The L2 motivational self system is a framework that incorporates two aspects of self theory from psychology and provides us with a relevant theoretical understanding for examining one factor related to learner beliefs. This theory was influenced by Markus and Nurius' (1986) 'possible selves theory' and has understanding L2 learner motivations at its heart. The crux of this theory is the concept of the 'ideal L2 self', a representation of an L2 self that learners envision themselves embodying in the future, meaning the kind of person they desire to become. If the kind of person they desire to become is a competent speaker of their target language(s), then that 'ideal self' would likely be a motivating factor in their language learning. The 'ought-to self' is another component of the self system. This, as Dörnyei (2009: 29) defines it, is 'the attributes that one believes one *ought to* possess to avoid possible negative outcomes'. Meaning other people's ideas or desires of what someone *should* become are exemplified through this component. These ideas and desires tend to be driven by influences from parents, peers or society. As Ryan and Dörnyei (2013: 95) explain, 'externally imposed factors connecting to career development and opportunities may form a significant part of the ought-to L2 self'. The last component of the L2 motivational self system is the 'L2 learning experience'. This is concerned with learners immediate decisions based on their motivations at a certain time in a certain circumstance or environment (Dörnyei, 2009). Although this component is not directly related to learners' future selves, their immediate learning situations do affect their motivation.

By understanding how 'future selves' relate to a particular learner, predictions can be made about the direction learners may take in an effort to realise a desired self or avoid an undesired one. In the case of undergraduate university students, this is particularly noteworthy, as the stage of life they are at is pivotal in determining the direction of their future. Thus, it is likely that ideas of who they would like to become and ideas of who they may feel they are expected to become could be in conflict. In this chapter, we focus on how motivations about an L2 self might influence participants' choices related to using the English Lounge.

(3) Previous learning experiences: *Eigo* and *eikaiwa*

As mentioned above, one factor that plays a role in shaping beliefs about learning is previous learning experiences (Little & Singleton, 1990). This may be due to various reasons: the assumption that the approach taken in a previous course of study is the 'only' way; the experience of success in a previous learning situation; or a previous negative experience with learning a language. In Japan, learning experiences immediately prior to starting university inevitably involve teaching methods heavily influenced by the required university entrance examinations. As communicative competence and speaking and listening skills are typically not part of university entrance exams, the language teaching approach often adopted is to teach English as an academic subject. In fact, as described in Chapter 3, the ideological distinction in Japan between English as an academic subject focusing on test preparation and grammar (*eigo*) and English as a communicative tool (*eikaiwa*) arguably permeates every sector of English education in the country (Hiramoto, 2013; McVeigh, 2004; Nagatomo, 2016), influencing educational reform and the experiences of Japanese English learners. Several qualitative and quantitative research studies have revealed additional evidence of this divergence in what many learners believe should be focused on in English classes and the realities of the *eigo*-dominated classroom (Falout *et al.*, 2008; Kikuchi, 2009; Kikuchi & Sakai, 2009). Students prioritising communicative ability in an international setting also foregrounds another assertion about the *eigo–eikaiwa* dichotomy: the idea of *eigo* being 'Japanese English', i.e. English purely for the purposes of exam taking inside Japan, and *eikaiwa* representing 'foreign English', i.e. English used for communication with others, primarily non-Japanese (McVeigh, 2004). This claim is supported by a dominant belief that *eikaiwa* should be taught by non-Japanese whereas *eigo* is solely the domain of the Japanese teacher of English (Lowe, 2017; Nagatomo, 2016).

A study by Miyahara (2015) into learner motivation and identity provided further examples of Japanese learners with a clear international posture (Yashima, 2013) expressing antipathy towards the *eigo* that they experienced in secondary education. Yashima (2013) describes three facets comprising an international posture: (1) an intergroup approach-avoidance tendency (i.e. the desire to interact with people from other countries/ethnic groups), (2) an interest in overseas work/activities and (3) an interest in global affairs. The learners in Miyahara's study exhibited beliefs that were coherent with an international posture and that stood in conflict with a test-oriented instrumentality promoted in their secondary education. It can therefore be argued that they had invested themselves in ideal L2 selves (Dörnyei, 2014) that were compatible with *eikaiwa*, i.e. using English to interact with the world beyond Japan. A key role of the English Lounge is affording learners opportunities to develop English (*eikaiwa*) as a tool for intercultural communication. Lounge users' experiences of *eigo* in secondary education and the nature of their language learning goals and ideal L2 selves may contribute to an investment in *eikaiwa* represented by their English Lounge participation. We were particularly interested to see whether the participants were able to reconcile both *eigo* and *eikaiwa* for a balanced and effective approach to language learning. This may entail drawing on previous knowledge in order to effectively communicate in the English Lounge. We also wanted to examine how *eigo-eikaiwa* related beliefs may have changed through the process of choosing to visit or to avoid the English Lounge.

(4) Language anxiety

Language anxiety can be defined as apprehension when using an L2 (Gardner & MacIntyre, 1993). It manifests itself as a 'fear of speaking; a fear of misunderstanding others; and a fear of being misunderstood' (Dörnyei & Ryan, 2015: 176), and undoubtedly impacts L2 performance. MacIntyre and Gregersen (2012: 103) write 'One of the most consistent findings in the SLA literature is that higher levels of language anxiety are associated with lower levels of language achievement', so it is a factor that needs to be carefully considered when supporting learners, especially in independent settings such as the English Lounge. Language anxiety is a complex construct, and researchers are unclear about how to conceptualise it. For example, should it be situated within the motivation literature, situated within the personality trait literature or viewed as an emotion (Dörnyei & Ryan, 2015)? We are not able to address this dilemma in this chapter, but considering its role as a factor within our context helped us to understand our learners' engagement (or disengagement) in the English Lounge. We could see from our data that beliefs that learners had about how languages are learnt, their previous experiences and other factors that influenced these beliefs affected their willingness to participate in the English Lounge. Importantly, these beliefs often stemmed from their levels of language anxiety. From our early observations of the English Lounge (see Chapter 4), we could see students on the peripheries of the lounge visibly anxious. Through interviews and examinations of participants' language learning histories, we were able to infer that beliefs, anxiety and lounge participation were linked in a dynamic way that warranted further theorising and exploration.

(5) Agency and interdependence

As explained in Chapter 3, agency is a capacity to act (Ahearn, 2001). Karp (1986) explores what distinguishes an 'actor' from an 'agent'.

According to Karp (1986), an actor is a person whose action is governed by or oriented towards rules. An agent, on the other hand, exercises power in order to bring about change or effects in the world (Karp, 1986). Actor and agent could be two aspects or two perspectives of the same person. So, what factors have influenced our participants' capacities to act or to exercise agency? Also, to what extent have these been informed by notions of independence, freedom, choice, ability, individual control and so on associated with British and American contexts (i.e. *independent agency*; Heine *et al.*, 1999)? Or have they been informed by parameters more associated with social relationships in Japanese contexts (Kitayama & Uchida, 2004)? Such expectations may include self-criticism, shame and apologies, self-discipline, effort, perseverance and interests of the wider group (i.e. *interdependent agency*; Heine *et al.*, 1999). Through interviews and analysis of participants' language learning histories, we found evidence of *interdependent* agency framing the beliefs, judgements, intentions and decisions of the students, shaping the psychology of the social structure of the English Lounge and influencing how students saw themselves within this milieu.

The Study

In order to explore how learner beliefs interact with the other four key factors that affect the use of the lounge, we established three research questions for this portion of the study:

(1) How might use of the English Lounge be explained according to five key factors?
- Beliefs.
- L2 motivational self system.
- Previous learning experiences.
- Language anxiety.
- Agency and interdependence.
(2) What connections exist between the five key factors?
(3) What do we learn about how beliefs and the other four factors interact with each other over time?

Analysis and Findings

Analysis (1): Narrative Analysis

The following sections are a summary of the findings from taking a narrative approach and applying the five factors within the analytic framework (see Chapter 4: Table 4.3) to the entire data. However, rather than only treating each factor separately, we also looked specifically at the interaction between the five factors that we identified. We completed this part of the analysis by looking at all the data pertaining to each participant, identifying the core beliefs, then linking those beliefs to emergent themes from the other four factors using colour coding.

Learner beliefs and the interaction with the other four factors

All of the participants gave clues to their core beliefs through the ways in which they described how they learnt languages and their opinions on the role(s) of the English Lounge and the people within it. Some of the core beliefs are complementary to each other, and others may be contradictory; some participants only expressed one core belief, others several. Clearly, this is a complex area as we also found that participants occasionally expressed a core belief, but indicated through their actions that they did not necessarily act on that belief. Some attempts to explore these connections and contradictions are made later in this chapter, but for now, this section is organised by the 14 core beliefs that surfaced, each of which is described in terms of how the other four factors played a role.

Core belief 1: Practising speaking is the most effective way to learn a language

All of the participants expressed this belief, but it often conflicted with opposing beliefs, suggesting that the participants were still transitioning predominantly from the *eigo* experiences of high school and entrance exams. In some cases, students expressed a resentment towards the *eigo* approach in high school; in other cases, the participants began to value the *eigo* experiences and appreciate that this knowledge could be applied to communication in the English Lounge.

Core belief 2: A thorough knowledge of grammar is needed before you can communicate effectively in the target language

Some of the participants believed that their English grammar or vocabulary skills were insufficient for communication. This had an effect on the anxiety they experienced when using English, which led to avoidance of the English Lounge.

Core belief 3: Accuracy is important when learning a language, but it is OK to make mistakes

Some participants expressed this belief in some ways even if they also exhibited conflicting behaviours such as being concerned about what other students thought about their English. Other participants expressed this opinion to counteract the extreme focus on *eigo* that they had previously experienced.

Core belief 4: Enjoyment and interest are the most important things when learning a language

Only two of the participants demonstrated that their beliefs were driven by positive or enjoyable experiences. Others expressed that interest was important but they did not show evidence of being guided by their interests when participating in the English Lounge.

Core belief 5: Teachers have an important role in ensuring that the language policy is maintained

This belief may indicate a lack of autonomy and an over-reliance on teachers to create suitable learning environments. Alternatively, this belief may stem from a sense of interdependent agency and the creation of an environment suitable for the good of the group. For a student to initiate taking an active role in promoting (or 'policing') the language policy, however, would be considered uncomfortable and inappropriate and would negatively impact the group harmony.

Core belief 6: It is important to be around other students who serve as role models for language learning

Many of the participants explained how other learners inspired or motivated them to use English and take a more proactive approach to their own language learning. Some of the younger students appeared to hold their seniors in high regard. This belief resulted in some of the participants feeling a responsibility for this role over time. On the negative side, this often caused more senior students to feel anxiety as they (in their own estimation) were not being good English language role models to the younger students.

Core belief 7: Students need to be autonomous; to take charge of their learning and follow a plan

Some students demonstrated a high level of awareness and control over their language learning. This was demonstrated through the activities they chose, including to intentionally *not* use the English Lounge as they had identified more appropriate activities for their language learning needs and personalities. The ideal L2 self appeared to contribute to this autonomy and desire to succeed, for example, the desire to be a 'serious student' who does not waste time chatting in a lounge, but instead makes regular appointments with learning advisors and lecturers.

Core belief 8: It is important to use available resources and strategies to make the most of the opportunities to use English

Some students discussed using other materials and services on or off campus, either used in combination with the English Lounge, or independently of it. This appeared to be one way in which *eigo* and *eikaiwa* were reconciled. For example, a student might spend time using a grammar book during quiet study time elsewhere in the Self-Access Learning Centre (SALC) and then practice using the structures at the English Lounge. Some participants overly relied on the English Lounge as the only source of language input, but this tended to be during an early phase of using the English Lounge before they started to reflect on the benefits of using the lounge (Point 2 on the trajectory – see Chapter 11: Table 11.2).

Core belief 9: Teachers have a role to play in socialising users into the conversation

Due to students' discomfort in joining established groups, insecurities about their English language abilities and the anxiety these issues might cause, most of the participants expressed the belief that one of the important roles of lecturers in the English Lounge was to invite students to join the group and to initiate the interactions within groups.

Core belief 10: Community is vital in sustaining the use of the social learning space

The participants who felt that being part of the community developed their confidence and sense of competence in English (see Chapter 15) believed it was important to create this supportive community. They also began to experience a collective sense of responsibility, i.e. interdependent agency, to invest in improving the space for other learners. This was then passed on to other students as they moved from year to year.

Core belief 11: English is a tool that facilitates intercultural communication

Some participants viewed English simply as a tool for communication, in contrast to others who were passionate about learning and understanding the language for its own sake. The students who viewed language as a tool were majoring in other languages and had had an opportunity to study abroad, where they used English in addition to the local languages (Chinese, Spanish, Portuguese). This had the effect of reducing anxiety since for those who held this belief, making mistakes is acceptable as the purpose is communication using whatever tools one has at one's disposal.

Core belief 12: Reaching 'native level' is a goal

For some of the participants, achieving 'native level' was a goal. In some cases, this resulted in anxiety due to the need for perfection, but in other cases, the ideal L2 self was so powerful that this goal was able to sustain motivation and efforts to use English at every opportunity, especially in the English Lounge.

Core belief 13: Confidence and personality play an important role in the language learning process

Many participants believed that personality type was important for language learning. There was a general assumption that extroversion was related to confidence and that this was helpful for the learning process. Many of the participants were able to develop their confidence either by exercising their natural tendencies towards extroversion or by projecting a more extrovert personality than usual in the English Lounge. There was a lot of evidence in the data of participants demonstrating an outgoing personality as part of their projected identity (see Chapter 11) even if their reflexive identity was rather introverted, shy or even anxious. Projecting a confident *image* seemed to be a successful strategy for many as it eventually had an effect on actual confidence levels.

Core belief 14: Sometimes you have to do things you don't want to do in order to progress in a language

There were some instances of participants forcing themselves to study something less enjoyable in order to develop their language skills. This was another example of reconciling *eigo* and *eikaiwa* where *eikaiwa* was generally more enjoyable than *eigo*. In other cases, students forced themselves to go to the English Lounge and 'push' themselves as they knew they needed to do more speaking practice outside of class.

L2 motivational self system and the interaction with learner beliefs

All of the participants gave insights into their desires and visions regarding how they saw themselves in the future, and the ways in which participants planned to achieve their visions drew upon their beliefs. Firstly, it is important to mention that all but one participant talked about their desire to live and work abroad/overseas, which is one component of the L2 motivational self system. This relates especially to *Core belief 11*, i.e. using English to communicate with others. Many participants gave specific details of plans to live abroad, work abroad and use English in their jobs (even if it was not clear what those jobs would be at the time). These participants spoke of their desire to be able to communicate with people from different countries and the role the English Lounge played in this.

Secondly, pressures related to achieving scores in tests, expectations from parents or from Japanese society (or even self-initiated pressures) were mentioned by several participants. This relates to the 'ought-to self' component of the L2 self system as well as to *Core belief 14*, i.e.

the belief that doing certain activities that they didn't necessarily enjoy was important. In fact, almost all of the participants made reference to aspects of their lives that they appeared to see as obligations influencing their futures. In terms of the use of the English Lounge, learners who saw their presence in the space as purely functional, were driven by 'ought-to self' pressures.

The most prominent theme related to future selves – the desire to live abroad – at times came hand in hand with the desire to use English for work in the future and beliefs about the best way to prepare for that experience. The following excerpt indicates how Mei (a Regular User [RU]) explained why she frequented the lounge; she believed that speaking to others would help her achieve her dream to work abroad:

> Hmm. First, I, I wanna work abroad. So, I have, I need to Spanish, no, no, English. And, um, English is use, use, useable so when, uh, if I speak English, I, I can, *nan darou* [what?] *ironna hito to shaberu koto ga dekiru, ironna sekai no hito no kyoutsuugo nanode…* [I can talk with many different people, because I will have a common language with people from around the world…] (Mei, RU, Interview 1)

Similarly, in the following excerpt we can see a connection between a belief Yuki had about language learning and her ideal L2 self. According to her, in order to be a language teacher she needed to be able to speak naturally. Regular attendance at the lounge would help Yuko to develop this fluency.

> At school, I want to be a Spanish and English teacher. So, I think speaking more naturally is important for the job. (Yuki, RU, Interview 2)

On the other hand, in the following excerpt, we see that Misa (an NU) focuses on exam study instead of engagement with the English Lounge even though her goal is also to live abroad as this links to her beliefs and her L2 ought-to self.

> Yeah, as I said, I wanted to go to America and for in order to go there, you need TOEFL score, and it's very important things to get in a school, American school. (Misa, NU, Interview 2)

Other participants conveyed stories of external pressures relating to their perceived obligations to family or Japanese society. These obligations related to their 'ought-to self' as well as to their 'interdependent agency' in the sense that they felt they should be acting for the good of their family or society. Thus, some decisions made can be seen to be connected with expectations held. This excerpt from an interview with Kyoji explains why students often stop using the English Lounge in their third and fourth years at the university; the pressure from society to start looking for a job is often more powerful than the desire to improve English communicative competence:

> That's also a big problem for me right now, I'm in the third grade right now, so university student usually start job hunting from third grade but I'm in Brazil so when I go back to Japan I have to start doing the interviews you know, but I really don't know what kind of sectors that I wanna work so. (Kyoji, YS Group, Interview 2)

It is very likely that students who choose to specialise in languages have hopes of improving and using those languages in their futures. As a result, these learners may be 'invested' in their target language. 'Investment', according to Norton (2013: 114–115), implies that learners 'take ownership over their meaning-making and re-imagine an expanded range of identities for the future'. However, we must remember that identities change over time and vary in different contexts (Dörnyei, 2001), hence the 'range of realities' is likely to impact learners' investment in the language and ideas about their future selves. Throughout the learning process, learners interact in different situations and thus adjust and reflect on their assumptions and ways of thinking based on their successes and failures, as shown by the research (e.g. Ellis, 2008; Mori, 1999; Wenden, 1999). This means learners' 'future selves' are always able to be altered or re-imagined based on their current learning experiences.

Whether or not participants had a clear picture of their future selves, it was certainly something they had given considerable thought to. Yashima *et al.* (2004) made the case that learners who can visualise their 'English-using selves' are more conscious of how they relate themselves to the world and thus are more motivated to communicate. It is difficult to know how strongly participants were motivated to become their future L2 selves in all their capacities, or the extent of the obligation they felt to follow external pressures influencing their lives. What can be understood through the interviews is that they were seriously considering their future selves, and this was reflected in the ways in which they used the lounge, in combination with their beliefs about learning.

Previous learning experiences, *eigo* and *eikaiwa* and the interaction with learner beliefs

As we analysed our participants' interviews, we found that the 'competing discourses' of *eigo* and *eikaiwa* (Nagatomo, 2016) were frequently tied to their wider beliefs about language learning. From our thematic coding, we discovered that most of our participants (11 out of 15) had referred in some way to their beliefs on the efficacy of *eigo* versus *eikaiwa* in language learning. We found this to be relevant to the existing literature in two main ways: (1) an incongruence between participants' language learning beliefs and the ideology of *eigo* and (2) a link between their focus on *eikaiwa* and 'international posture' (Yashima, 2013).

Several participants (8 out of 15) questioned to varying degrees the efficacy of their secondary English language education and its focus on *eigo*, as this excerpt indicates:

> In spite of studying for six years from junior high school, I could read but I couldn't speak at all. I thought that was not very good. (Translated from Japanese) (Mei, RU, Interview 1)

Mei, in particular, was quite critical in her evaluation of her high school English classes, stating that they lacked the 'practicality' (*jitsuyousei*) that she could get from the English Lounge. 'Practical', in this sense, appeared to mean the skills she needed in order to communicate with others in English. However, it could be argued that from the ideological perspective of *eigo*, Mei's high school classes *were* very practical, providing students with the tools required to pass the university entrance examinations. The issue then, is not one of 'practicality' *per se*, but a question of how students view the role of English in their lives and whether or not their goals are ideologically congruent with *eigo* in Japanese schools. In Mei's case, she prioritises English oral proficiency (*Core belief 1*) due to its utility in her future goal of speaking with 'people from different worlds' (Interview 1) as she travels and works overseas (*Core belief 11*).

Additionally, Kaede (RU, see case study in Chapter 7) had mixed feelings towards the *eigo* she had experienced in high school as it was linked to feelings of deficiency due to her lack of ability in test-oriented lessons, marking her as 'someone who can't do English' (*eigo ga dekinai hito*, Interview 1). These negative past experiences of *eigo* appeared to permeate Kaede's experiences in the English Lounge, further adding to the anxiety that she already felt as an introvert and a neophyte lounge user. In contrast, Sachiko (NU, see case study in Chapter 9) stated that her experiences of *eigo* in secondary education were positive and empowering.

> In the classes in high school, the teacher made us to read a lot and lot, and test many difficult words and phrases. Some of the students says it was really hard to do these all the times... But it was fun for me. (Sachiko, NU, Interview 2)

The prevalence of an international posture (Yashima, 2013) among all of our participants was relevant to the positioning of *eigo* as 'Japanese English' and *eikaiwa* as 'foreign English' (McVeigh, 2004). Although we were unable to ascertain the extent of participants' interest in global affairs, there was ample evidence to support the claim that almost all participants sought out interaction with non-Japanese people and desired overseas work or travel.

> I can't talk to non-Japanese, so. I like talking to other countries' people, but MULC [another study centre on campus for other languages] I don't like MULC, so I, I can only talk to them in SALC, so SALC is important for me. (Yuki, RU, Interview 1)

Here, the international posture that the *eikaiwa* of the English Lounge represents becomes clearer. The strong international posture found in almost all of the participants we spoke to may explain why the 'Japanese English' of *eigo* – focused primarily on test taking and sidelining intercultural communication (Fujimoto-Adamson, 2006) – was rejected in favour of developing proficiency in the 'foreign' *eikaiwa*. Just as in Miyahara's (2015) study, some English Lounge users saw opportunities for *eikaiwa* as being vital in achieving their personal goals, narrowing the gap between their current selves and their ideal L2 selves as users of English on an international stage. This international posture is reflected in the core beliefs that we identified among English Lounge users, both in terms of their language learning goal of intercultural communication (*Core belief 11*) and, in many cases, the means with which to achieve that goal through practicing speaking to develop English proficiency (*Core belief 1*).

One other interesting point was that in her second interview, Kaede indicated that she may have struck a balance between *eigo* and *eikaiwa* stemming from an overseas trip to develop her proficiency in Spanish.

Kaede: In the morning...
Interviewer: You learnt grammar.
Kaede: And speaking practice in the afternoon. That suited me. So I thought if I learn some phrases first, and then use them at the Yellow Sofas, I will learn English well that way.

(Kaede, RU, Interview 2)

Although the purpose of Kaede's Spanish study on her trip was more consistent with the ideology of *eikaiwa* rather than *eigo* in that it was geared towards developing communicative competence rather than test taking, this revelation highlights a shift in her beliefs about the role of grammar study. In terms of the purpose of *eigo* versus *eikaiwa*, Aspinall (2013: 147) claims that 'overlap between the two worlds does not exist'. While in ideological terms this may be true, through Kaede's evolving beliefs on language learning, it could be argued that we see an amalgamation of the approaches that she experienced in high school (*eigo*) and in the English Lounge (*eikaiwa*). Taking a more pragmatic approach to learning language, she was perhaps able to see past a black or white view of *eigo-eikaiwa* and pick and choose elements from each approach that she felt benefitted her development.

We also see a similar reconciliation between *eigo* and *eikaiwa* approaches in one of the senior YS Group members, Tomoya. His language learner history described how his language studies prior to university had been markedly orientated towards *eigo*, with his junior high and high school English classes being centred around the grammar-translation method. Subsequently, in his first interview, we observed a dramatic shift in the opposite direction where he spoke to us at length about the benefits of the *eikaiwa* approach he experienced at the English Lounge and the engaging and interactive nature of the space (see *Core beliefs 1 and 4*). *Eigo*, in contrast, was positioned negatively as Japanese students 'learn(ing) at the desk'. However, in his second interview, we heard that he had once again altered his opinion on the relative value of *eigo* and *eikaiwa*. Tomoya stated that although he saw the value of *eikaiwa* and the opportunities for output it provides and stated an intention to teach communicatively upon obtaining his teaching licence, he did not believe that this was the most beneficial contribution to his English competence. In actuality, he told us that the discrete grammatical knowledge and increased accuracy that had been developed in his *eigo*-dominant secondary school classes had been the factor that had been most valuable to him in his experiences as a language learner as it had provided a solid linguistic foundation upon which he was able to develop his communication skills. Here, we see examples of the core beliefs (2 and 3) of English Lounge users valuing grammatical knowledge and accuracy – but without sidelining the role of communicative interaction in English.

Language anxiety and the interaction with learner beliefs

Language anxiety manifested itself in the data in six ways, and we will outline these briefly in this section, making reference where relevant to the core beliefs.

(1) Fear of breaking into established groups

Two of the common beliefs (*Core beliefs* 5 and 9) are likely to have stemmed from a sense of interdependent agency and the cultural practice of needing to be part of a particular group in order to be able to enter it. As the English Lounge is perceived to be an international space where interaction with others – even people you do not know – is encouraged, this caused anxiety for many of the participants. This excerpt is from an interview with Yukari in Year 1:

> Because, um, I often come to SALC and see Yellow Sofas, but always same students are there, so I don't feel comfortable to join them. And if I started talking with them, I think it would be fine, but they all know each

other and I don't have any exchange student friends, so…. I…. don't feel comfortable to join people who all know each other and I don't know. (Yukari, NU, Interview 1)

(2) Fear of being judged by other students

This source of anxiety is linked to several beliefs (*Core beliefs 2, 3* and *12*). Firstly, beliefs related to the importance of accuracy (*Core belief 3*) and a thorough knowledge of grammar (*Core belief 2*) may result in a lack of confidence in one's abilities to speak English with others in the English Lounge. Some of the participants expressed crippling insecurities about their English levels and this made them feel anxious.

> There are many exchange students and foreigners (in the English Lounge), and also same age student who speak English very fluently, so it's like very stressful for me because I think, very, hmm, I think too much what people think, so yes, so stressful. (Misa, NU, Interview 1)

In some cases, students like Misa avoided using the English Lounge altogether, but others forced themselves to go as they believed that it offered worthwhile opportunities (*Core beliefs 1, 6, 8* and *14*). Secondly, a belief that it is important to reach what they perceived to be 'native-like' ability in English (*Core belief 12*) was a source of motivation for some, but a source of anxiety for others who began to realise that this may be an unachievable aim.

(3) Feeling of shame that their language skills are not better (felt by more senior students)

Beliefs related to role models (*Core belief 6*) acted as a motivator for many of the participants but simultaneously became a source of anxiety to students who felt pressure to be a good role model, while feeling that they lacked sufficient English proficiency to do so. This resulted in feelings of shame and possibly avoidance of the English Lounge.

> I'm afraid to go there because, um, I think my English skill is not enough to speak fluently. So, and I think, I'm sophomore now and it become more difficult to go there, so if I'm freshman, so 'I'm freshman, so please don't worry about my English skill' or something, I can say it, but I'm sophomore, so everyone think my English skill is maybe improved than freshman, so I'm worried about that. (Sayaka, NU, Interview 1)

(4) A personality trait of being shy or introverted/ making comparisons with others

Participants perceived the YS Group members and other students who used the English Lounge regularly to be 'positive', 'confident', 'active', 'talkative' and generally proactive about using English in the space. Sometimes, this led to the belief (*Core belief 13*) that it is necessary to be an extrovert in order to be a good language learner. Introversion is more common in Japan than extroversion (Carducci & Zimbardo, 1995), and the belief may be one reason why people tend not to develop high levels of English-speaking ability (Ortega, 2009). Some of the participants were able to reduce their anxiety about going to the English Lounge by always going with a more confident friend. Others felt anxiety as they perceived their friends and other members present in the lounge to be more confident and more suited to the English Lounge than they were. These two illustrative examples show this in our data:

> Spanish major students are a lot of, almost of them are outgoing people. They often go to the Yellow Sofa. (Yuki, RU, Interview 2)

> Uhhh I think the students that go to the other sofa and me ... want to improve our English level and the different point is they want to, they like talking, I think any language is okay for them, but for me I don't like talking. (Sachiko, NU, Interview 1)

(5) Insecurities about poor language skills or making mistakes

This type of anxiety is triggered by beliefs about the importance of accuracy (*Core belief 3*), the need for perfect grammar (*Core belief 2*) or the goal of developing perceived 'native-like compctcncc' (*Core belief 12*). Some participants described their lack of confidence due to an emphasis on accuracy and/or fear of making mistakes. Sachiko, as we see in the following excerpt, has a fear of making mistakes combined with a preference for being alone, and has consequently never used the English Lounge:

> One of the reasons is that I am afraid of making mistakes and another one is I don't like being with anybody.... I still have no confidence with talking, talking in English. (Sachiko, NU, Interview 1)

(6) Institutional markers (e.g. test score, streams)

Poor results on tests or being streamed into a low-level class might mean that students feel insecure about their language skills (*Core beliefs 2 and 3*). An example of this in the data comes from the first interview with Kaede (an RU) where she explained how she had been labelled and streamed in high school as a 'person who can't "do" English' and this had initially affected her confidence to go to the English Lounge.

Adaptive interdependent agency and the interaction with learner beliefs

One adaptive way that interdependent agency manifested itself was the manner in which members of the YS Group interacted with others who did not use the lounge so often. We found evidence that they recognised that others felt a sense of trepidation when it came to sitting with them, and they took steps to ameliorate these fears, so as to grow the community and make it more useful to the wider body of students (*Core belief 10* – belief in the benefit of a community). In addition to the above, we also found that the YS Group members were each engaging in a variety of activities aimed at enhancing both the membership and the usefulness of the community. Crucially, these activities were framed in the language of 'for us', rather than 'for me'. This likely stemmed from their belief that using the language is important for language development (*Core belief 1*), and that as senior students, they could motivate others by being role models (*Core belief 6*).

Analysis (2): A Threaded Analysis

The results of the analysis described in the previous section not only took each factor as a starting point but also attempted to comment on the interplay between the factors. It is difficult to show all of the interactive parts, but in the following two sections, we return to the data and visually represent the nature of the connections between factors.

A threaded analysis (Davis & Sumara, 2006) allowed us to visually present the data in order to see the presence of the five factors as they occurred within the three groups of participants – the 15 individuals – and over at least a two-year period. Although there is a range of sub-categories within each factor, we selected the ones that appeared in our data most frequently. Based on the presence of these factors in our data, we established whether the belief was generally helpful/positive or unhelpful/negative for our participants' language learning. Table 13.1 is the key to reading the threaded visualisation of our analysis. The first row (shaded light grey) under each of the factors is largely to be seen as the presence of helpful or positive elements influencing language learning through using the target language, for example using English at the English Lounge. The second row (shaded dark grey) contains elements that are largely considered to be unhelpful or negative in terms of using the English Lounge. The third row (hatched shading) indicates that both factors were evident in the data. A question mark (Row 4) is used when it is unclear, and N/D (Row 5) is used if there is insufficient data to make an assumption about this factor. In order to show the temporal nature of the presence of the factors, we examined the data for evidence from Year 1 and Year 2 of the study and also from prior to the study, which could have been prior to starting at the university or soon after joining the university.

The analysis was done by four members of the research team. Firstly, we held a pre-analysis meeting where we agreed on the procedures and examined all of the data for a sample of three participants together. By finding evidence in the data, we were able to shade the boxes appropriately to best summarise the presence of each factor. Secondly, as this was

Understanding Learner Beliefs and Individual Differences in a Social Learning Space   143

Table 13.1 Key for reading the threaded analysis

	Beliefs
	Beliefs helpful for language learning
	Beliefs may be hindering language learning
	Evidence of both
?	Unclear
N/D	No (or insufficient) data
	L2 self-system
	Desire to use English in the future
	Ought to self / external pressures
	Evidence of both
?	Unclear
N/D	No (or insufficient) data
	Eigo-eikaiwa distinction
	Reconciles *eigo* and *eikaiwa*
	Overcommitment to *eigo* or *eikaiwa*
	Evidence of both
?	Unclear / no data
N/D	No (or insufficient) data
	Language anxiety
	Positive experience / may look back on an anxious time, but has moved on
	Negative experience / still experiences language anxiety
	Evidence of both
?	Unclear
N/D	No (or insufficient) data
	Agency and Interdependence
	Adaptive approach to interdependent agency
	Maladaptive approach to interdependent agency
	Evidence of both
?	Unclear
N/D	No (or insufficient) data

time-consuming, we divided up the data and did an analysis of several of the remaining participants each. We did this analysis individually through close reading of all the data. Thirdly, we met again one week later to discuss our analysis in depth and finalise the results. Table 13.2 shows the results of our analysis after the discussion process.

Interpretation of threading: Patterns?

YS Group

As can be seen from the clusters of light grey shading around the YS Group, our threaded analysis revealed a number of trends indicating generally helpful beliefs and other factors related to language learning. We found that the YS Group members shared an adaptive set of language learning beliefs. We also found evidence that the person they desired to become was shaping their motivation to engage with the area, which is in keeping with the ideal L2 self model of language learning motivation.

In terms of the *eigo* versus *eikaiwa* dichotomy, we found that the majority of students had reconciled communication-oriented learning with the forms of study more traditional to the Japanese context. They did not then view their language learning experience solely one way or

Table 13.2 Threaded analysis representing factors, participants and time

Group	YS Group					Regular Users					Non-Users			
Participants	Kyoji	Kokon	Sina	Suzuka	Tomoya	Kaede	Mei	Rintaro	Ririka	Ryuno-suke	Yuki	Misa	Sachiko	Sayaka	Yuka
Previous beliefs			?	N/D	N/D			N/D	N/D	N/D	?				N/D
Beliefs year 1													?		
Beliefs year 2				N/D				N/D					?		
Previous L2 self		N/D		N/D				N/D	N/D	N/D	?	N/D	?		
L2 self year 1									N/D						
L2 self year 2				N/D	N/D				N/D						
Previous eig-eik			N/D				N/D	N/D		?		?			N/D
Eig-eik Year 1										?		?			
Eig-eik Year 2										?		?			
Previous anxiety		N/D				N/D	N/D	N/D		N/D				?	
Anxiety year 1															
Anxiety year 2							?		N/D						
Previous Int agen	N/D		N/D	N/D	N/D		N/D	N/D	N/D	N/D			?	?	N/D
Interdp Year 1									N/D				?		
Interdp Year 2				N/D	N/D			?	N/D			?	?		

the other. Most notably here, no student expressed a preference for *eigo* over *eikaiwa*, and this is particularly interesting because our analysis revealed a number of these same students had valued *eigo* at the expense of *eikaiwa* prior to joining the university. The strongest trend, however, was in the area of anxiety, or specifically a lack of anxiety, for while many of the participants described having felt some sense of anxiety upon encountering and getting used to the space, they had all since adapted by the time of their first interview, and no longer held any apprehensions over using it at all.

Finally, while one student felt some reluctance to taking on the role of *senpai*, we found strong evidence of adaptive interdependent agency, insofar as every member of the YS Group had taken ownership of the space and formed a tight-knit community within it. Crucially, this close-knit community seemed to impart a sense of obligation, and all members of the YS Group described actively implementing a number of strategies aimed at making the space more useful and approachable to those outside their immediate sphere; in particular, they all noticed and were attempting to ameliorate the invisible barrier that many students from the other groups we analysed described as serving as an impediment to their entering the space.

Regular Users

From our threaded analysis of data from the RUs, we noticed that these learners had largely adaptive beliefs that may have helped them to continue to develop as L2 users, such as an openness to communicating with others in English. This can be seen most clearly in their first-year interviews, with four out of six learners exhibiting predominantly positive beliefs and the remaining two learners displaying a mixture of beliefs that may have both helped and hindered their language learning. However, arguably the strongest indicator of the nature of the RUs is when we look at the findings related to their L2 selves. All but one learner (where data was unclear) show evidence of having a clear sense of an ideal future L2 self that they draw on for language learning motivation. We can also observe that, for the most part, this strong presence continues into the second-year interview findings. In the case of *eigo* and *eikaiwa*, our findings are rather mixed. In many cases, we did not have enough data to note any patterns related to *eigo* or *eikaiwa*. We found that half of the RUs had a reasonably balanced view on these different approaches to learning English and saw the benefits of both. In the case of anxiety, we were not able to identify any particularly strong patterns from our data. However, we did notice that even though most of the RUs in their first year at university dealt with their anxiety relatively successfully, for some of them, their anxiety surfaced once more in their second year due to the perceived expectation that they should have achieved a higher level of proficiency by that time. Finally, when analysing our data for adaptive or maladaptive manifestations of interdependent agency, such as wanting to join a space but feeling unable to do so due to not feeling a part of the group occupying it, we found that a slight trend towards adaptive interdependence existed in the first-year interviews but that this appeared to weaken over time.

Non Users

Although in many cases there was too little data to be able to discern any particular trends in the NU data, from the threading we are able to observe a few interesting points at a glance. Firstly, three out of four of the participants (Sachiko's data was unclear) possessed helpful beliefs related to language learning. Secondly, three out of four of the participants had a positive L2 self image in Years 1 and 2 of the study. Thirdly, language anxiety was present in all four participants. Finally, we can see that there was evidence of maladaptive interdependent agency in all four participants, mainly related to the perception that it is not possible to join groups of unknown people for language practice, even in the context of a designated English Lounge.

Analysis (3): Visual Representations of Nested Beliefs

In order to visually explore relationships between the factors, we also created diagrams which represented how beliefs interacted with other factors. The purpose of this kind of diagramming is to show that there are 'levels of complex organization' (Davis & Sumara, 2006: 91) between various factors, in this case, the core beliefs and other individual differences. The nested analysis incorporated the interview data from both years of the study and the language learning histories. Taking beliefs as a starting point, the other four key factors were nested within that in order to show the connections. Admittedly, this representation oversimplifies the relationships and the dynamics by making them appear static. In addition, it does not include all of the potential factors that could be present as we had to be selective in order for our analysis to be possible at all. Nevertheless, if we keep in mind that this is only part of the story, it allows us to make sense of the connections in a different way and add to our understanding of how beliefs and other individual differences affect the ways in which participants view and use the English Lounge. Due to space restrictions, we are only sharing the nested visualisations for three participants (one from each group). Figure 13.1 shows the core beliefs of an RU, Kaede, as we interpreted them in the data. Each textbox represents one of Kaede's core beliefs. Within each of these core beliefs, we can see how the other factors interact. For example, *Core belief 3* is that accuracy is important, but it is OK to make mistakes when speaking English. The factors nested within this core belief show how this is evident in her views on grammar, and these beliefs probably stem from her

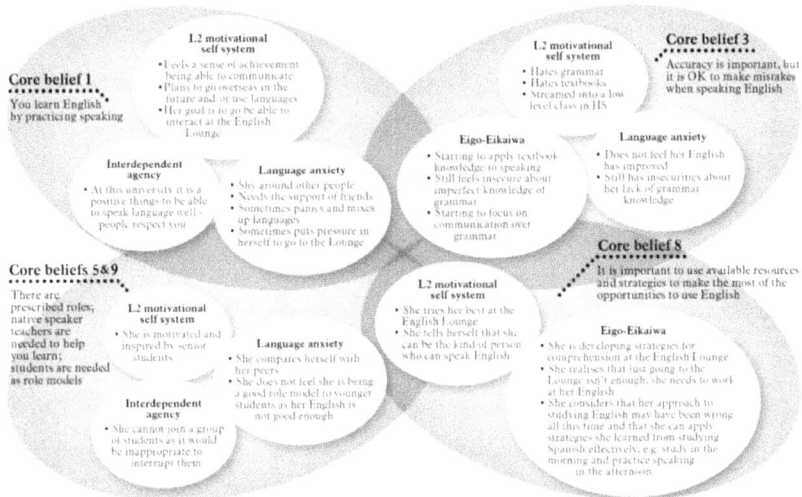

Figure 13.1 Kaede's (RU) core beliefs and nested factors

previous experience of being labelled as someone who was not good at English (grammar). Kaede's approach to developing English proficiency is to focus on the development of communication skills. However, by nesting the ideas, we can also see the conflict between belief and action. For example, Kaede still feels insecure about her (perceived) poor grammar, and this contributes to her language anxiety. Nevertheless, she is starting to apply strategies to make links between what she is learning and her communication practice. Patterns can also be seen for three more of Kaede's core beliefs. Figures 13.1–13.3 show how the nesting varies from person to person, as examples of Kyoji (a YS Group member) and Misa (an NU of the lounge) show.

Conclusions

The analysis of beliefs and other individual difference factors has been the focus of this chapter, and our three levels of analysis have allowed us to reach certain conclusions. These conclusions are summarised here, but the pedagogical implications are presented in Chapter 16. As we have seen, each of the key factors (learner beliefs, L2 motivational self system, previous learning experiences/*eigo-eikaiwa*, anxiety, interdependent agency) plays a role in the ways in which the participants use the English Lounge and indeed in whether they choose to go there at all. We identified 14 core beliefs expressed in one way or another by the participants. Many of the beliefs were complementary, others conflicting (e.g. a participant who values interaction in the target language, but also thinks grammatical accuracy is necessary before one is able to speak), but discovering these conflicts helped us to understand the complex nature

148 Part 3: Exploring Concepts Through the Research

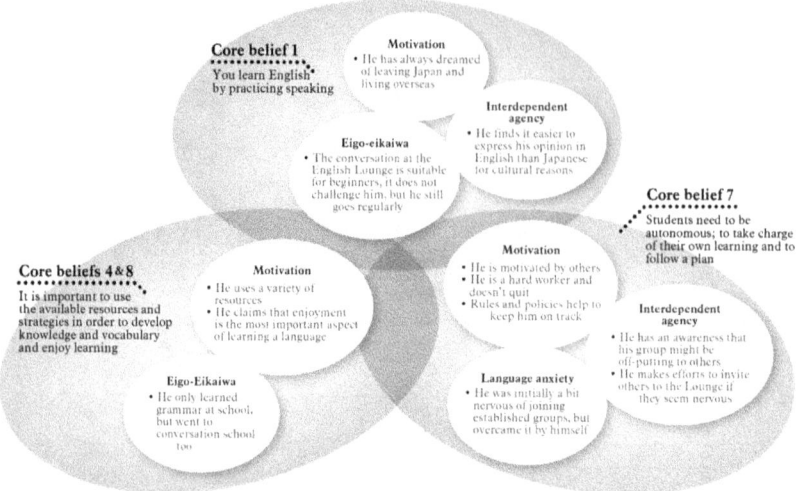

Figure 13.2 Kyoji's (YS Group) core beliefs and nested factors

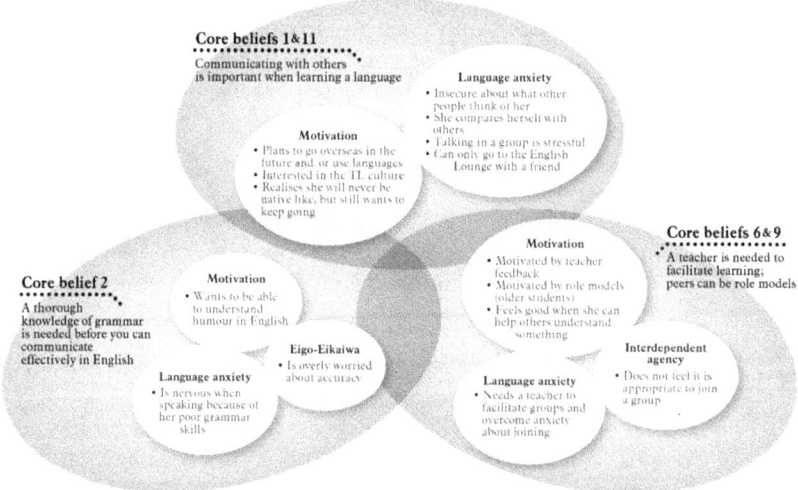

Figure 13.3 Misa's core beliefs and nested factors

of the beliefs. All 14 beliefs could be considered helpful for language learning. However, as we have seen, not only were beliefs and actions often misaligned, but also the interplay between beliefs and other factors (particularly *eigo-eikaiwa*, language anxiety and interdependent agency) caused barriers for English Lounge use.

From the perspective of the L2 motivational self system, many of the participants saw the English Lounge as a place that allowed them to become a version of their ideal selves. Visions of ideal L2 selves became more specific over time and this often had an effect on the ways in which RUs and YS Group members used and viewed the English Lounge. NUs chose other activities which contributed to visions of their future selves; as we saw in Chapter 11, the presence of the lounge itself, even when they actively chose not to use it, enhanced their identities as learners.

Eigo-eikaiwa is an interesting and contextually relevant concept which allowed us to uncover our participants' beliefs from another perspective. All of the participants had experienced a high school system which drew almost exclusively on *eigo*. This shared experience and the new opportunities the English Lounge afforded our participants who frequented it meant that their views on *eigo* and *eikaiwa* shifted throughout their time at the university. It was common for participants to experience a period when *eigo* was referred to in negative terms and almost rejected for a while. Later, many of the participants reconciled *eigo* and *eikaiwa* and made use of the English Lounge and other opportunities in a way that was helpful for language learning.

Language anxiety was a key reason why some participants chose to avoid the English Lounge. In fact, most of the participants had experienced some anxiety at one time or another, but many had managed to reduce it or overcome it in various ways, such as developing a projected identity (see Chapter 11), relying on social support from friends or lecturers or making use of the English Lounge as a habit or a goal.

Interdependent agency is also culturally relevant and we were able to see from the data that an adaptive view of one's role in the society of the English Lounge could lead to benefits from the point of view of language learning. Adaptive views manifested themselves as willingness to join a group of strangers in order to practice speaking English; taking ownership of the space and making attempts to make it a better place for others; and making others feel welcome in the space.

Of course, a space such as the English Lounge is far more complex than this chapter suggests. We chose only five individual difference factors and conducted only a partial analysis for practical purposes, but we were already able to see some of the main areas of influence. We reflect in more depth on our methods, limitations and possible courses of action for future research in Chapter 14.

14 Lessons Learnt from the Research Methods Applied in This Project

Jo Mynard, Daniel Hooper and Phoebe Lyon

In this chapter, we reflect on the ways in which we approached the research, and examine what we learnt and how helpful these methods were in allowing us to answer our research questions. We also offer some practical advice and guidelines for others wishing to investigate the dynamics of social learning spaces elsewhere. Throughout this project, we were specifically interested in whether the lounge/space itself had any kind of impact on user identity, beliefs or community membership, and this chapter allows us to share our views on whether this research was done effectively, or whether other approaches could have worked better. We will also return to our broader questions about how this research has contributed to our knowledge of the wider learning ecology and learning spaces elsewhere. To recap, our overall research questions were:

(1) What happens in the English Lounge? i.e.:
    (a) What communities formed in the space?
    (b) How do different students perceive and use the space?
    (c) Why do some students choose *not* to use the space?
(2) What is the relationship between the English Lounge and language learner identity?
(3) How do learner beliefs affect participation in the space?
(4) What other factors affect the ways in which participants view and use (or avoid) the English Lounge?

Reflecting on Our Methods

Focus 1: Data collection

Observation study

This initial part of the project began with the overarching question 'What happens in the English Lounge?' and we were able to broadly answer this question by way of an initial observation study. We would certainly recommend this approach as a starting point for other researchers interested in exploring a social learning space. The main reason that we benefited from starting with an observation study is that it allowed us to put aside our preconceived notions of what was occurring in the space and instead draw on the results of systematic observations using a framework. Our observations and the discussions we engaged in during the observation period also allowed us to strengthen our subsequent research foci. We used Spradley's (1980) observation framework as a starting point and augmented it with aspects of the psychological processes that we were interested in exploring in more depth. If we were to repeat the observation study, we would consider appointing two researchers per observation session (or one researcher and one research assistant). As there is so much going on in a social learning space, it is difficult to notice everything, so having two researchers would allow for not only the potential to capture more episodes, but also the opportunity to discuss what was happening as part of the interpretation process. In our case, although we only had one researcher per observation session, we each typed up the raw field notes as soon as possible after the observation took place. We would also recommend including a map of the area in the observation guide where the observers can write rough notes and timestamps (Chapter 4: Figure 4.1).

Interviews

The three sub-questions relating to what was occurring in the English Lounge were more difficult to answer by way of observation alone. Although we were able to observe generally what was happening in the English Lounge, we could not understand the nature of the communities that had formed, students' perceptions of the space or the views of Non Users from observations alone. In order to answer research Questions 1a–c, we found that semi-structured interviews were generally an effective method as they not only allowed us to explore our research questions, but they also allowed for other themes to emerge. However, there were some challenges related to the scope of the project. We had a range of research questions and were interested in several themes, so the interviews needed to address all of these. In addition, there were seven interviewers, so we needed to ensure that the questions were somewhat consistent. We overcame these challenges in two ways. Firstly, we jointly constructed a bank of interview questions that addressed all aspects of the research and indicated which questions were essential for all of us to ask. Secondly, we conducted mock interviews with each other prior to the real ones in order to become familiar with the questions and also to gain an understanding of how it would feel to be a participant attempting to answer the questions. These steps ensured that the interviews generally went smoothly. We inevitably failed to collect sufficient data for all of the research questions for various reasons such as students having insufficient experience or an interviewer not probing persistently, but we attempted to mitigate this by sharing the interview transcripts and our interpretations with the participants and inviting them to add or change anything. As learners' engagement with a social learning space is likely to be mediated by their evolving learner identities (Murray *et al.*, 2018), it was important that we examined participants' language learning histories in order to understand the potential impact of past experiences on their English Lounge usage. The language learning histories (Murphey & Carpenter, 2008) supported the interviewers in the second round of interviews and should ideally have also been used in the first year of the project.

Focus 2: Data analysis

We qualitatively analysed the data collected from the observations, interviews and language learning histories using different methods from different perspectives in sub-teams, which also had its benefits and challenges. We will discuss these according to each type of analysis we undertook: a narrative analysis of case studies, a typological analysis and an interpretative analysis. One general challenge relates to the amount of data that needed to be analysed and the scope of the project; the same qualitative data needed to be coded several times depending on the different research questions being considered. This process involved several rounds of organising the data into relevant themes and identifying emergent patterns. Since coding requires personal judgement, we moderated this process discursively with others in the research team (Hammond & Wellington, 2013). We also found that the qualitative analysis software programme HyperResearch helped us to organise this process and keep the coding separate for different aspects of the project.

Case studies

We decided to include intact case studies to ensure that the individual stories of the participants were not lost with the levels of data analysis that were occurring. In addition, these case studies informed the results of all four research questions. Unlike the other research methods where we analysed data discursively in sub-teams, the case studies were written as narratives by one of the researchers. The researcher responsible for writing a given narrative had conducted both interviews, developed a rapport with the individual participant and made reflective notes on the data throughout the project. Although the narrative case studies were written by one researcher, these chapters drew on data and interpretations provided by all seven of the researchers. The benefit of this is that the case studies could be more detailed and draw on multiple perspectives, but consequently were not considered to be 'pure' interpretative narratives as the authors incorporated interpretations made by all of the team members. One challenge with case study research in general is that it has the danger of presenting a 'distorted picture' (Simons, 2009: 24) as it presents 'events in time' when the participants and context may have changed since the research was conducted. When examining qualitative interview data, one must also take into account the widely recognised assertion that the interview interaction is essentially co-constructed between interviewer and interviewee (Mann, 2016). This means that one cannot assume that interview data represents objective 'truths' simply uncovered by targeted questioning, but rather information that is shaped by the multiple and shifting identities of both interlocutors. In addition, the stories are complicated and are affected by researcher interpretations, possibly by the research project itself and the dialogue between the research team members. We are part of the community that we are researching and we, as educators, are invested in creating a positive learning environment for the students using the space that we are researching. Advice we would give others is to acknowledge that any interpretations and interventions will inevitably influence the space under investigation, so try to be as transparent as possible throughout the project.

Typological analysis

A typological analysis (Ayres & Knafi, 2008) was the term we used to mean the analysis we did according to different predetermined frameworks for investigating community (Research Question 1) and identity (Research Question 2). Benson *et al.*'s (2013) framework for identity was easy to apply and ensured that we investigated many facets of the participants' identities in a systematic way. Although not originally envisioned, a trajectory emerged from our interpretations that was very helpful for seeing at a glance how students in our institution navigated their way through the use of a social learning space, and the role that identity played in this process. We have not applied this trajectory to other spaces within our institution; however, drawing on other work being done by some of our colleagues at our institution (e.g. Kanai & Imamura, 2019; Watkins, 2019), we can certainly see similarities and applications. In addition, we would also be interested in seeing how Benson *et al.*'s (2013) framework applies to other social learning spaces in other institutions, and whether similar trajectories are found elsewhere.

The second framework we applied was the well-established communities of practice (CoP) model. As this is such a well-known and robust model, and relatively easy to apply, we also recommend this to other researchers. It is important, however, to mention that this kind of analysis represents a mere 'snapshot' of a given community at one fixed point in time. CoPs by their nature are in constant flux, meaning that member interviews conducted a year later are likely to illustrate a markedly different picture to the one we have described here. We believe, therefore, that carrying out longitudinal research describing participants' engagement with the CoP over the course of their entire university career would provide valuable and well-rounded insights into the workings and roles of a dynamic community.

Interpretative analysis

One approach we could have taken for this project could have been to *only* carry out an interpretative analysis, or to carry out the interpretative analysis first and then decide which factors to explore in more depth and which framework (if any) would be appropriate. There is no one best way to approach this, but we feel that our research benefited from both the interpretative analysis *and* the typological analyses. The main reason for this was that we began with specific research questions about identity and community, but we were also curious to see what other factors contributed to the overall dynamics of the space. Nevertheless, we were unable to capture the full story. For practical reasons, we were not able to study *all* of the interacting factors, but we wanted to be able to at least understand the roles that *some* of them played. We applied three strategies in order to make the process manageable. Firstly, we began with a thematic interpretative analysis of *part* of our data and then applied it to the rest as a practical way to approach the analysis. Secondly, we chose only five factors to focus on; these had emerged prominently in our thematic analysis and were the most important for our particular area of focus. Thirdly, we presented key ideas as tables, figures, diagrams and lists where our interpretations of aspects of the data could be visualised, and patterns and connections identified. Although we acknowledge that this approach is limited and we could not appreciate the full influence of a wide range of influencing factors, we recommend these three strategies to other researchers mainly for practical purposes. If time permitted and we were to continue the analysis, or extend the project, we would include a focus on how the learners engaged with a wider range of interacting factors. For example, further analysis could include other individual differences such as personality, autonomy, strategies, self-regulation, creativity and other factors. In addition, the factors we chose are a lot more complex than we have been able to show. For example, we only used the second language (L2) motivational self system for our analysis, but we could have looked into intrinsic and extrinsic motivation, amotivation and other features of self-determination theory (Deci & Ryan, 1985), including the basic psychological needs sub-theory components of autonomy, competence and relatedness.

Our main advice for future researchers would, again, depend on the initial research questions. If researchers are planning to attempt to answer specific questions about identity and community (for example), the frameworks we selected could be usefully applied. However, if the research question is much more open, time is limited and/or there are fewer researchers, then just an interpretative analysis might be sufficient. Although simplistic, Appendix 4 shows some of the main research preparation considerations which could guide the process.

Examining connections and dynamics

As we discussed earlier, it is challenging to study a social learning environment where there are so many factors at play interacting dynamically at different levels. Taking a more longitudinal approach to the study was appropriate for us in order to attempt to capture some of the connections and changes associated with learner beliefs and other individual difference factors. By looking at connections between these factors, we were able to see how these affected the use (or avoidance) of the English Lounge (Research Questions 3 and 4). However, this process might have been more robust had we considered taking a complex dynamic systems (CDS) approach. This would have allowed us to observe how the agents (i.e. the learners) engaged with the various processes and individual difference factors and how these affected their use of the English Lounge. However, this would have entailed taking a CDS approach from the beginning of the study. In our case, we had already collected the data by the time we started to consider CDS, so it would have been challenging to reframe the study midway through.

Complex dynamic systems theory (CDST)

Social science research is increasingly being influenced by complexity theory as a way to incorporate insights from multiple approaches. In the field of L2 acquisition, taking a complexity perspective allows us to take various individual differences, affect, context, cognition and interrelationships into account when considering how languages are learnt (Mercer, 2011). CDS have been defined as 'large networks of components with no central control, and simple rules of operation [which] give rise to complex collective behaviour, sophisticated information processing, and adaptation via learning or evolution' (Mitchell, 2009: 13). CDST in the field of language education attempts to account for all of the interacting parts and behaviours within an environment (Larsen-Freeman & Cameron, 2008). Using a CDS perspective is one way to attempt to capture the dynamics and motivations of the agentive users in the lounge. CDST is only beginning to make its mark in research related to learning spaces, but we can refer to the findings of studies conducted within a social learning space at Okayama University in Japan; Murray (2018: 102) considers such environments to be 'self-enriching complex dynamic ecosocial systems' as the studies indicated the learners (as active agents) engaged with various interacting factors.

MacIntyre *et al.* (2014) offer the following advice to researchers considering taking a CDS approach: (1) a CDS approach should be integrated into the research process at the beginning stages; (2) researchers should examine the interplay between factors; (3) the system being investigated needs to be defined; (4) researchers need to design research questions that focus on the process rather than the product; and (5) they should ensure that research methods investigate dynamic accounts of learning. In order for us to have been able to take a CDS approach, we would have needed to take a different starting point when examining the data in order to do this sufficiently well. It would require 'taking a human agent as the starting point, and looking at how the interactions between their various psychological elements, and the learning space and other human members therein gave rise to some phenomenon (such as continued, active participation in the learning space)' (Richard Sampson, personal communication).

A CDS approach acknowledges that there are 'large networks of components with no central control' (Mitchell, 2009: 13) which can make research very challenging. Although many scholars have written about the nature of taking a CDS approach, few studies have actually attempted to analyse phenomena this way because of the complexity and the potential scale of such an analysis. Taking a CDS approach to the entire study could have allowed us to explore the interconnectedness of identity, community, beliefs and other factors, and if we were to do a similar project in the future, we may take this approach. However, as we began with specific questions about identity and community membership, there is a strong argument for taking the approach we did in order to draw on previous academic work, situate our project within the field and systematically analyse our data for a deep understanding of those two areas. A follow-up project could certainly take CDS as a starting point. For researchers wishing to investigate the dynamics of a social learning community elsewhere, our advice would be to begin with research questions, conduct an observation study and then decide which approach to take (see Appendix 4). A CDS approach may indeed lead to a richer and more multifaceted reading of the data worth the time investment.

Part 4
Implications for the Field

15 Summary of the Findings

Jo Mynard, Phoebe Lyon, Phillip Taw and Daniel Hooper

In this chapter, we conclude by briefly summarising our findings from the four studies we have described in this book in order to highlight some of the key themes and bring them together. We comment on how this project is situated within the larger research agenda of the Self-Access Learning Centre (SALC) as a whole and on how our findings are applicable to other social learning spaces. Finally, we give brief details of some of the related projects in progress, and outline the next steps.

Brief Summary of Our Findings

From our observation study (see Chapter 4), we were able to systematically observe what was happening in our space and identify key behaviours exhibited by different participants within the English Lounge. From our interviews, and drawing on the participants' language learning histories, we were able to gain a greater depth of understanding of the complex dynamics of the space from the three perspectives we chose: identity, communities of practice (CoP) and beliefs and other interacting factors.

Identity

In Chapter 11, we explored identity, and our research was guided by a pre-existing framework (Benson *et al.*, 2013). One thing we noticed was that over time, Regular Users (RUs) and the Yellow Sofa (YS) Group members overcame initial anxieties about using the space, and many developed confidence in their language skills. We found that the English Lounge may be one space where they could project identities that helped them to overcome insecurities they may have previously felt about their English abilities. We suggested a trajectory of behaviours and identities that shift over time (Table 11.2). We included Non Users as part of this trajectory should they choose to use the English Lounge, but in this project we learnt a lot about the important role that identity has in their conscious decision *not* to use it. The students in this group showed a deep understanding of themselves as learners and carefully considered what learning activities would be appropriate for learners like them. Some Non Users perceived the users of the English Lounge to be confident and proficient students who were part of a group and not very serious about studying English (this stems from their beliefs about what a good student 'does'). Whereas we saw that YS Group members and RUs tended to project an identity when using the English Lounge, the Non Users did not do this. We could suggest that projecting an identity when using the lounge is a helpful strategy and also one way of expressing learner autonomy; to be aware of different identities is one indication of learner autonomy (Benson & Cooker, 2013b).

Communities of Practice

In Chapter 12, we examined the interview data from the perspective of CoP and found evidence of *domain*, *community* and *practice*.

Domain

Our research findings suggest that a domain existed at the time of the study due to the consistent characteristics of members and certain shared beliefs about the community. For example, the members of the CoP valued actual communicative language use (*eikaiwa*) over declarative language knowledge (*eigo*). A number of participants belonging to the CoP (i.e. the YS Group) also shared a desire to gain membership of an international imagined community of English users and often exhibited traits that were congruent with an international mindset. These beliefs were heavily influenced by their past and present language learning experiences as well as being linked to their perceived future second language (L2) selves.

Community

We saw the YS Group members inhabiting (willingly or otherwise) the role of exemplars for newer users of the English Lounge. In some cases, this role of exemplar was found to be similar to that of a near peer role model (NPRM) (Murphey, 1998) and could also be tied to a *senpai–kohai* dynamic common in Japanese society. We saw older YS Group members appearing to accept an 'old-timer' *senpai* role, taking responsibility for socialising new members. In addition, newer RUs recognised their responsibilities in a future *senpai* role in the lounge as they moved into their second year. There was also, however, signs of members using their agency to resist certain cultural expectations related to *senpai–kohai* relations.

Practice

Examples of practice in the English Lounge included awareness of certain recurring problems in the community and central members sometimes taking steps to negotiate those problems internally. For example, some new users of the English Lounge were intimidated by the YS Group, and members took steps to deal with that in order to sustain the community. Another example of practice was the creation of artefacts such as the Study Group by some of the YS Group members. Some of the YS Group members also provided feedback to the SALC director about concerns over the layout of the lounge and about people not adhering to the language policy. These are all examples of 'horizontal accountability', where the community deals with issues by working together and customising responses to their needs, rather than 'vertical accountability', i.e. the SALC imposing measures/policies in a top-down fashion.

Learner beliefs

In Chapter 13, we explored four key factors nested within learner beliefs: L2 motivational self system, *eigo-eikaiwa*, language anxiety and interdependent agency. Each of these key factors interacted with participants' beliefs and played a role in the ways in which the participants used the English Lounge and indeed in whether they chose to go there at all. *All* 14 core beliefs identified in the data could be considered helpful for language learning given the right conditions. However, the ways in which other factors interacted with the beliefs sometimes meant that there was a mismatch between belief and action, or that the belief was realised in a way that was *not* helpful for language learning (e.g. that a thorough knowledge of grammar is needed before someone is able to speak the target language effectively). In addition, there were some beliefs that would be considered very helpful for language learning (e.g. it is important to use available resources and strategies to make the most of the opportunities to use English), but were not widely shared among the participants. In terms of the other factors, almost all of the participants held an image of an ideal L2 self which was helpful and motivating and something to be cultivated. Views on *eigo* and *eikaiwa* shifted throughout the participants' time at the university, and many RUs and YS Group members were able to reconcile the two. Most of the participants had experienced language anxiety in relation to the lounge, and many students had overcome it or reduced its impact by relying on friends, developing a projected identity or making their use of the lounge a habit. Although interdependent agency was a barrier for many, the students who took ownership of the space and made it better for others demonstrated how it could also be an advantage overall.

Intersection of the themes

Each of the research perspectives has added to our understanding of the learners who study in and around the English Lounge. Through this project, it has become clear that the factors affecting how individuals act within the learning space are extremely complex. Individual differences, cultural contexts and previous experiences inevitably affect beliefs about learning in general and about the role of the English Lounge. These beliefs play a role in how a person behaves and uses (or avoids) the English Lounge. The experience of using the English Lounge – even on the peripheries – shapes beliefs through observation and interaction with other people. Depending on a multitude of factors, learners' experiences of using and observing the lounge govern whether they decide to initially avoid or use the English Lounge, return to it again or eventually become part of the CoP. In terms of identities, these may shift depending on the experiences and observations of the individuals. In some cases, students develop a strong identity as someone who does not use the English Lounge; in other cases, students project a more confident 'self' in order to overcome anxiety or be seen to be confident and friendly to other users. So, how do we respond to these findings? In the next section, we will discuss some implications for practice.

Linking the Findings to the Wider Learning Ecology and Other Settings

In this chapter, we have commented on the findings related to each of the key themes we investigated. We will now return to our meta research questions and look more holistically at how our understanding of learners' participation in the English Lounge links to the wider learning ecology, and what we have learnt about social learning spaces in general. The meta-questions for the ethnographic study were:

(5) How does an understanding of psychological phenomena benefit users and potential users?
(6) What do we learn that can be applied to the study of social learning spaces elsewhere?
(7) How can language learners best be supported as they navigate the complex processes of language learning within a wider ecology of learning opportunities?

Taking an ecological view of learning, we can say that individuals construct their own array of learning environments (Benson, 2017) and social networks that support learning (Menezes, 2011; Palfreyman, 2014; Van Lier, 2004). Engaged learners draw upon their own agency to 'not only choose but also create their own learning activities by choosing to pursue lines of activity that they find worthy and meaningful' (Barron, 2010: 114). The environments and social networks that learners draw upon are found not only within classroom settings, but also increasingly in outside classroom settings (online and offline) where language learning or language use can take place. As we mentioned previously, in a generally monolingual culture such as Japan, opportunities for practicing languages in everyday life in the physical environment are scarce. Because of this, there is an argument to be made for the provision of spaces dedicated to language practice for people learning languages, such as the English Lounge described in this study. What we have seen through the analysis of the data is that the YS Group members and RUs viewed the English Lounge as an important space as part of their overall learning ecology. During the interviews, the participants made connections between classroom learning and speaking English in the lounge; between learning English in high school and speaking English in the lounge; between using English in the lounge and also in other contexts; and about travelling and working in places in the future that would provide further opportunities to use English. For these participants, the English Lounge is an obvious part of their learning ecologies. For the Non Users, even though the lounge is not currently part of their chosen repertoire of spaces that offer language learning opportunities, the data suggests that in many cases, it has the potential to become part of their future learning ecologies under the right conditions. However, in order for this to happen, there may be a need for interventions which will be suggested in Chapter 16.

Looking again at Research Question 5 – How does an understanding of psychological phenomena benefit users and potential users? – we can say that our understanding of the benefits perceived by YS Group members and RUs helps us to support more potential users though awareness raising and other interventions (see Chapter 16). The interventions specifically draw on our understanding of identity, community and beliefs and other individual difference factors. In addition, we are better able to support the goals of the YS Group members and the RUs. By understanding their motives, goals and their psychological processes, we can further empower them to take ownership of the space and to overcome the kinds of insecurities that surfaced in the study, for example the anxiety they feel when taking on a new *sempai* role.

Turning to Research Question 6 – What do we learn that can be applied to the study of social learning spaces elsewhere? – we can say that the study of one micro learning space can give us insights into part of a learner's ecology, the psychological processes of the learners and also the role that others play in the process of learning. Although researchers elsewhere would need to conduct their own research in order to understand the contextual and psychological factors that affect their particular learners and learning spaces, there are some findings that are likely to be widely applicable. For example, based on this ethnographic study and other research, we would suggest that any institutional language learning programme should provide a social learning space outside the classroom for practicing the target language. In addition to the potential benefits that we already discussed in Chapter 2, some of the particular benefits we have seen through the analysis of our data are as follows:

- A social learning space has the potential to help learners to develop speaking confidence and to reduce language anxiety.

- It can foster a sense of belonging to a community which is important for sustained language learning over time.
- There will be opportunities to be exposed to NPRMs which is a motivating factor.
- There will be opportunities for learners to intentionally project new identities in ways which are helpful for sustained learning.
- There will be opportunities for learners to undertake a leadership role and to be role models to other learners.

Finally, how can language learners best be supported as they navigate the complex processes of language learning within a social learning space? Murray *et al.* (2014: 95) also found that 'the meanings learners attach to a place will shape practices'. In the social learning space in their study, interventions were implemented to make newcomers – who had previously formed incorrect assumptions about the purpose of the space – feel comfortable and welcome. As we have seen in our study, not all learners were drawn to the English Lounge for a number of reasons, but we recommend that learners are made aware of some of the reasons that using a social learning space may be beneficial for them. In addition, in Chapter 16 we describe some interventions that might make joining such a space easier for them.

Next Steps

This ethnographic study has given us invaluable insights into the dynamics of the English Lounge, but there is plenty of room for further research. For example, the project spanned two years, but we are planning to continue to track some of the participants for longer to see if any further shifts occur with regard to identity, community and beliefs. One of the features of this kind of research is that by conducting in-depth interviews and belonging to the environment that we are studying, we are likely to have influenced the participants in various ways. One example of this was with some of our Non Users starting to use the English Lounge, and this could have been because of our research. We are particularly interested to see how the beliefs and identities of formerly Non Users develop over time.

Secondly, the CoP at the time of the study (the YS Group) represented a group of participants who significantly influenced the space. As these members graduate or develop different priorities as they progress through their university careers, the English Lounge will begin to change as well. New members will inevitably form a new CoP, and they may have different characteristics from the ones we have described here. The YS Group in this study had the experience of using a previous facility. Over time, students will no longer have had experience of using the previous conversation lounge, which is likely to have an effect on how they view the current English Lounge. We will continue to observe the space and will consider a replication study in the future.

Interestingly, despite the ubiquity of social media, technological support for learning or as a tool for accessing or facilitating the use of the English Lounge is not something that emerged from our ethnographic study. Nevertheless, colleagues at our institution are investigating the affordances of technology for self-directed learning (Mynard & Yamamoto, 2018; Peeters & Mynard, 2019; Viberg *et al.*, 2018) and the research so far indicates that Kanda University of International Studies (KUIS) students would respond well to technology tools that could blend online with offline interaction in some way. Technology tools may create digital pathways to offline interaction, for example in a social learning space, and this is an area of interest for future research. There may even be technological solutions to helping students to overcome their anxieties and negative beliefs, or gain access to a CoP in a social learning space in a culturally appropriate way.

As we previously explained, follow-up studies and interventions have begun. In addition, we are looking in depth at other spaces and features of the SALC, for example, student perceptions of our advising service (Shelton-Strong, 2018); language choice within a student-led study buddy group (Kanai & Imamura, 2019); participation in student-led learning communities (Watkins, 2019); the extent to which key areas of the SALC are autonomy supportive (Mynard & Shelton-Strong, 2019); the effect our SALC curriculum has on learning (Noguchi *et al.*, 2018); leadership among SALC peer advisors (Knight & Mynard, 2018); and learner perceptions of the English language practice service 'The Conversation Desk' (Kushida, 2018). Studying a particular area or service in depth is certainly useful for understanding our space and our learners; however, as we mentioned in Chapter 14, we are aware of the importance of looking at the entire SALC rather than just the various components in isolation. A larger research project (Asta & Mynard, 2018; Mynard & Shelton-Strong, 2019; Yarwood *et al.*, 2019) is attempting to see the connections and evaluate the extent to which our SALC supports learners' basic psychological needs (competence, autonomy and relatedness) within a self-determination theory framework (Deci & Ryan, 1985) and the conditions necessary for them to thrive.

16 Implications and Practical Interventions

Jo Mynard, Daniel Hooper,
Phoebe Lyon and Phillip Taw

Several practical interventions can be considered as a result of this project. This chapter has been written with our context in mind, but the activities could be adapted to other social learning spaces elsewhere. However, we recommend that interventions draw on research done in specific contexts as some of the issues that arose in our study might not necessarily apply to others. The purpose of our proposed interventions might be (1) to support the students who are already making effective use of a social learning space by raising awareness of what they are doing and why, and (2) to make a social learning space a more accessible space for students at the university who do not currently use the space but might want to. The overall purpose is to promote learner autonomy: a sense of awareness and control over one's language learning (Benson, 2011b). In this chapter, we suggest interventions related to identity, community and beliefs in turn.

Implications Related to Identity

In this section, we will share two possible interventions related to identity: (1) sharing findings and raising awareness of strategies and (2) providing hands-on learner development.

(1) Sharing findings and raising awareness of strategies

The results of this study have highlighted the importance of sharing findings with both students and the greater population. In our case, it has been beneficial to raise awareness of the trajectory of behaviours and shifting identities with colleagues at the university so that teachers can support students and also conduct related future research to further develop our understanding. In addition, sharing some of the case studies with students has helped to raise their awareness of how people feel when they use the English Lounge and what strategies they use. This may, in turn, alleviate any concerns or feelings of trepidation they might have entering such a space. Finally, raising awareness in learners about the role of their identities may help them to achieve a better understanding of themselves and adopt different identities when using the English Lounge, if they choose to do so.

(2) Hands-on learner development

Another possible aspect to consider relates to training students to develop alternative projected identities when using a target language (TL). This may help them to mitigate the contextual and social challenges of talking to strangers and/or overcoming the fear of being judged on their linguistic performance. Workshop activities might include discussing example student cases (or extracts from the case studies in this book) and having students share their own experiences. For example, in Chapter 10, Sayaka described how her 'English' identity gave her more confidence:

> One of the reasons why Sayaka enjoyed speaking English was that it made her feel like a different person. She found it hard to explain, but she called it a *'fresh feeling'*. When she listened to recordings of herself speaking, she felt that the person wasn't her. When asked which she preferred, she said it was hard to choose because English was difficult for her, but she would say the *English Sayaka* because she was more positive and brave. The *Japanese Sayaka* had a fear of speaking English and was hesitant to go to the English Lounge, but once she started trying to speak English, she gained confidence and a belief that she was capable.

> **S:** It's kind of strange but when I'm Japanese me, I feel I'm afraid to speak English, so I can't go Yellow Sofa or SALC so much, but when I turn to speak English, like switch, yeah, I don't know, it's strange but I feel confidence. Maybe 'I can speak English!', or like that.

Possible discussion questions:

- How confident do you think Sayaka felt about using the English Lounge?
- What do you think are the differences between the 'two Sayakas'?
- Why do you think Sayaka feels different when she speaks English in the English Lounge?
- How different do you feel when you use other languages?

A follow-up activity could be to create an imagined identity that could be adopted in the context of the conversation lounge, discuss it with classmates, then make a plan to intentionally adopt it and report back on how successful it was.

Implications Related to Communities of Practice (CoPs)

Although CoPs often develop and thrive without support, Wenger *et al.* (2002: 12) are clear in asserting the need for institutions to 'cultivate communities of practice actively and systematically, for their benefit as well as the benefit of the members and communities themselves'. Several practical interventions could be considered related to the findings from the CoP study: (1) provide various opportunities for student ownership in the Self-Access Learning Centre (SALC); (2) support interest-based communities; (3) empower student leaders with the authority to influence the English Lounge; and (4) provide multiple opportunities for student input.

(1) Provide various opportunities for student ownership in the SALC

The CoP emerged naturally in the English Lounge, so to a certain extent the conditions were already present to encourage student ownership and leadership. However, we observed both positive and negative effects. As an asset of the space, the members of the CoP, the Yellow Sofa (YS) Group members, acted as near peer role models (NPRMs) that allowed other users of the lounge to imagine their possible future selves. On the flip side, as mentioned in Chapter 12, some visitors to the English Lounge felt intimidated by such a strong presence in the space, even though the members of the CoP did not intend to project an unwelcoming atmosphere.

An intervention that some of the participants of our study mentioned was that rather than one central community, we might create the conditions for many communities to emerge, each with distinct characteristics. One thing that staff working in a social learning space might do is create events and meetups in the space at the start of the academic year to help potential members meet like-minded fellow students. This will also remove the social barriers that many students experience when talking to strangers. Equally important is to create other spaces within the self-access centre or other social spaces where natural communities might emerge. This can be through the arrangement of furniture clusters conducive to encouraging groups to meet, or by actively hosting regular events in the same location each time so that potential community members will know where to find each other.

(2) Support interest-based communities

In addition to examining communities in a social learning space, there is a need to look at communities that are emerging in other spaces in the self-access centre or surrounding spaces and understand the factors that contribute to their success (cf. Kanai & Imamura, 2019; Watkins, 2019). For example, in our case, we have seen in other groups that have formed in other areas of the SALC that when a community forms based on shared interests, the participants' anxiety about using the TL is reduced. The SALC is actively promoting and supporting an increasing number of learning communities where students come together to learn something they are passionate about *through* English, which is an encouraging development. Wenger *et al.* (2002) state that opening up dialogue between 'insider' and 'outsider' voices from different groups is often required to raise awareness of new possibilities for evolving CoPs, and we feel this could certainly be the case for the English Lounge CoP. In the case of the YS Group, the shared purpose they had related to promoting the use of English, but as one of the participants of our study mentioned, there could be merit in helping these core members to also think about interest-based activities that might make their group more accessible. This might also serve the purpose of making the interactions less superficial, as well as providing a needed linguistic challenge for students with higher language skills and/or scaffolding the experience of lower-level learners. These activities could include, for example, themed discussions or screenings of documentaries or films with follow-up discussions. However, the ideas need to come from the students themselves in order to promote ownership and autonomy. The SALC staff might be the catalyst if they provide encouragement, access to facilities and help when required.

(3) Empower student leaders with the authority to influence the learning space

In our case, the YS Group members became aware of their influence on the dynamics of the English Lounge, yet they lacked the experience and authority to act on their observations. As a practical measure, since we were able to identify the likely CoP even before the data collection phase, the core members of the community could have been made aware of strategies of inclusion. They could have been assisted in reflecting on their impact on the space and their potential effects on other students (if they were not already aware) and also in developing skills for how to change the dynamics from an intimidating space to a welcoming one. Members of the YS Group acknowledged an awareness of their presence and its effect on other visitors to the lounge, and they made attempts to resolve or mitigate some of the issues. This shows that they had a desire to include others. It would be even more effective if members of staff could raise awareness of techniques they may not have been aware of, in addition to applying their own ideas.

This kind of staff assistance might also be a useful approach to help regular visitors transition into being CoP members. Wenger *et al.* (2002) recognise the challenge of core member turnover and emphasise the importance of community coordinators finding new candidates for central roles in the group. Some of our participants expressed a heightened sense of anxiety as their roles shifted over time. For example, in our study, some Regular Users (RUs) expressed disappointment in themselves as *senpais* due to their own perceptions of lack of progress. Although members of the YS Group may have a positive influence as NPRMs, some RUs may potentially be discouraged because they may not see themselves as being able to bridge the gap from being an RU to becoming a core member of the CoP. There are 11 trained learning advisors working in the SALC who play a crucial role in facilitating dialogues related to these kinds of insecurities and helping RUs to develop confidence and to manage the transition. However, this is not to say that learners' trajectories within CoPs must be defined only as inward bound. Wenger (1998) and Fenton O'Creevy *et al.* (2014) illustrate the plethora of potential learner trajectories within CoPs, many of which do not result in full participation. Some learners or 'tourists' will only engage with a community on a very superficial level, whereas 'sojourners' will be more invested in community practices and identities but are fundamentally just 'passing through' (Fenton O'Creevy *et al.*, 2014: 44). As the context of the English Lounge is a four-year university, this concept of transience is especially salient and therefore needs to be recognised by the social learning space and CoP stakeholders. More specifically in terms of managing a social learning space, Murray and Fujishima (2016b) emphasise the importance of recognising learner diversity and allowing for users to participate according to varied levels of engagement.

(4) Provide multiple opportunities for student input

In order to encourage student ownership and investment, it is important for staff working in a self-access centre or social learning space to create multiple opportunities for student input, not only via an annual survey, but also through regular discussion groups. Sharing the summaries from these discussions through posters, newsletters and social media could engage the larger community in debates about appropriate ways to run and access social learning spaces. This could increase horizontal accountability.

Implications Related to Beliefs

In this section, we will share four suggested implications emerging from the findings on learner beliefs: (1) awareness raising of the connections between beliefs, actions and possible outcomes; (2) awareness raising of misaligned beliefs; (3) awareness raising of how other factors affect beliefs; and (4) awareness raising of lesser-known beliefs and associated actions that could be helpful.

(1) Awareness raising of existing beliefs, actions and possible outcomes

Students may not be consciously aware of their beliefs or the role that these beliefs play in their learning. In order to raise awareness of the role of beliefs, it might be useful to offer workshops. These could involve discussing sample beliefs (both helpful and unhelpful) that students often express (see Chapter 4: Table 4.3, or the description of core beliefs in Chapter 13 for ideas). The next step would be to look at the links between someone's beliefs and their subsequent action. A workshop activity could include prediction, e.g. 'Yuko believes that you need to have perfect grammar before you can practice speaking English. What action do you think Yuko will take to improve her speaking?'. After that, students could discuss possible outcomes of this action, e.g.

Belief: Yuko believes that you need to have perfect grammar before you can practice speaking English.
Likely action: Yuko will not use the English Lounge. Instead, she will work alone on her grammar until she thinks she knows it perfectly.
Possible outcomes: Yuko will become bored learning grammar by herself. She will not be able to use the grammar in conversation if she doesn't practice with others. Yuko will feel excluded from the community at the English Lounge.

After this activity, a discussion could involve giving Yuko advice that could help her develop her speaking skills in English. Finally, students could complete a questionnaire helping them pinpoint their own beliefs and discuss actions and outcomes with other students. Further activities related to beliefs and action are provided by Gregersen and MacIntyre (2014).

(2) Awareness raising of misaligned beliefs

In the foregoing example, the beliefs and actions may be aligned, but as our research discovered, beliefs and subsequent actions may be misaligned, e.g.

Belief: Hiroki believes that using English is very important in order to improve his speaking fluency.
Action: Hiroki watches a lot of English movies in order to improve his speaking skills.
Possible outcomes: Hiroki's listening skills will probably improve a lot. Hiroki has a lot of knowledge of movies and plenty to talk about. Hiroki might find it difficult to speak fluently because he never practices.

A workshop activity could involve discussion, prediction, advice giving, self-analysis and goal setting.

(3) Awareness raising of how other factors affect beliefs

As we have seen from our findings, other factors are tightly connected to learner beliefs and might also be explored in workshop activities.

The factors we explored in this book are the second language (L2) motivational self system, previous learning experiences/*eigo-eikaiwa*, language anxiety and interdependent agency. An example of beliefs and actions related to the L2 motivational self system is given below that could be analysed in a workshop. In addition, it is useful to give students opportunities to activate their own ideal future L2 self visions and consider how their beliefs and actions support them.

Beliefs and visions: Chihiro wants to live and work in the United States in the future. She imagines herself working for an international company and living in a big city. In her vision, she speaks English every day with her international friends and colleagues. She believes that creating opportunities for joining an English-speaking international community, even when she is still a student, is important.

Current actions: Chihiro has started a learning community which meets every week to talk about international current issues in English. She also uses social media to connect with international friends in English.

Possible outcomes: Chihiro will feel confident using English with an international community. Chihiro will make international friends.

(4) Awareness raising of lesser-known beliefs and associated actions that could be helpful

Potentially helpful beliefs (see the list of core beliefs in Chapter 13 for ideas) and actions can be discussed in workshops in order to encourage learners to confront their own beliefs and even consider alternatives. For example, you could ask students the degree to which they agree with the following statements related to language learning. Responses could be 'not at all', 'I have never thought about it', 'I agree a little', 'I agree completely!' and could be discussed with classmates:

- Enjoyment and interest are the most important things when learning a language.
- It is important to be around other students who are role models.
- Students need to be autonomous, to take charge of their learning and to follow a plan.
- It is important to use the available resources to make the most of the opportunities to use English.
- Being part of a community of learners is very important.
- Sometimes you have to do things you don't want to do in order to progress in a language.

A follow-up discussion could include matching actions and outcomes in a similar way to the activities previously described.

Alternatively, a similar workshop activity could present students' actions, where participants match an action with an associated probable

Table 16.1 An exercise to match actions with beliefs

Action	Belief
1. Miru listens to English podcasts every day.	A. Enjoyment and interest are the most important things when learning a language.
2. Teru practises speaking English at the English Lounge every day.	B. Lots of English input is important for developing listening skills.
3. Satomi makes a plan for her English learning and follows it. She checks her progress regularly.	C. It is important to practise using English to become more fluent.
4. Hiro doesn't study English, but he watches a lot of fun YouTube videos every day that teach him about programming.	D. Students need to be autonomous; to take charge of their learning and follow a plan.

belief from a list similar to that shown in Table 16.1. As a follow up, students could discuss the extent to which they engage in these activities and whether they align with their beliefs.

There may be a role for explicit instruction too. For example, teachers could reconcile the concept of the *eigo–eikaiwa* dichotomy by giving suggestions about how a conversation lounge could represent a place where students can comfortably practice the language they have learnt in class, in school or from grammar books. Related required activities could even be set for homework, for example:

Assignment: Have a 15-minute conversation with someone in English using some of the new language or information you have learnt in class this week. Record the conversation (with permission) and write a reflection on how well you felt you were able to express your ideas.
Planning:
- Think about a specific language point or knowledge you have learnt in class this week that you would like to practice (e.g. grammar, vocabulary, expressions or content knowledge).
- How do you plan to use your new language or knowledge in conversation with others?
  - Place:
  - Person:
  - Time/date:
  - Topic:
- How will you start the conversation?
- Make a note of some examples or questions that you could use to help you keep the conversation going.

General Implications and Outcomes of Our Study

As mentioned earlier, we are in the process of sharing some of the results of this study with lecturers and learning advisors at our institution. The information will help them understand students' needs and actions and prepare them to support the learners in accessing and benefitting from the English Lounge. In addition, we have involved lecturers and senior students in follow-up interventions, some of which have become research projects that build on the knowledge we gained from the ethnographic study described in this book. The process of sharing has extended the impact of our research and has resulted in a general sense of shared investment in making the space as beneficial as possible for our students. For example, one large group of researchers (including student research assistants) are conducting a large-scale evaluation of the learning environment as a space to learn and practice English using a self-determination theory perspective (Asta & Mynard, 2018; Mynard & Shelton-Strong, 2019; Yarwood *et al.*, 2019). Some colleagues are doing activities such as awareness raising and goal setting in their classrooms and at first-year student orientation camps, which has had a noticeable effect on the actions and attitudes of their students, many of whom have increased their use of the English Lounge. We have facilitated two group discussion activities with all the lecturers working with students in the SALC to offer an opportunity to consider their roles and share ideas for supporting students. Our research and suggestions from lecturers in discussions such as these have led to an updated version of the guidelines for lecturers who are on duty in the English Lounge. We have tried to communicate two things in particular to lecturers: that they have an important role to play in helping to maintain the English Language environment by communicating the policy and rationale to students, by using only English in the space and through gentle reminders to users of the space to respect the policy. Even though lecturers have a range of beliefs about language policies, it is important to be consistent in our message. The following extract is from the guidelines provided for lecturers related to maintaining an English environment (Figure 16.1).

The other point that we have tried to stress in communications and discussions with lecturers is the role that they can play in (1) helping students to overcome their anxiety about using English and (2) reducing anxiety and socialising students into the English Lounge. We know from our research that feelings of anxiety about using English and joining a conversation in progress with people they do not know are the biggest obstacles deterring students from initially going to the English Lounge. The guidelines in the SALC handbook help to clarify the reasons why the lecturers' role in socialising students into the lounge and helping to reduce anxiety are important. This is followed by a list of ways in which they might consider interacting with students in the English Lounge (compiled based on ideas shared by lecturers and students) (Appendix 5).

Final Words

Looking back on the two-year project, we reflect on what we have learnt. We started the project with some rather vague plans and

How strict should we be?

Language policy is a tricky issue which polarises students and staff alike. Even in small teams, opinions on how to encourage an English environment span the length of a continuum (Figure 16.1 below). Some people feel strongly that the policy should be strictly enforced and the space should be policed. Others feel strongly that we should have no intervention beyond providing a space, i.e. English use should be driven by student self-regulatory processes. There is no easy answer, but based on our research, experience and observations, we take **position B** on the continuum below.

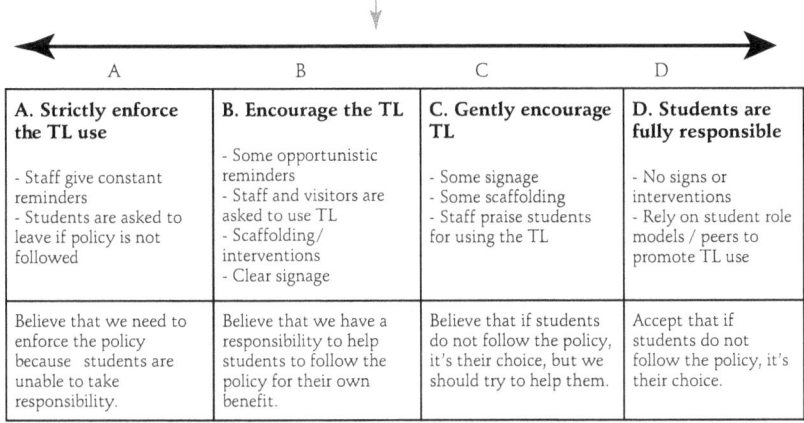

A. Strictly enforce the TL use	B. Encourage the TL	C. Gently encourage TL	D. Students are fully responsible
- Staff give constant reminders - Students are asked to leave if policy is not followed	- Some opportunistic reminders - Staff and visitors are asked to use TL - Scaffolding/interventions - Clear signage	- Some signage - Some scaffolding - Staff praise students for using the TL	- No signs or interventions - Rely on student role models / peers to promote TL use
Believe that we need to enforce the policy because students are unable to take responsibility.	Believe that we have a responsibility to help students to follow the policy for their own benefit.	Believe that if students do not follow the policy, it's their choice, but we should try to help them.	Accept that if students do not follow the policy, it's their choice.

Approaches to Providing a TL Environment in a SALC

Figure 16.1 Language policy guidelines for teachers (SALC Handbook, 2019, Section 2, KUIS 8 Language Policy)

unsubstantiated assumptions, but we now feel a sense of accomplishment as we are able to describe the dynamics of the English Lounge with confidence. We understand how it functions as a community for many of the students who use it; we are also more aware of our students and their language learning beliefs and identities. This information will be used in our own context to encourage increased participation in the English Lounge while also improving the area for current and future users. This includes both how the lounge is used and how comfortable students feel in the space. Our hope is that anyone who has similar aims will find this book useful. We are heartened to see the other research projects by colleagues and students that are in progress in the SALC which overlap with our research, and we hope this will continue. One last point to make is that although we have been studying *student* CoP, the authors of this book are also a CoP. We benefited from a shared purpose and a sense of responsibility for completing the project. The dynamics of the team contributed greatly to the success of this longitudinal study through the culmination of ideas, drawing on our different backgrounds and expertise. Our hope is that we can inspire other researchers to investigate the fascinating area of the learning dynamics of other social language learning spaces and possibly develop their own CoP through the process.

Appendices

**Appendix 1: Observation Guidelines
(Adapted from Spradley, 1980)**

    Observer:
    Date:
    Start time:
    Finish time:
    Other teachers on duty:
    Presence of international students:
    Where the observer is sitting:

(1) SPACE: Layout of the physical setting; rooms, outdoor spaces, etc.
    (a) Are the chairs and tables arranged as normal, or are there any changes?
    (b) Is the weather affecting the environment?
    (c) Is the lighting affecting the environment?
    (d) Is the temperature affecting the environment?
(2) ACTORS: The names and relevant details of the people involved.
    (i) Who appears to be 'members' of the in-group? (names or descriptions)
        (a) Where are they sitting exactly?
        (b) How are they sitting?
        (c) What are they wearing?
    (ii) Do you have any observations about in-group members? e.g. age, gender, ethnicity, social class or physical appearance.
        (a) Describe other groups/individuals present.
        (b) Where are they sitting exactly?
        (c) How are they sitting?
        (d) What are they wearing?
    (iii) Do you have any observations about other students? e.g. age, gender, ethnicity, social class or physical appearance.

Appendix 2: Interview Procedure and Questions

Aims:

- To understand the communities existing in the lounge.
- To understand what role (if any) the English Lounge plays in the identity construction of student users of the lounge.
- To understand the role of beliefs in how the students conceptualise the role of the lounge.

Participants:

(1) Students who use the English Lounge as a default place to situate themselves while on campus. (Core Community of Practice [CoP] members)
(2) Students who go regularly to the lounge (at least once a week) but who are not part of the CoP group. (Regular Users)
(3) Non Users of the English Lounge. (Non Users)

(1) Preliminaries

- Greeting/ice-breaker/How was lunch?/How has your day been so far?/Are Tuesdays busy generally for you?/Oh, nice bag! I love the colours! etc.
- Ask them to read the statement about the research and sign the consent form.
- Thank them by saying something like 'Thank you so much for helping us with our research. We really want to hear students' honest opinions as it will help us to help future students'.
- Establish what they call the space 'What do you usually call the English Lounge area of the Self-Access Learning Centre (SALC)?' *(Then refer to this term throughout)*

(2) Warm up
(This can vary. The purpose is to help the student relax – these questions might not be needed if the preliminaries have done the trick.)

- The centre is so busy today! Why do you think it's popular with students? What's the best way to learn languages? *(Easy question and also investigates beliefs)*
- Could you just talk me through a typical day at the university for you? *(Warm up)*
- How much time would you say you spend at the lounge each day?

**(3) Perceived purpose of the lounge/the space
Key questions to ask everyone:**

- How would you describe the English Lounge to someone who has never been there?
- What is the main purpose of the lounge for you and your friends? *(Pick up: other purposes)*

Other optional questions. Keep going until you are comfortable that you understand how the student views the space and its purpose.

- How soon after you became a student did you begin using the lounge? Can you give your first impressions of the space? *(Experience)*
- Have your impressions changed since the move to the new building?
- What phrases best describe the space?
- What metaphor would you use to describe the space?
- Would you recommend the lounge to other friends? Why?/Why not?
- Has the way you used the lounge changed over time?
- Do you see the space as a community?
- Do you come to spend time in the space or to spend time with specific people?

OR (for Non Users)

- Have you ever been to the lounge?
- Yes – What did you do?/What happened there?/How did you feel?
- No – Can you tell me more about the reasons for not going?

Other optional questions. Keep going until you are comfortable that you understand how the student views the space and its purpose and the reasons why they don't go.

- Would you recommend the lounge to other friends? Why?/Why not?
- What are some reasons why students choose not to go the lounge?

**Transition: OK, let's talk a bit about how you feel in the lounge.

(4) Reflexive identities/How does the student view himself/herself as an English user? Does the lounge have a role to play?

- How do you feel when you use English? *(Pick up on whether the lounge contributes to this feeling)*
- How do you feel when you are in the lounge? Is this different from when you are at home/in class/outside university/when you were at high school?

Or

- Many people have different identities for different parts of their lives (maybe give personal example). How about you? Which identity do you have when you are in the lounge?

Other optional questions. Keep going until you are comfortable that you understand how the student perceives their English user identity and whether being in the lounge contributes in some way.

- Has your participation/role/behaviour in the lounge changed over time? Tell me more about...
- Have your feelings about using English changed since using the Yellow Sofas?

**Transition: OK, let's talk about ways to learn English.

(5) Questions getting at learning beliefs

- How do you learn best?
- How do you like to learn English?
- What kind of student are you?

Other optional questions. Keep going until you are comfortable that you understand how the student views language learning.

- How would you describe yourself as a language learner? *(Background/self)*
- What is the best way to learn languages?

**Transition: OK, let's talk about students who use the lounge.

(6) Imagined identities/Projected identities/What image does the student try to project in the lounge?

- What kind of students typically use the lounge? *(Opinion/demographic)*
- Are there different kinds of students there? What have you noticed?
- What kind of student are you?
- How would people view you and your friends?

Other optional questions. Keep going until you are comfortable that you understand how the student projects their identity in the lounge.

- Do you think you will continue using the lounge as much next year, or the year after?
- Are you and your friends part of this group? Why/Why not?
- What is the role of teachers in the lounge?

**Transition: OK, let's talk a bit about the future.

(7) **Future projections/How does the lounge fit into their views of future learning/English user identity?**

- Do you think you will continue using the lounge as much next year, or the year after?
- Do you think you will change the way you use the lounge in the future?

Other optional questions. Keep going until you are comfortable that you understand how the student conceptualises their future lounge use as part of their English user identity.

- Why are you learning English?
- What do you want to do in the future?
- Do you think you would like to work in an English environment in the future?

OR (for Non Users)

- Do you think you will ever go to the lounge? What are the reasons?
- What would make this space feel more comfortable for you?
- What other ways would you like to try to use English outside of class?
- What do you want to do in the future?

Other optional questions. Keep going until you are comfortable that you understand how the student conceptualises their future and their future English user identity.

- Why are you learning English?
- Do you think you would like to work in an English environment in the future?
- In what kinds of situations do you want to be able to use English?

For CoP members only

(8) CoP/What behaviours and views indicate membership of the community?

- You use the lounge often. What makes you keep coming back?
- Who is in your closest circle of friends at the lounge?
- What do you all have in common? *(Pick up how teachers and other lounge users are viewed in relation to these members)*

Other optional questions. Keep going until you are comfortable that you understand how the student views the behaviour and beliefs of being a member of a CoP.

- What do you learn by being at the lounge regularly?
- Have new members joined your close group this year?
- How did it happen?

(9) Finally

- Well, I've asked all my questions. Thank you so much for the very useful information. I hope it will help us to help students.
- Do you have anything else you want to say about the centre or anything else? Thank you very much for your time.

Appendix 3: My Language Learning History

Write a paper about your language learning history from when you began learning English to the present. Feel free to write as much as you like (but do not write for more than 30 minutes). You can write in English or Japanese (or a mixture). Please don't worry about any grammar or spelling mistakes. I am more interested in your ideas.

Please send it to me by email. Some questions you *may* want to answer in your story (you don't have to answer all of these questions):

- How did you learn English in junior high school and high school?
- What positive and negative experiences did you have and what did you learn from them?
- What were you expecting before you came to the university?
- What were you surprised about in your university classes?
- What were you surprised about in the SALC?
- How have you changed your ways of language learning since coming to the university?
- What are the things that you found especially helpful?
- What are the areas that you still want to improve in?
- How do you think your next three years will be?
- What are your language learning plans and goals after graduation?
- What advice would you give to this year's first-year students?

Adapted from Murphey and Carpenter (2008): http://www.veramenezes.com/nar_tim.htm

Appendix 4: Research Preparation Suggestions

1. Decide the parameters of the social space to investigate.
Conceptual: Define the space.
Physical: Draw a map of the space.

2. Write down the overall purpose of the project.
Is it simply to understand phenomena, or is there an overlying pedagogical purpose? e.g. To understand what is happening in the space so that we can help support students in developing speaking confidence in the target language.

3. Draft some possible research questions. Examples:

Questions related to purpose and usage, e.g.:

Who is the space designed for? What is the intended purpose of the space? What happens in the space?

Questions related to community and membership, e.g.:

Who uses the space? Why do they use it? Which target users do not use the space? What are some reasons they do not use the space?

Questions related to psychological processes, e.g.:

Identity	*Beliefs*	*Language anxiety*
What is the relationship between L2 identity and use of the space? (How) do identities shift through continued use of the space?	What are some of the core learner beliefs of the regular uses of the space? (How) do learner beliefs shift through continued use of the space?	How comfortable do learners feel using the target language in general? How does the space help or hinder comfortable target language use?

4. Conduct a systematic observation study.

5. Do some further background reading of the existing literature as necessary.

6. Decide the research approach, e.g.

Pre-existing framework **Benefits**	*Interpretative* **Benefits**	*Complex Dynamic Systems*
May be easier if time is short; allows for comparisons; focussed and manageable. **Drawbacks:** May not adequately fit your context; the focus may be too narrow.	Broader scope, allows for relevant themes to emerge; **Drawbacks:** Analysis can take a long time.	**Benefits:** Examination of multiple interconnected agents affecting learning. **Drawbacks:** Analysis can take a long time; you will need to decide which agents to include.

7. Refine the research questions.

8. Decide on methods, e.g. interview, surveys

Appendix 5: Guidelines for New Teachers on Duty in the English Lounge (SALC, 2019: Section 2)

Some guidelines for new teachers on duty in the English Lounge

For teachers on duty in the lounge, thank you for signing up to do duty in this area and for helping us to provide a safe and supportive space for Kanda University of International Studies (KUIS) learners to practice using English. For other teachers, please keep these points in mind when you pass through the lounge – even if you are not on duty.

(1) Students use this space for a variety of reasons:

- Students want to make friends and feel part of a community.
- Students want to develop confidence and fluency in using English in a safe and supportive environment.
- Students need help with homework assignments that require them to talk to other people in English.
- Students want to talk to teachers and international students in order to expand their understanding of the world.

(2) Although you will meet many KUIS students who seem confident English users, these are a minority and most of our students feel anxious and insecure when using English, or are hesitant to talk to people they do not know. When you are on duty in the lounge, be aware that you become part of an important experience for our learners.

(3) Some guidelines for new teachers

Approachability and visibility

- Please make sure you are visible when you are on duty. Feedback from students indicated that teachers on duty should sit at one of the sofas nearest the central area.
- As with all other users in this space, please use English at all times.
- Please seek out opportunities to talk to students. This could range from simply making eye contact and saying 'hello' to taking a more proactive role, e.g. asking 'What are you working on today?'
- Be proactive at inviting students to join conversations, our research indicates that being welcomed into a group by a teacher is really appreciated by anxious students and can make a *huge difference* in students' decisions to come back.
- Avoid bringing your laptop with you or appearing busy with marking – even if you plan to stop when students arrive – as this will give the impression that you are too busy to talk to students.
- Be aware of 'hovering' students. Often, these students have summoned the courage to venture upstairs and just need a little more encouragement to sit down and join a conversation.

What to talk about

- Feel free to use props, games, etc., to facilitate discussions. For example, having magazines or some photos nearby helps with starting conversations.
- Be patient and keep in mind that learners may be insecure or have limited English skills. Start with some easy topics until you get a sense of a student's level of English or level of confidence.
- Don't be afraid to talk about deeper topics with students when they seem ready. Challenge them to think about serious issues.
- Try to listen more than you speak (and be comfortable with silence as students formulate what they want to say).

Managing groups

- Feel free to move light furniture to accommodate students in a group if needed.
- If the group gets too big, feel free to have them break up into smaller groups allowing more opportunities for students to participate.
- Invite quiet students to share their opinions. You might find that they are just waiting to be asked, however…
- Some students just want to observe until they are ready to participate. Read their body language and don't put them under pressure.

Promoting learner autonomy

- Encourage students to lead discussions, choose topics and invite others into the group.
- Invite students to think about their participation and how they might improve next time 'How did you feel about your speaking today?/ Will you do anything different next time you come?'
- Encourage students to make a habit of coming back to the English Lounge, for example a particular day or time each week.

Don't get too personal

- There are various ways you can communicate your professional distance but still be friendly and approachable, e.g. stay away from overly personal conversations and avoid making comments that are too personal. If you are uncomfortable with where the discussion is going, make a joke and steer it back to academic or other appropriate topics (e.g. 'maybe that's something you can talk about later. So, has anyone got any ideas for things to do during the holidays?').
- Be careful about adding students to your social media networks. It might be safer to make an account just for student contacts.

References

Acuña González, E., Avila Pardo, M. and Holmes Lewendon, J.E. (2015) The SAC as a community of practice: A case study of peer-run conversation sessions at the Universidad del Caribe. *Studies in Self-Access Learning Journal* 6 (3), 313–321.
Adamson, J.L., Brown, H.G. and Fujimoto-Adamson, N. (2012) Revealing shifts and diversity in understandings of self-access language learning. *Journal of University Teaching & Learning Practice* 9 (1). See http://ro.uow.edu.au/jutlp/vol9/iss1/5
Ahearn, L.M. (2001) Language and agency. *Annual Review of Anthropology* 30 (1), 109–137.
Allhouse, M. (2015) Room 101: A movement towards social learning spaces? A survey of SAC managers in UK higher education. *Studies in Self-Access Learning Journal* 6 (1), 124–137.
American Anthropological Association (2018) American Anthropological Association Statement on Ethnography and Institutional Review Boards. See https://www.americananthro.org/ParticipateAndAdvocate/Content.aspx?ItemNumber=1652 (accessed 1 June 2019).
American Psychological Association (2019) *Personality*. See https://www.apa.org/topics/personality. Accessed October 2019.
Aspinall, R.W. (2013) *International Education Policy in Japan in an Age of Globalization and risk*. Leiden: Global Oriental.
Asta, E. and Mynard, J. (2018) Exploring basic psychological needs in a language learning center. Part 1: Conducting student interviews. *Relay Journal* 1 (2), 382–404.
Ayres, L. and Knafl, K.A. (2008) Typological analysis. In L.M. Given (ed.) *The SAGE Encyclopedia of Qualitative Research Methods* (pp. 901–902). Thousand Oaks, CA: Sage.
Balçikanli, C. (2018) The 'English Café' as a social learning place. In G. Murray and T. Lamb (eds) *Space, Place and Autonomy in Language Learning* (pp. 61–74). Abingdon: Routledge.
Bandura, A. (1977) Self-efficacy: Toward a unifying theory of behavioral change. *Psychological Review* 84 (2), 191–215.
Barron, B. (2010) Conceptualizing and tracing learning pathways over time and setting. *National Society for the Study of Education* 109 (1), 113–127.
Bartlett, K. (2016) Japanese teachers' attitudes towards incorporating CLT in the high school English language classroom: An ethnographic study. *Kwansei Gakuin University Humanities Review* 21, 93–104.
Bax, S. (2003) The end of CLT: A context approach to language teaching. *ELT Journal* 57 (3), 278–287.
Bell, J.S. (2002) Narrative inquiry: More than just telling stories. *TESOL Quarterly* 36 (2), 207–213.
Benson, P. (2001) *Teaching and Researching Autonomy in Language Learning*. Harlow: Pearson.

Benson, P. (2011a) Language learning and teaching beyond the classroom: An introduction to the field. In P. Benson and H. Reinders (eds) *Beyond the Language Classroom* (pp. 7–16). Basingstoke: Palgrave Macmillan.

Benson, P. (2011b) *Teaching and Researching Autonomy in Language Learning*. New York: Routledge.

Benson, P. (2017) Language learning beyond the classroom: Access all areas. *Studies in Self-Access Learning Journal* 8 (2), 135–146.

Benson, P. and Lor, W. (1999) Conceptions of language and language learning. *System* 27 (4), 459–72.

Benson, P. and Reinders, H. (eds) (2011) *Beyond the Language Classroom*. Basingstoke: Palgrave Macmillan.

Benson, P. and Cooker, L. (2013a) The applied linguistic individual: Gaining perspective. In P. Benson and L. Cooker (eds) *The Applied Linguistic Individual: Sociocultural Approaches to Identity, Agency and Autonomy* (pp. 178–186). Sheffield: Equinox.

Benson, P. and Cooker, L. (2013b) The social and the individual in applied linguistics research. In P. Benson and L. Cooker (eds) *The Applied Linguistic Individual: Sociocultural Approaches to Identity, Agency and Autonomy* (pp. 1–16). Sheffield: Equinox.

Benson, P., Barkhuizen, G., Bodycott, P. and Brown, J. (2013) *Second Language Narratives in Study Abroad*. London: Palgrave Macmillan.

Bibby, S., Jolley, K. and Shiobara, F. (2016) Increasing attendance in a self-access language lounge. *Studies in Self-Access Learning Journal* 7 (3), 301–311.

Block, D. (2003) *The Social Turn in Second Language Acquisition*. Edinburgh: Edinburgh University Press.

Block, D. (2007) *Second Language Identities*. London: Continuum.

Bouchard, J. (2017) *Ideology, Agency, and Intercultural Communicative Competence: A Stratified Look into EFL Education in Japan*. Singapore: Springer Nature.

Brooks, J., McCluskey, S., Turley, E. and King, N. (2015) The utility of template analysis in qualitative psychology research. *Qualitative Research in Psychology* 12 (2), 202–222.

Burke, M., Hooper, D., Kushida, B., Lyon, P., Mynard, J., Sampson, R. and Taw, P. (2018) Observing a social learning space: A summary of an ethnographic project in progress. *Relay Journal* 1 (1), 209–220.

Butler, J. (1997) *Excitable Speech: A Politics of the Performative*. New York: Routledge.

Canagarajah, A.S. (1996) From critical research practice to critical research reporting. *TESOL Quarterly* 30, 321–331.

Canale, M. and Swain, M. (1980) Theoretical bases of communicative approaches to second language teaching and testing. *Applied Linguistics* 1 (1), 1–47.

Carducci, B.J. and Zimbardo, P.G. (1995, November) Are you shy? *Psychology Today* 28, 34–40.

Chen, A. and Mynard, J. (2018) Student perceptions of the English Lounge after a layout change. *Relay Journal* 1 (1), 221–235.

CLAIR (Council of Local Authorities for International Relations) (2018). JET Programme [PDF file]. See http://jetprogramme.org/wp-content/themes/biz-vektor/pdf/ninyo/JET-pamphlet-en.pdf (accessed June 2018).

Clandinin, D.J. and Connelly, F.M. (1994) Personal experience methods. In N.K. Denzin and Y.S. Lincoln (eds) *Handbook of Qualitative Research* (pp. 413–427). London: Sage.

Cook, M. (2009) Factors inhibiting and facilitating Japanese teachers of English in adopting communicative language teaching methodologies. *K@TA* 11, 99–116. See http://jurnalmanajemen.petra.ac.id/index.php/ing/article/viewFile/17887/17815 (accessed April 2018).

Cook, M. (2012) Revisiting Japanese English teachers' perceptions of communicative, audio-lingual, and grammar translation (yakudoku) activities: Beliefs, practices, and rationales. *The Asian EFL Journal Quarterly* 14 (2), 79–98.

Cooker, L. (2010) Some self-access principles. *Studies in Self-Access Learning Journal* 1 (1), 5–9.

Cooker, L. and Torpey, M. (2004) From self-direction to self-access: A chronicle of learner-centred curriculum development [Special issue]. *The Language Teacher: Perspectives on Self-Access* 28 (6), 11–16.

Cotterall, S. and Reinders, H. (2000) Fortress or bridge? Learners' perceptions and practice in self access language learning. *The TESOLANZ Journal* 8, 23–38.

Croker, R. and Ashurova, U. (2012) Scaffolding students' initial self-access language centre experiences. *Studies in Self-Access Learning Journal* 3 (3), 237–253.

Davis, B. and Sumara, D. (2006) *Complexity and Education: Inquiries into Learning, Teaching and Research*. Mahwah, NJ: Lawrence Erlbaum.

Davis, B. and Sumara, D. (2008) Complexity as a theory of education. *Transnational Curriculum Enquiry* 5 (2), 33–44.

Davis, P. and Holdom, S. (2008, July 8) The Language Café. Paper presented at Languages in Higher Education Conference: Transitions and Connections, York, UK. See https://www.llas.ac.uk/resources/paper/3230.html

Dean, E. and Sugiura, R. (2017) Creating an international communication lounge at Tokai University Sapporo. *Journal of Higher Education, Tokai University (Hokkaido Campus)* 17, 9–23.

Deci, E.L. and Ryan, R.M. (1985) *Intrinsic Motivation and Self-Determination in Human Behavior*. New York: Plenum.

Dewaele, J.M. (2002) Psychological and sociodemographic correlates of communicative anxiety in L2 and L3 production. *International Journal of Bilingualism* 6 (1), 23–38.

Dewaele, J.M. and Furnham, A. (2000) Personality and speech production: A pilot study of second language learners. *Personality and Individual Differences* 28 (2), 355–365.

Dewey, J. (1997) *Experience and Education* (First Touchstone edn). New York: Touchstone.

Dofs, K. and Hobbs, M. (2011) *Guidelines for Maximising Student Use of Independent Learning Centres: Support for ESOL learners*. Christchurch & Auckland, New Zealand: Ako Aotearoa, National Centre for Tertiary Teaching Excellence. See https://ako.ac.nz/assets/Knowledge-centre/RHPF-s0914-Guidelines-for-maximising-student-use-of-Independent-Learning-Centres/8c57188af2/guidelines-for-maximising-student-use-of-independent-learning-centres.pdf (accessed February 2019).

Dörnyei, Z. (2001) *Teaching and Researching Motivation*. Harlow: Longman.

Dörnyei, Z. (2005) *The Psychology of the Language Learner: Individual Differences in Second Language Acquisition*. Mahwah, NJ: Lawrence Erlbaum Associates.

Dörnyei, Z. (2007) *Research Methods in Applied Linguistics*. Oxford: Oxford University Press.

Dörnyei, Z. (2009) The L2 motivational self system. In Z. Dörnyei and E. Ushioda (eds) *Motivation, Language Identity and the L2 Self* (pp. 9–42). Bristol: Multilingual Matters.

Dörnyei, Z. (2014) Future self-guides and vision. In K. Csizér and M. Magid (eds) *The Impact of Self-Concept on Language Learning* (pp. 7–18). Bristol: Multilingual Matters.

Dörnyei, Z. and Ryan, S. (2015) *The Psychology of the Language Learner Revisited*. New York: Routledge.

Edlin, C. (2016) Informed eclecticism in the design of self-access language learning environments. *Studies in Self-Access Learning Journal* 7 (2), 115–135.

Eikaiwa gakkou no jios ga hasan shinsei fusai 75 oku en (2010, April 21) *Asahi Shimbun*. See http://www.asahi.com/special/playback/TKY201004210222.html (accessed November 2018).

Ellis, R. (2008) Learner beliefs and language learning. *The Asian EFL Journal* 10 (4), 7–25.

Everhard, C.J. (2013) Exploring a model of autonomy to live, learn and teach by. In A. Burkert, L. Dam and C. Ludwig (eds) *The Answer is Autonomy: Issues in Language Teaching and Learning* (pp. 25–39). Canterbury: IATEFL.

Falout, J., Murphey, T., Elwood, J. and Hood, M. (2008) Learner voices: Reflections on secondary education. In K. Bradford Watts, T. Muller and M. Swanson (eds) *JALT2007 Conference Proceedings* (pp. 231–243). Tokyo: JALT.

Firth, A. and Wagner, J. (1997) On discourse, communication, and (some) fundamental concepts in SLA research. *Modern Language Journal* 81 (3), 285–300.

Foucault, M. (1986) Of other spaces. *Diacritics* 16 (1), 22–27.

Fujimoto, M. (2016) Management of L-café. In G. Murray and N. Fujishima (eds) *Social Spaces for Language Learning: Stories from the L-Café* (pp. 31–39). London: Palgrave Macmillan.

Fujimoto-Adamson, N. (2006) Globalization and history of English education in Japan. *Asian EFL Journal* 8 (3), 259–282.

Fukuba, S. (2016) My critical thoughts on the English Café and the L-café. In G. Murray and N. Fujishima (eds) *Social Spaces for Language Learning: Stories from the L-Café* (pp. 105–109). London: Palgrave Macmillan.

Gao, X. (2009) The 'English-corner' as an out-of-class learning activity. *ELT Journal* 63 (1), 60–67.

Gardner, D. and Miller, L. (1999) *Establishing Self-Access: From Theory to Practice*. Cambridge: Cambridge University Press.

Gardner, R.C. and Lambert, W.E. (1959) Motivational variables in second-language acquisition. *Canadian Journal of Psychology* 13 (4), 266–272.

Gardner, R.C. and MacIntyre, P.D. (1993) A student's contribution to second language learning. Part II: Affect variables. *Language Teaching* 26, 1–11.

Gee, J.P. (1996) *Social Linguistics and Literacies: Ideology in Discourses* (2nd edn). London: Taylor & Francis.

Gillies, H. (2007) SAL for everyone? Motivation and demotivation in self-access learning. *Studies in Linguistics and Language Teaching* 18, 117–137.

Gillies, H. (2010) Listening to the learner: A qualitative investigation of motivation for embracing or avoiding the use of self-access centres. *Studies in Self-Access Learning Journal* 1 (3), 189–211.

Glasgow, G.P. (2013) The impact of the new national senior high school English curriculum on collaboration between Japanese teachers and native speakers. *JALT Journal* 35 (2), 191–204.

Goffman, E. (1959; republished 1990) *The Presentation of Self in Everyday Life*. New York: Anchor.

Gorsuch, G. (2000) EFL educational policies and education cultures: Influences on teachers' approval of communicative activities. *TESOL Quarterly* 34 (4), 675–710.

Gregersen, T. and MacIntyre, P.D. (2014) *Capitalizing on Language Learners' Individuality: From Premise to Practice*. Bristol: Multilingual Matters.

Haghirian, P. (2010) *Understanding Japanese Management Practices*. New York: Business Expert Press.

Hamaguchi, E. (1985) A contextual model of the Japanese: Toward methodological innovation in Japan studies. *Journal of Japan Studies* 11, 281–321.

Hammond, M. and Wellington, J. (2013) *Research Methods: The Key Concepts*. London: Routledge.

Harré, R. (2001) *Metaphysics and Narrative: Singularities and Multiplicities of Self*. Amsterdam: John Benjamins.

Hatch, J.A. (2002) *Doing Qualitative Research in Education Settings*. Albany, NY: State University of New York Press.

Heine, S.J., Lehman, D.R., Markus, H.R. and Kitayama, S. (1999) Is there a universal need for positive self-regard? *Psychological Review* 106, 766–794.

Hino, Y. (2016) The dark side of the L-café. In G. Murray and N. Fujishima (eds) *Social Spaces for Language Learning: Stories from the L-Café* (pp. 100–104). London: Palgrave Macmillan.

Hiramoto, M. (2013) English vs English conversation: Language teaching in modern Japan. In L. Wee, R.B.H. Goh and L. Lim (eds) *The Politics of English: South Asia, Southeast Asia and the Asia Pacific* (pp. 228–248). Amsterdam: John Benjamins.

Ho, K.M. (2016) L-café: The international home. In G. Murray and N. Fujishima (eds) *Social Spaces for Language Learning: Stories from the L-Café* (pp. 91–95). London: Palgrave Macmillan.

Hobbs, M. and Dofs, K. (2018) Spaced out or zoned in? An exploratory study of spaces enabling autonomous learning in two New Zealand tertiary learning institutions. In G. Murray and T. Lamb (eds) *Space, Place and Autonomy in Language Learning* (pp. 201–218). Abingdon: Routledge.

Holec, H. (1981) *Autonomy and Foreign Language Learning*. Oxford: Pergamon.

Holliday, A. (1994) *Appropriate Methodology and Social Context*. Cambridge: Cambridge University Press.

Hones, S. and Law, G. (1989) First reading: Second thoughts on English studies in the Japanese college curriculum. *Keisen Jogakuen College Bulletin* 1, 1–24.

Hooper, D., Mynard, J., Sampson, R. and Taw, P. (2019) Shifting identities in a social learning space. *Learner Development Journal* 3.

Horwitz, E.K. (1987) Surveying student beliefs about language learning. In A. Wenden and J. Rubin (eds) *Learner Strategies in Language Learning* (pp. 119–132). New York: Prentice Hall.

Horwitz, E.K. (1988) The beliefs about language learning of beginning university foreign language students. *Modern Language Journal* 72 (3), 283–294.

Hosoki, Y. (2011) English language education in Japan: Transitions and challenges (I). *Kokusai Kankeigaku Bulletin* 6 (1), 199–215.

Huang, J. and Benson, P. (2013) Autonomy, agency and identity in foreign and second language education. *Chinese Journal of Applied Linguistics* 36 (1), 7–28.

Hughes, L.S., Krug, N.P. and Vye, S.L. (2012) Advising practices: A survey of self-access learner motivations and preferences. *Studies in Self-Access Learning Journal* 3 (2), 163–181.

Humphries, S. and Burns, A. (2015) 'In reality it's almost impossible': CLT-oriented curriculum change. *ELT Journal* 69 (3), 239–248.

Igarashi, M. (2016) Writing tutorials at the L-café. In G. Murray and N. Fujishima (eds) *Social Spaces for Language Learning: Stories from the L-Café* (pp. 50–59). London: Palgrave Macmillan.

Imamura, Y. (2018) Adopting and adapting to new language policies in a self-access centre in Japan. *Relay Journal* 1 (1), 197–208.

Ishikawa, Y. (2012) The influence of learning beliefs in peer-advising sessions: Promoting independent language learning. *Studies in Self-Access Learning Journal* 3 (1), 93–107.

Johnson, K.E. and Golombek, P.R. (2002) Inquiry into experience: Teachers' personal and professional growth. In K.E. Johnson and P.R. Golombek (eds) *Teachers' Narrative Inquiry as Professional Development* (pp. 1–14). Cambridge: Cambridge University Press.

Johnston, S. and Ochitani, M. (2008) Nuanced communication in a writing center in Japan. *The Writing Lab Newsletter* 33 (4), 5–8. See http://writinglabnewsletter.org (accessed March 2018).

Kachru, B.B. (1985) Standards, codification, and sociolinguistic realism: The English language in the outer circle. In R. Quirk and H. Widdowson (eds) *English in the World: Teaching and Learning the Language and Literature* (pp. 11–30). Cambridge: Cambridge University Press.

Kanai, H. and Imamura, Y. (2019) Why do students keep joining Study Buddies? A case study of a learner-led learning community in the SALC. *Independence* 77, 31–34.

Kanda University of International Studies (2016) English Lounge: Yellow Sofas. See http://kuis8.com/spaces/lounge/. Accessed October 2019.

Kanno, K. (2010) An English speaking space outside the classroom: The English Lounge at Soka Women's College. *Soka Joshi Tanki Daigaku Kiyo* 41, 95–117.

Karp, I. (1986) Agency and social theory: A review of Anthony Giddens. *American Ethnologist* 13 (1), 131–137.

Kato, S. and Mynard, J. (2016) *Reflective Dialogue: Advising in Language Learning*. New York: Routledge.

Kikuchi, K. (2009) Listening to our learners' voices: What demotivates Japanese high school students? *Language Teaching Research* 13 (4), 453–471.

Kikuchi, K. and Sakai, H. (2009) Japanese learners' demotivation to study English: A survey study. *JALT Journal* 31 (2), 183–204.

Kitayama, S. and Uchida, Y. (2004) Interdependent agency: An alternative system for action. In R. Sorrentine, D. Cohen, J.M. Olson and P. Wanna (eds) *Culture and Social Behaviour: The Ontario Symposium* (Vol. 10; pp. 137–164). Mahwah, NJ: Erlbaum.

Kiyota, A. (2018) Emotions in the process of generating, protecting and sustaining L2 learning motivation in low-proficiency learners. *Journal of Language Learner Development* 1, 36–50.

Knight, K. and Mynard, K. (2018) Language learner autonomy and student leadership within and beyond the classroom: How do SALC student leaders conceptualize leadership? *Studies in Linguistics and Language Teaching* 29, 19–48.

Kurihara, N. (2008) Classroom anxiety: Changes in student attitudes in an English oral communication class in a Japanese senior high school. *The Language Teacher* 32 (1), 3–10.

Kurokawa, I., Yoshida, T., Lewis, C.H., Igarashi, R. and Kuradate, K. (2013) The Plurilingual Lounge: Creating new worldviews through social interaction. *International Journal of Intercultural Relations* 37 (1), 113–126.

Kushida, B. (2018) Motivational factors in students' non-use of a conversation practice center. *Studies in Linguistics and Language Teaching* 29, 49–70.

Kuwada, B. (2016) L-café: The source of my motivation to study English. In G. Murray and N. Fujishima (eds) *Social Spaces for Language Learning: Stories from the L-Café* (pp. 119–123). London: Palgrave Macmillan.

Kuwayama, T. (1992) The reference: Other orientation. In N. Rosenberger (ed.) *Japanese Sense of Self* (pp. 122–251). New York: University of Cambridge Press.

Lamb, M. (2013) The struggle to belong: Individual language learners in situated learning theory. In P. Benson and L. Cooker (eds) *The Applied Linguistic Individual: Autonomy, Agency and Identity* (pp. 32–45). Sheffield: Equinox.

Lantolf, J.P. (2000) Introducing sociocultural theory. In J.P. Lantolf (ed.) *Sociocultural Theory and Second Language Learning* (pp. 1–26). Oxford: Oxford University Press.

Lantolf, J.P. and Thorne, S.L. (2006) *Sociocultural Theory and the Genesis of Second Language Development*. Oxford: Oxford University Press.

Larsen-Freeman, D. and Cameron, L. (2008) *Complex Systems and Applied Linguistics*. Oxford: Oxford University Press.

Lave, J. and Wenger, E. (1991) *Situated Learning: Legitimate Peripheral Participation*. New York: Cambridge University Press.

Law, G. (1995) Ideologies of English education in Japan. *JALT Journal* 17 (2), 213–224.

LeBane, M.C., Shilling, M. and Harris, A. (2016) Promoting independent English language learning within an Asian tertiary institution: The Lingnan experience. *Studies in Self-Access Learning* 7 (3), 322–330.

Lewis, T. (2014) Learner autonomy and the theory of sociality. In G. Murray (ed.) *Social Dimensions of Autonomy in Language Learning* (pp. 37–59). Basingstoke: Palgrave Macmillan.

Li, L.C., Grimshaw, J.M., Nielsen, C., Judd, M., Coyte, P.C. and Graham, I.D. (2009) Evolution of Wenger's concept of community of practice. *Implementation Science* 4 (1), 11. https://doi.org/10.1186/1748-5908-4-11

Lightbown, P.M. and Spada, N. (2010) *How Languages are Learned* (3rd edn). Oxford: Oxford University Press.

Little, D. and Singleton, D. (1990) Cognitive style and learning approach. In R. Duda and P. Riley (eds) *Learning Styles: Proceedings of the First European Seminar. 26–29 April, 1987, Nancy, France* (pp. 11–19). Nancy, France: University of Nancy.

Liyanage, I. and Bartlett, B. (2013) Personality types and languages learning strategies: Chameleons changing colours. *System* 41, 598–608.

Lowe, R. (2017) The 'native speaker' frame: Issues in the professional culture of a Japanese tertiary EFL program. Unpublished doctoral dissertation, Canterbury Christ Church University.

Machida, T. (2019) How do Japanese junior high school teachers react to the teaching English in English policy? *JALT Journal* 41 (1), 5–26.

MacIntyre, P.D. and Gregersen, T. (2012) Affect: The role of language anxiety and other emotions in language learning. In S. Mercer, S. Ryan and M. Williams (eds) *Language Learning Psychology: Research, Theory and Pedagogy* (pp. 103–118). Basingstoke: Palgrave.

MacIntyre, P.D., Dörnyei, Z. and Henry, A. (2014) Conclusion: Hot enough to be cool: The promise of dynamic systems research. In Z. Dörnyei, P.D. MacIntyre and A. Henry (eds) *Motivational Dynamics in Language Learning* (pp. 419–429). Bristol: Multilingual Matters.

Malcolm, D. (2011) Learner involvement at Arabian Gulf University Self-Access Centre. *Studies in Self-Access Learning Journal* 2 (2), 68–77.

Mann, S. (2016) *The Research Interview: Reflective Practice and Reflexivity in Research Processes*. London: Palgrave Macmillan.

Markus, H. and Nurius, P. (1986) Possible selves. *American Psychologist* 41 (9), 954–969.

Matsuda, A. (2011) 'Not everyone can be a star': Students' and teachers' beliefs about English teaching in Japan. In P. Seargeant (ed.) *English in Japan in the Era of Globalization* (pp. 38–59). Basingstoke: Palgrave Macmillan.

Matsuura, H., Chiba, R. and Hilderbrandt, P. (2001) Beliefs about learning and teaching communicative English in Japan. *JALT Journal* 23 (1), 69–89.

Mayeda, A., MacKenzie, D. and Nusplinger, B. (2016) Integrating self-access center components into core English classes. *Studies in Self-Access Learning Journal* 7 (2), 220–233.

McVeigh, B. (2002) *Japanese Higher Education as Myth*. New York: Routledge.

McVeigh, B. (2004) Foreign language instruction in Japanese higher education: The humanistic vision or nationalistic utilitarianism? *Arts and Humanities in Higher Education* 3 (2), 211–227.

Menezes, V. (2011) Affordances for language learning beyond the classroom. In P. Benson and H. Reinders (eds) *Beyond the Language Classroom* (pp. 59–71). Basingstoke: Palgrave Macmillan.

Mercer, S. (2011) The self as a complex dynamic system. *Studies in Second Language Learning and Teaching* 1 (1), 57–82.

MEXT (2014) Report on the future improvement and enhancement of English education (Outline): Five recommendations on the English education reform plan responding to the rapid globalization. See http://www.mext.go.jp/en/news/topics/detail/1372625.htm (accessed June 2018).

MEXT (2017) Gaikokugo kyouiku niokeru shingakushuushidouryouyou no enkatsu na jisshi ni muketa ikousochi [Transition towards the smooth implementation of the new course of study in foreign language education] [PDF file]. See http://www.mext.go.jp/b_menu/shingi/chousa/shotou/123/shiryo/__icsFiles/afieldfile/2017/06/28/1387431_11.pdf (accessed July 2018).

Miles, M.B. and Huberman, A.M. (1984) *Qualitative Data Analysis: A Sourcebook of New Methods*. London: Sage.

Miles, M.B. and Huberman, A.M. (1994) *Qualitative Data Analysis: An Expanded Sourcebook* (2nd edn). London: Sage.
Miller, A.L. (2013) For basketball court and company cubicle: New expectations for university athletes and corporate employees in Japan. *Japanese Studies* 33 (1), 63–81.
Miller, E.R. (2014) *The Language of Adult Immigrants: Agency in the Making*. Bristol: Multilingual Matters.
Ministry of Economy, Trade and Industry (2019) Foreign language conversation schools. See www.meti.go.jp/statistics/tyo/tokusabido/result/result_1/xls/hv15601j.xls - 2019-02-18 (accessed 20 March 2019).
Mitchell, M. (2009) *Complexity: A Guided Tour*. Oxford: Oxford University Press.
Miura, Y. (2016) How I got involved with the L-café. In G. Murray and N. Fujishima (eds) *Social Spaces for Language Learning: Stories from the L-Café* (pp. 110–113). London: Palgrave Macmillan.
Miyahara, M. (2015) *Emerging Self-Identities and Emotions in Foreign Language Learning: A Narrative-Oriented Approach*. Bristol: Multilingual Matters.
Miyake, K. (2016) My life in the L-café from different angles. In G. Murray and N. Fujishima (eds) *Social Spaces for Language Learning: Stories from the L-Café* (pp. 86–90). London: Palgrave Macmillan.
Mori, Y. (1999) Epistemological beliefs and language learning beliefs: What do language learners believe about their learning? *Language Learning* 49 (3), 377–415.
Morita, N. (2004) Negotiating participation and identity in second language academic communities. *TESOL Quarterly* 38, 573–603.
Morrison, B. (2005) Evaluating learning gain in a self-access language learning centre. *Language Teaching Research* 9 (3), 267–293.
Moscovici, S. (1984) *Social Representations*. Cambridge: Cambridge University Press.
Murphey, T. (1998) Motivating with near-peer role models. *On JALT97: Trends & Transitions* 201–205.
Murphey, T. and Arao, H. (2001) Reported belief changes through near peer role modeling. *TESL-EJ* 5 (3). See http://tesl-ej.org/ej19/al.html
Murphey, T. and Carpenter, C. (2008) The seeds of agency in language learning histories. In P. Kalaja, V. Menezes and A.M.F. Barcelos (eds) *Narratives of Learning and Teaching EFL* (pp. 17–35). New York: Palgrave Macmillan.
Murray, G. (2008) Communities of practice: Stories of Japanese EFL learners. In P. Kalaja, V. Menezes and A. Barcelos (eds) *Narratives of Learning and Teaching EFL* (pp. 128–140). Basingstoke: Palgrave Macmillan.
Murray, G. (2014a) Exploring the social dimensions of autonomy in language learning. In G. Murray (ed.) *Social Dimensions of Autonomy in Language Learning* (pp. 3–11). Basingstoke: Palgrave Macmillan.
Murray, G. (ed.) (2014b) *Social Dimensions of Autonomy in Language Learning*. Basingstoke: Palgrave Macmillan.
Murray, G. (2017a) Autonomy in the time of complexity: Lessons from beyond the classroom. *Studies in Self-Access Learning Journal* 8 (2), 116–134.
Murray, G. (2017b) Autonomy and complexity in social learning space management. *Studies in Self-Access Learning Journal* 8 (2), 183–193.
Murray, G. (2018) Self-access environments as self-enriching complex dynamic ecosocial systems. *Studies in Self-Access Learning Journal* 9 (2), 102–115.
Murray, G. and Fujishima, N. (2013) Social language learning spaces: Affordances in a community of learners. *Chinese Journal of Applied Linguistics* 36 (1), 141–157.
Murray, G. and Fujishima, N. (2016a) Exploring a social space for language learning. In G. Murray and N. Fujishima (eds) *Social Spaces for Language Learning: Stories from the L-Café* (pp. 1–12). London: Palgrave Macmillan.
Murray, G. and Fujishima, N. (2016b) *Social Spaces for Language Learning: Stories from the L-Café*. London: Palgrave Macmillan.

Murray, G. and Fujishima, N. (2016c) Understanding a social space for language learning. In G. Murray and N. Fujishima (eds) *Social Spaces for Language Learning: Stories from the L-Café* (pp. 124–146). London: Palgrave Macmillan.

Murray, G. and Lamb, T. (eds) (2018) *Space, Place and Autonomy in Language Learning*. Abingdon: Routledge.

Murray, G., Fujishima, N. and Uzuka, M. (2014) The semiotics of place: Autonomy and space. In G. Murray (ed.) *Social Dimensions of Autonomy in Language Learning* (pp. 81–99). Basingstoke: Palgrave.

Murray, G., Fujishima, N. and Uzuka. M. (2018) Social learning spaces and the invisible fence. In G. Murray and T. Lamb (eds) *Space, Place and Autonomy in Language Learning* (pp. 233–246). Abingdon: Routledge.

Mynard, J. (2016) Self-access in Japan: Introduction. *Studies in Self-Access Learning* 7 (4), 331–340.

Mynard, J. (2019) Advising and self-access learning: Promoting language learner autonomy beyond the classroom. In H. Reinders, S. Ryan and S. Nakao (eds) *Innovations in Language Learning and Teaching: The Case of Japan*. Basingstoke: Palgrave Macmillan.

Mynard, J. and Yamamoto, K. (2018) User perceptions of an app for managing self-directed language learning. *Relay Journal* 1 (2), 405–428.

Mynard, J. and Shelton-Strong, S.J. (2019) Evaluating a Self-Access Centre: A Self-Determination Theory Perspective. Paper presented at the 53rd International Association of Teachers of English as a Foreign Language annual conference, Liverpool, UK, 2–5 April, 2019.

Nagatomo, D.H. (2012) *Exploring Japanese University English Teachers' Professional Identity*. Bristol: Multilingual Matters.

Nagatomo, D.H. (2016) *Identity, Gender and Teaching English in Japan*. Bristol: Multilingual Matters.

Nakamoto, N. (2016) The door to the L-café, the door to the world. In G. Murray and N. Fujishima (eds) *Social Spaces for Language Learning: Stories from the L-Café* (pp. 80–85). London: Palgrave Macmillan.

Navarro, D. and Thornton, K. (2011) Investigating the relationship between belief and action in self-directed language learning. *System* 39, 290–310.

Nemoto, A.K. (2018) Getting ready for 2020: Changes and challenges for English education in public primary schools in Japan. *The Language Teacher* 42 (4), 33–35.

News from the SALC (2016a) SALC survey results (3): How did the respondents rate the various areas? [web log post]. See https://salcnews.wordpress.com/2016/12/23/salc-survey-results-3-how-did-the-respondents-rate-the-various-areas/ (accessed February 2019).

News from the SALC (2016b) SALC survey results (4): The Conversation Lounge (yellow sofas) [web log post]. See https://salcnews.wordpress.com/2016/12/23/salc-survey-results-4-the-conversation-lounge-yellow-sofas/ (accessed February 2019).

Nishino, T. (2008) Japanese secondary school teachers' beliefs and practices regarding communicative language teaching: An exploratory survey. *JALT Journal* 30 (1), 27–50.

Nishino, T. (2011) Japanese high school teachers' beliefs and practices regarding communicative language teaching. *JALT Journal* 33 (2), 131–155.

Noguchi, J. (2015) 'I'm a SALCer': Influences of identity on fear of making mistakes. *Studies in Self-Access Learning Journal* 6 (2), 163–175.

Noguchi, J., Mynard, J., Curry, N. and Watkins, S. (2018) Students' perceptions of the impact of a self-directed learning skills training program on language learning. *Studies in Linguistics and Language Teaching* 29, 91–118.

Norton, B. (2000) *Identity and Language Learning* (1st edn). London: Longman.

Norton, B. (2001) Non-participation, imagined communities and the language learning classroom. In M.P. Breen (ed.) *Learner Contributions to Language Learning: New Directions in Research* (pp. 151–171). Harlow: Longman.

Norton, B. (2013) *Identity and Language Learning: Extending the Conversation* (2nd edn). Bristol: Multilingual Matters.

Nunan, D. (1997) Designing and adapting materials to encourage learner autonomy. In P. Benson and P. Voller (eds) *Autonomy and Independence in Language Learning* (pp. 192–203). Harlow: Pearson.

Oblinger, D. (ed.) (2006) *Learning Spaces*. Boulder, CO: EDUCAUSE.

OECD (2015) Education policy outlook: Japan [pdf file]. See http://www.oecd.org/education/Japan-country-profile.pdf (accessed June 2018).

Ortega, L. (2009) *Understanding Second Language Acquisition*. London: Hodder Education.

Oxford, R.L. (2003) Toward a more systematic model of L2 learner autonomy. In D. Palfreyman and R. Smith (eds) *Learner Autonomy Across Cultures* (pp. 75–91). Basingstoke: Palgrave Macmillan.

Palfreyman, D.M. (2014) The ecology of learner autonomy. In G. Murray (ed.) *Social Dimensions of Autonomy in Language Learning* (pp. 175–191). Basingstoke: Palgrave Macmillan.

Peeters, W. and Mynard, J. (2019) Peer collaboration and learner autonomy in online interaction spaces. *Relay Journal* 2 (2), 450–458.

Reinders, H. (2012) The end of self-access? From walled garden to public park. *ELT World Online* 4, 1–5.

Reinders, H. and Benson, P. (2017) Research agenda: Language learning beyond the classroom. *Language Teaching* 50 (4), 561–578. https://doi.org/10.1017/S0261444817000192

Ritchie, J. and Spencer, L. (1994) Qualitative data analysis for applied policy research. In A. Bryman and R.G. Burgess (eds) *Analyzing Qualitative Data* (pp. 173–194). London: Routledge.

Rose, H. (2007) Jump-starting student motivation to use self-access learning facilities: A case-study of a class's use of a free-conversation area. *The Journal of Kanda University of International Studies* 19, 171–188.

Rose, H. and Elliott, R. (2010) An investigation of student use of a self-access English-only speaking area. *Studies in Self-Access Learning Journal* 1 (1), 32–46.

Ryan, S. and Dörnyei, Z. (2013) The long-term evolution of language motivation and the L2 self. In A. Berndt (ed.) *Fremdsprachen in der Perspektive lebenslangen Lernens* (pp. 89–100). Frankfurt: Peter Lang.

Sakui, K. (2004) Wearing two pairs of shoes: Language teaching in Japan. *ELT Journal* 58 (2), 155–163.

Sakui, K. and Gaies, S. (1999) Investigating Japanese learners' beliefs about language learning. *System* 27, 473–492.

SALC (2018) *Mission*. Self-Access Learning Center, Kanda University of International Studies, Japan. See https://www.kandagaigo.ac.jp/kuis/salc/aboutthesalc/mission.html (accessed 1 November 2019).

SALC (2019) *SALC Handbook*. Self-Access Learning Center, Kanda University of International Studies, Japan.

Sampson, E.E. (1985) The decentralization of identity: Toward a revised concept of personal and social order. *American Psychologist* 40, 1203–1211.

Sampson, R.J. (2016) *Complexity in Classroom Foreign Language Learning Motivation: A Practitioner Perspective from Japan*. Bristol: Multilingual Matters.

Sato, K. and Kleinsasser, R.C. (2004) Beliefs, practices, and interactions of teachers in a Japanese high school English department. *Teaching and Teacher Education* 20, 797–816.

Seargeant, P. (2008) Ideologies of English in Japan: The perspective of policy and pedagogy. *Language Policy* 7, 121–142.

Sherry, M. (2008) Identity. In L.M. Given (ed.) *The SAGE Encyclopedia of Qualitative Research Methods* (pp. 414–416). Thousand Oaks, CA: Sage. http://dx.doi.org/10.4135/9781412963909.n206

Shelton-Strong, S.J. (2018) How are Learning Advisors and Advising Sessions Perceived by Learners Who Attend Them? Paper presented at the Japan Association for Self-Access Learning Conferences, Kumamoto, Japan, 15 September 2018.

Simons, H. (2009) *Case Study Research in Practice*. London: Sage.

Sinclair, B. (1999) Wrestling with a jelly: The evaluation of learner autonomy. In B. Morrison (ed.) *Experiments and Evaluation in Self-Access Language Learning* (pp. 95–110). Hong Kong: HASALD.

Spradley, J.P. (1980) *Participant Observation*. New York: Holt, Rinehart & Winston.

Stephens, M.A. (2002) Eigo versus eikaiwa: The interference of written English on the pronunciation of EFL learners in Japan. *Studies in Language and Literature* 22 (1), 87–111.

Stubbings, B. (2007, September 25) Is it all over for Nova? *The Japan Times*. See https://www.japantimes.co.jp/community/2007/09/25/issues/is-it-all-over-for-nova/#.XSACB-gza02 (accessed November 2018).

Suzuki, H. and Roger, P. (2014) Foreign language anxiety in teachers. *JALT Journal* 36 (2), 175–199.

Tahara, M. (2016) Creating the L-café: An administrator's standpoint. In G. Murray and N. Fujishima (eds) *Social Spaces for Language Learning: Stories from the L-Café* (pp. 14–20). London: Palgrave Macmillan.

Tahira, M. (2012) Behind MEXT's new course of study guidelines. *The Language Teacher* 36 (3), 3–8.

Takeuchi, H. (2015) Peer tutoring in Japan: A new approach for a unique educational system. *Studies in Self-Access Learning Journal* 6 (1), 112–119.

Tanaka, T. (2009) Communicative language teaching and its cultural appropriateness in Japan. *Doshisha Studies in English* 84, 107–123. See https://doors.doshisha.ac.jp/duar/repository/ir/14214/020000840005.pdf

Tanaka, K. and Ellis, R. (2003) Study abroad, language proficiency, and learner beliefs about language learning. *JALT Journal* 25, 63–85.

Tangonan, D. (2016) Defining experience through the L-café. In G. Murray and N. Fujishima (eds) *Social Spaces for Language Learning: Stories from the L-Café* (pp. 96–99). London: Palgrave Macmillan.

Tanimoto, Y. (2016) Fulfilling time at the L-café. In G. Murray and N. Fujishima (eds) *Social Spaces for Language Learning: Stories from the L-Café* (pp. 114–118). London: Palgrave Macmillan.

Taylor, C. (2014) The transformation of a foreign language conversation lounge: An action research project. *Bulletin of Shotoku Gakuen University (Faculty of Foreign Languages)* 53, 1–16. See http://www.shotoku.ac.jp/data/facilities/library/publication/gaigo53-1.pdf (accessed February 2019).

Taylor, C., Beck, D., Hardy, D., Omura, K., Stout, M. and Talandis, G. (2012) Encouraging students to engage in learning outside the classroom. In K. Irie and A. Stewart (eds) Proceedings of the JALT Learner Development SIG Realizing Autonomy Conference, [Special issue] *Learning* 19 (2), 31–45.

Thomson, C.K. and Mori, T. (2015) Japanese communities of practice: Creating opportunities for out-of-class learning. In D. Nunan and J.C. Richards (eds) *Language Learning Beyond the Classroom*. ESL & Applied Linguistics Professional Series (pp. 272–281). New York: Routledge.

Thompson, G. and Atkinson, L. (2010) Integrating self-access into the curriculum: Our experience. *Studies in Self-Access Learning Journal* 1 (1), 47–58.

Thornton, K. (2015) Sharing stories of practice in self-access facility design and management. *Studies in Self-Access Learning Journal* 6 (2), 216–218.

Thornton, K. (2016) Promoting engagement with language learning spaces: How to attract users and create a community of practice. *Studies in Self-Access Learning Journal* 7 (3), 297–300.

Thornton, K. and Noguchi, N. (2016) Building a picture of usage patterns in a language learning space: Gathering useful quantitative and qualitative data. *Studies in Self-Access Learning Journal* 7 (4), 412–425.

Toohey, K. (1998) Breaking them up, taking them away: ESL students in grade 1. *TESOL Quarterly* 32, 61–84.

Triandis, H.C. (1995) *Individualism and Collectivism*. Boulder, CO: Westview Press.

Tsukamoto, M. (2013) The implementation of "English Communication I": Incorporating the new Course of Study for senior high schools in Japan. *Seinanjo Gakuin Daigaku Kiyo* 17, 67–77.

Uchida, C. (2016) Optimizing affordances: Developing a 'digital habitat' for the L-café. In G. Murray and N. Fujishima (eds) *Social Spaces for Language Learning: Stories from the L-Café* (pp. 69–78). London: Palgrave Macmillan.

Underwood, P. (2012a) Teacher beliefs and intentions regarding the instruction of English grammar under national curriculum reforms: A theory of planned behaviour perspective. *Teaching and Teacher Education* 28, 911–925.

Underwood, P. (2012b) The course of study for senior high school English: Recent developments, implementation to date, and considerations for future research. *Toyo Eiwa University, Jinbun Shakaikagaku Ronshu* 30, 115–145.

Ushioda, E. (2014) Context and complex dynamic systems theory. In Z. Dornyei, P.D. MacIntyre and A. Henry (eds) *Motivational Dynamics in Language Learning* (pp. 47–54). Bristol: Multilingual Matters.

Uzuka, M. (2016) Five years at the L-café: The secret of its success. In G. Murray and N. Fujishima (eds) *Social Spaces for Language Learning: Stories from the L-Café* (pp. 21–30). London: Palgrave Macmillan.

van Lier, L. (2004) *The Ecology and Semiotics of Language Learning: A Sociocultural Perspective*. Boston, MA: Kluwer Academic.

Verhoeven, L. and Vermeer, A. (2002) Communicative competence and personality dimensions in first and second language learners. *Applied Psycholinguistics* 23, 361–374.

Viberg, O., Laaksolahti, J., Mynard, J. and Mavroudi, A. (2018) Assessing the potential role of technology in promoting self-directed language learning: A collaborative project between Japan and Sweden. *Relay Journal* 1 (2), 346–359.

Victori, M. and Lockhart, W. (1995) Enhancing metacognition in self-directed language learning. *System* 23 (2), 223–234.

Vygotsky, L. (1987) *The Collected Works of L.S. Vygotsky: Vol 1. Problems of General Psychology*. New York: Plenum.

Wada, M. (1987) *Kokusaika jidai ni okeru eigokyouiku: Mombusho English fellows no ashiato [English Education in an International Era: Footprints of Mombusho English Fellows]*. Kyoto: Yamaguchi Shoten.

Watkins, S. (2019) Investigating Interest-based Learning Communities Outside the Classroom: Research in Progress. Presentation given in the SALC department meeting, 28 March 2019.

Weedon, C. (1997) *Feminist Practice and Poststructuralist Theory* (2nd edn). London: Blackwell.

Wenden, A. (1999) An introduction to metacognitive knowledge and beliefs in language learning: Beyond the basics. *System* 27 (4), 435–441.

Wenger, E. (1998) *Communities of Practice: Learning, Meaning, and Identity*. New York: Cambridge University Press.

Wenger, E. (2010) Communities of practice and social learning systems: The career of a concept. In C. Blackmore (ed.) *Social Learning Systems and Communities of Practice* (pp. 179–198). London: Springer.

Wenger, E. and Snyder, W.M. (2000, January) Communities of practice: The organizational frontier. *Harvard Business Review*. See https://hbr.org/2000/01/communities-of-practice-the-organizational-frontier (accessed February 2018).

Wenger, E., McDermott, R. and Snyder, W.M. (2002) *Cultivating Communities of Practice: A Guide to Managing Knowledge*. Boston, MA: Harvard Business School Press.

Wenger-Trayner, E. and Wenger-Trayner, B. (2015) Communities of practice: A brief introduction [PDF file]. See http://wenger-trayner.com/wp-content/uploads/2015/04/07-Brief-introduction-to-communities-of-practice.pdf (accessed November 2017).

Werner, R.J. and Von Joo, L. (2018) From theory to practice: Considerations in opening a new self-access center. *Studies in Self-Access Learning Journal* 9 (2), 116–134.

Yarwood, A., Lorentzen, A., Wallingford, A. and Wongsarnpigoon, I. (2019) Exploring basic psychological needs in a language learning center. Part 2: The autonomy-supportive nature and limitations of a SALC. *Relay Journal* 2 (1).

Yashima, T. (2009) International posture and the ideal L2 self in the Japanese EFL context. In Z. Dörnyei and E. Ushioda (eds) *Motivation, Language Identity and the L2 Self* (pp. 144–163). Bristol: Multilingual Matters.

Yashima, T. (2013) Individuality, imagination and community in a globalizing world: An Asian EFL perspective. In P. Benson and L. Cooker (eds) *The Applied Linguistic Individual: Sociocultural Approaches to Identity, Agency and Autonomy* (pp. 46–58). Sheffield: Equinox Publishing.

Yashima, T., Zenuk-Nishide, L. and Shimizu, K. (2004) The influence of attitudes and affect on willingness to communicate and second language communication. *Language Learning* 54 (1), 119–152.

Index

access (to a space)   3, 4, 17, 21, 25, 28, 169
access (to comunity)   17, 26, 27, 28, 26, 111, 116, 139-140, 166, 169
accountability (vertical/horizontal)   123, 161, 170
advisor / learning advisor / advising   6, 103-4, 132, 165, 170
agency   16, 35-36, 43, 46-47, 103, 126, 129, 132-133, 135, 139, 141, 145-149, 160-161, 172,
anxiety / language anxiety   18-19, 21, 23-25, 34, 46-47, 61, 67, 71, 90, 102, 107, 119, 121, 126, 129, 131-133, 139-140, 145-149, 163, 174
avoidance/non-use of lounge   18, 23, 26, 78-79, 87, 103-107, 129, 131, 132, 140-141, 146, 149, 162
awareness raising   17-18, 24, 163, 166-167, 169, 170-173, 174,

beliefs   11, 32, 43, 45, 46, 47, 52, 59, 69, 104, 105, 114, 117, 125-132, 134-149, 160-162, 170-173
belonging   25, 27, 36, 106, 167

case study research   44, 153
choice (of activity) / choising activity   6, 7, 13, 18, 19, 22, 23, 24, 25, 35, 93, 128, 130, 132, 147, 149, 159, 162, 163, 165, 175,
classroom learning   68, 163
communicative ability / communicative competence   27, 30-35
community of practice   4, 6, 11, 15, 25, 28, 39, 44-45, 51, 97, 107-112, 114, 116-124, 151-154, 159-160, 162, 164-165, 168-170, 175, 177, 180-181
community of practice   51, 97, 108-109, 111-112, 117, 119-124, 133, 153, 160-161, 164, 168, 170, 177, 183
complexity theory   14, 155-156
confidence   18, 22-24, 27, 30, 54, 56-57, 59, 61, 65-67, 78-82, 86-88, 90, 97-98, 99, 101-103, 105-107, 133-134, 140-141, 159, 163, 167, 170, 183-184
conversation lounges / English lounges   3-13, 17-19, 22-23, 26-29, 32, 35-36, 37-41, 43- 47, 51-74, 76-80, 82-83, 86-90, 93-135, 137-142, 146-152, 155, 159-171, 173-175, 177-178, 183-184
conversation schools (eikaiwa) / extracurricular education   8, 29-30, 35-36, 46-47, 64

decor   21
disappointment   18, 26, 54,

ecology / ecological perspective   4-5, 13, 27, 150, 162-163
eigo/eikaiwa   32-33, 35-36, 46-47, 68-71, 115, 169, 126, 128-129, 133-134, 136-139, 144-145, 147-149, 160-161, 172-173
empowerment   6, 71, 137, 163, 168-170
environmental factors   12-28, 54, 94-95, 116, 117, 132, 155, 162-164, 174-175
ethnography   10, 15, 37, 44, 94

fear of taking risks / risk taking   21, 74, 86, 87, 90, 105, 167 future career   35-36, 62, 63-64, 70, 72-73, 77, 82, 84, 102, 98, 100, 101, 102, 103, 104, 127, 115-116, 127, 128, 134-136, 137-138, 163, 172,

grammar   30, 31, 32, 34, 36, 47, 51, 67, 69-70, 71, 84, 87, 103, 114, 128, 131, 133, 138-139, 140, 141, 146-147, 161, 171, 173

identity   16, 41, 43, 45, 57, 61, 63, 64, 68, 69, 71, 76-77, 79, 82, 85-86, 93-107, 108-109, 110, 113, 114, 115, 134, 149, 153, 154, 156, 159-160, 161, 162, 166-167
ideologies of language learning   21, 31-32, 128, 137, 138
imagined communities   71, 116-117, 160
interdependence   14, 35-36, 47, 111, 120, 124, 129-130, 132, 133, 135, 139-142, 145, 146, 148, 149, 161
international posture   96, 105, 116, 128, 137-138
interpretative analysis   45-47, 125, 152, 154-155
interventions   166-175
Interview methods   10-11, 41, 43, 94-95, 96, 125, 146, 151-154, 164

Japanese education system   23, 29-36, 51, 67-68, 83-84, 114-115, 128-129, 131, 137-139. 149

kohai/junior   34, 76, 120
kohai/senpai (seniority-based relationships) (senior/junior)   34, 61, 66-67, 71, 74, 76, 98, 99, 102, 119-121, 132, 145, 160, 169-170

L2 motivational self system / L2 self   20, 23, 24-25, 35-36, 46-47, 66, 70, 90, 112, 115-118, 120, 127-129, 132-136, 138, 144-146, 148-149, 154, 160-161, 172
language learning history   43, 44, 58, 63, 67-68, 94, 139, 152, 181-182

language policy / policy   22, 28, 38, 54, 56, 122-123, 132, 161, 174, 175   /
other policy: 24
layout (of a space) (furniture)   21, 38, 54, 55, 73-74, 99, 122, 161, 168
leadership   16, 20, 25, 54, 99, 106, 110, 112, 164, 168-170
learner autonomy   6, 13-14, 15-16, 16-17, 19, 21, 22, 23, 24, 63, 103, 105, 111, 127-128, 132, 154, 160, 166, 169, 172, 184

making friends   16, 52, 54, 55, 61, 73, 101, 183
making mistakes   62, 74, 76, 85, 87-88, 89-90, 122, 131, 133, 141, 147
metaphor   63, 178
motivation   17, 20, 12, 23-26, 35-36, 45, 52, 59-63, 66, 82, 85, 87, 90, 98, 100-102, 104, 112-114, 116-118, 126-128, 132, 134, 136, 140, 142, 144-145, 154, 155, 164
multilingual space   22, maybe N/A

narrative research   43-45, 94, 96-97
native speakers / near native speakers   21, 31-32, 52, 62-63, 80-81, 100-101, 106, 118, 132
native-like level (attainment)   78, 80, 101, 133, 141
near peer role models / role models   26, 66, 90, 112, 160,168,
nesting   146-148
non-English majors   70, 74, 80, 133, 141

observation (study)   38, 39-41, 150-151, 176

peripherality   25, 27, 109-111
personality (and language learning)   56, 59, 79, 80, 101, 104, 113, 126, 129, 134, 140

reconciliation of beliefs   69, 71, 129, 133-134, 139, 144, 149, 161, 173

responsibilty   14, 16, 21, 23, 27, 28, 35, 71, 98, 99, 106, 120, 123, 132, 133, 160
role models (near peer role models)   26, 66, 80, 90, 112, 160, 168

secondary education   29, 31-35, 114-115, 128-129, 137, 139
self-access centre / SALC   3-4, 6-7, 11, 13-26, 23-24, 26-27, 29, 41, 47, 51-52, 54, 56-58, 61, 68, 74, 79-82, 84-86, 89, 93, 95, 103-105, 119, 118-119, 121-123, 133, 138-139, 143, 159, 161, 169-170, 174-175, 178, 180, 183, 187, 189
senpai/senior   34, 61, 66-67, 119-120
social learning   3-6, 8-23, 25-30, 32, 35-38, 48, 73, 108-109, 112, 124, 125-126, 150-153, 155, 159, 164-166, 170, 172,

social learning space   3-5, 9, 11-30, 35-38, 48, 73, 93, 96, 107-109, 111-112, 117, 124-125, 150-153, 155-156, 159, 162-166, 168, 170,
social skills   16, 76-77
socialising / meeting friends   23, 25, 52, 55, 56, 60, 73, 76, 97, 99, 101
sociocultural theory   14, 126
student ownership (of a SALC)   19, 47, 161, 168, 170
study abroad   16, 20, 66, 70-72, 74-77, 84, 95-96, 98, 102-103, 113, 116, 133-135

target language/culture   3, 8 ,12-13, 22, 29, 47, 70-71, 79, 96, 116-117, 127, 131, 136, 142, 147, 163, 167
tasks   24, 66, 126
teacher's role   20-21, 24-25, 32, 80, 132-133,
threading / threaded analysis   142-144

For Product Safety Concerns and Information please contact our EU Authorised Representative:

Easy Access System Europe

Mustamäe tee 50

10621 Tallinn

Estonia

gpsr.requests@easproject.com

www.ingramcontent.com/pod-product-compliance
Lightning Source LLC
Chambersburg PA
CBHW070608300426
44113CB00010B/1459